THE GERMAN REVOLUTION OF 1848–49

The German Revolution of 1848–49

WOLFRAM SIEMANN
Professor of Modern and Contemporary History
University of Munich

Translated by Christiane Banerji

St. Martin's Press
New York

THE GERMAN REVOLUTION OF 1848–49

Copyright © 1985 by Suhrkamp Verlag
English translation copyright © 1998 by Macmillan Press Ltd

St. Martin's Press, Scholarly and Reference Division, 175 Fifth Avenue, New York, N.Y. 10010

First published in the United States of America in 1998

This book is printed on paper suitable for recycling and made from fully managed and sustained forest sources.

Printed in Hong Kong

ISBN 0–312–21694–7 clothbound
ISBN 0–312–21695–5 paperback

Library of Congress Cataloging-in-Publication Data
Siemann, Wolfram.
[Deutsche Revolution von 1848/49. English]
The German revolution of 1848–49 / Wolfram Siemann ; translated by Christiane Banerji.
p. cm. — (European studies series)
Includes bibliographical references and index.
ISBN 0–312–21694–7. — ISBN 0–312–21695–5 (pbk.)
1. Germany—History—Revolution, 1848–1849. I. Title.
II. Series.
IN PROCESS
943'.076—dc21   98–21100
                                                                          CIP

Contents

List of Tables

List of Figures

List of Abbreviations

AfS	*Archiv für Sozialgeschichte*
FBPG	*Forschungen zur Brandenburgischen und Preußischen Geschichte*
GG	*Geschichte und Gesellschaft*
HZ	*Historische Zeitschrift*
MEW	*Marx–Engels Werke*
MÖStA	*Mitteilungen des Österreichischen Staatsarchivs*
NPL	*Neue Politische Literatur*
SOWI	*Sozialwissenschaftliche Informationen für Unterricht und Studium*
VSWG	*Vierteljahrschrift für Sozial- und Wirtschaftsgeschichte*
ZfG	*Zeitschrift für Geschichtswissenschaft*

Foreword to the English Edition

Wolfram Siemann's history of the German revolution of 1848–9 is the best single volume treatment of the events of those extraordinary years, something which was immediately recognized when the original German version of this book was published in 1985.

It is by German standards a short book. Siemann does not, for example, seek to match the detail of Veit Valentin's massive narrative of the revolutions.[1] Indeed, there is not a great deal of narrative in Siemann's book. What there is focuses mainly on the outbreak and ending of the revolution. There are many books, English as well as German, which tell one more about the political course of the revolution, especially about the ultimately unsuccessful attempt by the German National Assembly to create a constitutional and national state.[2] There is a large literature looking at the regional, even local, impact of the revolution. There are studies of particular social groups and how they acted during the revolutionary period.[3] There are books which place the revolutions in a longer time-frame, including works by Siemann himself.[4] Finally, there are studies of the revolutions of 1848–9 at a European level.[5]

Yet none of this literature treats the revolution in the innovative and comprehensive way that Siemann does. Siemann has a good deal to say about the politics of the revolution, in particular the work of the German National Assembly. However, the political aspects of the revolution are placed firmly in a broader context which takes account of social and economic history. Siemann also broadens and differentiates between the various notions of revolutionary politics.

In many treatments of the 1848 revolutions, the 'masses' enter at the beginning and the end. They enter as the crowds and popular movements which bring governments down in March 1848. They are seen again in the form of the doomed 'second revolution' of spring 1849, the repression of which signalled the end of the revolution. In the intervening period they are largely treated as 'noises offstage', disrupting the work of the politicians in the various parliaments and ministries. The inability of these institutions to find a legitimate place for popular movements, indeed the increasing fear and anxiety of politicians about a continuing, radicalizing revolution, is rightly regarded as crucial to the success of counter-revolution. Nevertheless, to see popular movements as a threat is to see them from the outside, through the eyes of the parliamentarians and ministers, or more broadly from a bourgeois perspective. Alternatively, when historians sympathetic to the popular revolution write about 1848–9, they tend to do so in terms of categories such as the 'people' or the 'working class' and to consider the political, 'official' side of the revolution as a betrayal of that popular or class movement. From either point of view, the revolution was a failure and there was a gulf between the political and the popular levels. The way in which the revolution itself failed and was repressed, together with the fact that the 'national question' was later to be 'solved' in a quite different way, favoured these polarized ways of first remembering and then writing the history of the revolution, something Siemann outlines in his introduction.

Siemann's major achievement is to overcome that gulf and, by so doing, to offer us a very different picture and interpretation of the revolution. Siemann has taken into account much recent research into subjects such as popular protest and mentality, work which has generally had a fairly fragmented character and has not been closely related to conventional political history. He has then synthesized that research by deploying the idea of a crisis of modernization. He has also fitted these subjects into a history of the revolution by distinguishing between different levels of action.

The benefits of this novel approach are to be seen immediately in the first section of the book on structures and crises: Siemann describes a society in a crisis of modernization. He begins with a survey of the major social groups. In socio-economic terms what was of central importance was the combination of population growth and increasing commercialization of production but without the emergence of significant large-scale or technologically advanced forms of production. Siemann goes on to consider how various groups acted collectively – through formal association or informal protest – as well as the methods by which the state sought to control such action.

These problems grew more acute during the mid 1840s, years of high food prices and increased misery. Finally, Siemann points to significant European dimensions. Germany was politically the product of a European peace settlement. The civil war in Switzerland and the widespread belief that crisis in France meant crisis throughout Europe provided political models and perceptions which are vital to an understanding of the revolution in Germany. Thus, before considering the outbreak of revolution Siemann has pointed to socio-economic problems, collective movements, types of political understanding and modes of governmental control which make that outbreak, even if unpredictable and surprising, more than a bolt of lightning from a clear blue sky.

When Siemann comes to the revolution itself he develops the idea of levels of action. This enables him to do justice to a great range of subjects and offers the opportunity to show how these different levels interact. The five levels distinguished are: popular movements; association and communication; the elected assemblies; the newly constituted governments; and the old political order. Initially, there was something of a sequence to these levels. Popular movements in March/April 1848 led to the collapse of restrictions on assembly, association and freedom of communication. That in turn led to the election of constituent assemblies in most states as well as a German National Assembly. It also resulted in members of the political opposition forming new ministries. Meanwhile, the princes and their officials, civil and military, held on to various kinds of power and sought to reassert their own position. However, after the initial phase of the revolution these levels operated simultaneously and in increasingly complex relationships to one another. Finally, Siemann makes the point, vital but neglected in most studies, that one should also look at the places where the revolution *did not take place* – the 'quiet zones'.

By making these distinctions Siemann is able to produce a comprehensive account of the revolution. The distinctions draw attention to levels of action other than those of popular movements and elected assemblies which have been the main focus of historical study. Indeed, some of the most striking and novel passages in the book deal with such subjects as the emergence of a new public sphere dominated by regular meetings, an expanding range of associations and the publication of a huge range of newspapers, periodicals, pamphlets and posters.

Siemann shows that the course of the revolution was not determined just by conflicts between different levels of action (for example, the 'people' against the 'politicians') or between different groups within one level (for example, between urban and rural movements, journeymen and masters, radicals and liberals), although these were important. There were also contradictions within particular levels or groups. Liberals in state ministries defended their powers against liberals in state parliaments and both defended their state concerns against their counterparts in the National Assembly. Artisans made progressive political demands but allied them to backward-looking social and economic programmes. Conversely, different levels of action could reinforce one another. The old order, for example, was reluctant to act against elected assemblies so long as it felt these could draw upon organized popular support.

The subject of counter-revolution and the issue of 'failures' is also one to which Siemann makes an original contribution. By doing justice to the variety of group interests and levels of action Siemann can argue that the simple dichotomy of success/failure is inadequate to grasp the full meaning of the revolution. Drawing on his own research into policing, Siemann demonstrates that the post-1848 order was more effectively policed than before 1848 and by a more modern, bureaucratized system of states. At the same time, the consequences of revolution included greater economic freedom and a politicization of German society in ways that could not be reversed but also that could not have been anticipated before 1848. In these complex ways the revolution helped shape the modernization of Germany.

The book will convey to the English reader a great deal of recent research on the German revolutions of 1848–9. However, this is much more than a work of synthesis. Above all, Wolfram Siemann has written a book which, by dint of an original interpretation framework, does justice to the complexity of the German revolution of 1848–9, and which makes clear the significance of that revolution to a longer term understanding of modern German history.

November 1997   JOHN BREUILLY

Notes

1. Veit Valentin, *Geschichte der deutschen Revolution von 1848–49*, 2 vols (Berlin, 1930–1).
2. Such as Frank Eyck, *The Frankfurt Parliament, 1848–49* (London, 1968).
3. For a recent outstanding work in English with both a regional and socio-political focus see Jonathan Sperber, *Rhineland Radicals: The Democratic Movement and the Revolution of 1848–1849* (New Jersey, 1991).

4. Wolfram Siemann, *Vom Staatenbund zum Nationalstaat. Deutschland 1806–1871* (Munich, 1995).
5. Jonathan Sperber, *The European Revolutions, 1848–1851* (Cambridge, 1994) is a good recent example and can be used in addition to Siemann's references by English readers looking for further literature on the 1848–9 revolutions beyond Germany.

Introduction – Coming to Terms with the German Revolution of 1848–9: Repression and Identification

To a large degree, the history of the German revolution of 1848–9 is the history of its repression and the attempts made to come to terms with it, and this process had already begun during the revolution itself. Three social groups in particular undertook these tasks: the participants and witnesses at the time of the revolution, the ruling élites after the revolution and, finally, historians: the professional trustees of the past.

For the post-revolutionary governments the events of 1848–9 were an aberration, an accident, a 'mad year', whose consequences had to be reversed as quickly and effectively as possible. To a great extent German political life was paralysed by the decade of systematic reactionary policies which followed the revolution, unprecedented numbers of people were forced to emigrate, and a climate of intimidation and persecution was created, to which opposition members of every hue were subjected.[1] The unbridled police-state activity seen during this decade, which has always been underestimated, left more lasting traces on the political culture of the second half of the century than the fact of the failed revolution itself. As late as 1886, in his memoirs on the consequences of post-revolutionary policies, the Saxon National Liberal, Karl Biedermann, concluded that, 'a reaction swept through the whole of Germany, assaulting the nation's finest feelings in a methodical, merciless manner that had never before been encountered, not in the 1820s, nor the thirties or the forties; a reaction whose effects the usually mild-mannered Dahlmann denounced with the bitter words, "Injustice has lost all sense of shame." '[2] This was the perception of an attempt to deal with the revolution, which was calculated to repress this year in the political consciousness altogether. It is for this reason that this quotation belongs at the beginning of this volume.

Participants in the revolution and its witnesses, including Biedermann and Dahlmann, were caught between two opposing lines of fire. On the one hand, they were potential victims of the reactionary policies; Biedermann, for example, lost his Leipzig Chair in 1853, following his involvement in a press trial. On the other hand, however, they laid themselves open to charges of failure, treason or political *naïveté*. The apportioning of blame, the retribution and the myth-making began as early as 1848, at the same time as the governments were beginning to reassert themselves. A comprehensive account of the history of the Frankfurt National Assembly by the constitutionalist deputy Rudolf Haym was first published in the autumn of 1848. Bearing the subtitle *A Report from the Party of the Centre-Right*, it 'blamed' the failure of the Frankfurt constitution on what Haym saw as lack of moderation on the part of the parliamentary liberal and democratic minority factions.[3]

Those at whom the censure was aimed, on the other hand, issued frequent warnings that all the '*Märzerrungenschaften*' – the achievements of March 1848 – would be gambled away by the indecision and over-scrupulousness of the majority. In this regard one need only turn one's attention to the minority factions' numerous 'emergency motions' and the 'parliamentary questions' recorded in the shorthand report of the Paulskirche debates. Clearly, the theory of a split in the middle classes already enjoyed currency in the reappraisals of the revolution which started to take place even before the revolution was over.

Not just during the period of reaction, but long after the unification of the *Reich* in 1871, it remained unwise to openly declare oneself a 'forty-eighter'. In Heinrich Mann's novel *Der Untertan (The Underling)*, published in parts in 1914, the Wilhelmine middle classes are embodied in the figure of the nationalist opportunist Diederich Heßling, who is able both economically and socially to outmanoeuvre 'old Buck', the democrat of 1848. The admittedly exaggerated portrayal in this novel reflected the tendency either to repress the revolution entirely, or to integrate only isolated parts of it into the prehistory of the *Kaiserreich*. Leading Paulskirche deputies, such as its Parliamentary President, Eduard von Simson, or Georg Beseler, mentor of the discussions on the Basic Rights, regarded Bismarck as the executor of the aims of the 1848 revolution. A reductive historical picture was drawn in which the middle classes were portrayed as the major social driving force and national unity as the true message of 1848. Rather than resign themselves to the fact that it was not possible to achieve freedom and unity without power, it was said, some of the 'failures' had sold themselves to the doctrine of *realpolitik*. During the most reactionary period – 1853 – Ludwig August von Rochau published the programme which ensured the ideological success of this kind of assessment of the revolution.[4]

Most historians also dealt with the revolution in this manner; frequently because they were forced to do so. The public academic interpretations of some of the more famous among them – Georg Waitz, Johann Gustav Droysen or Friedrich Christoph Dahlmann – were understandably restrained. A state post as university professor and academic theory were too closely interwoven to allow comprehensive research into the revolution to take place.

It was the trial for high treason of the liberal Heidelberg historian and former Paulskirche deputy, Georg Gottfried Gervinus, which brought home to his dismayed colleagues the limitations that politics could place on their research. In his measured analysis, Gervinus had concluded that the tenor of modern history was leading irresistibly to the participation of the 'masses'. 'The emancipation of all those who are oppressed and suffering is the call of the century.'[5]

Contemporary observers were well aware of the exemplary function of the court case: 'This trial is about whether it will continue to be possible to write history in Germany, a country famous for its scholarship.'[6] Badenese courts sentenced Gervinus to imprisonment at a first hearing, but subsequently quashed the verdict on formal grounds. Gervinus was never acquitted, however, and his licence to teach at a university was revoked.

The limitations on university history could hardly have been more clearly shown. A chair of revolutionary history, such as that held by Alphonse Aulard at the Sorbonne in Paris from 1886 onwards, would have been inconceivable under the conditions in German universities in the second half of the century. The prevailing tenor of national historiography was German unity. The revolution as an independent theme remained a delicate subject until the early *Kaiserzeit*, especially since the Kaiser himself, as Prince William, had held the military supreme command when the campaign for the Imperial Constitution was put down in the summer of 1849.

Those authors who freed the revolution from its reduction to a middle-class national basis, and who sought to grasp its underlying economic and social causes, did so not from an academic post, but from exile. They included Friedrich Engels, who published a series of articles on 'Revolution and Counterrevolution in Germany' in the *New York Daily Tribune* between August 1851 and September 1852.[7]

Others, such as the historian and titular professor, Wilhelm Zimmermann, paid with their removal from office. In 1848 Zimmermann published an analysis of the revolution as a visible sign of the emancipatory process.[8] In 1851 he lost his post at the Stuttgart *Oberrealschule*.

Just as the political movement split into parties in 1848, so too did the historical assessment of the revolution – both initially and in the long term. This was highlighted with particular clarity during the celebrations to mark its fiftieth anniversary in 1898. In the *Reichstag* debate of 18 March 1898, emotions ran high when the Berlin barricade battles of March 1848 were discussed. In response to the barricaders' supporters from the ranks of the Social Democrats (Bebel) and from the South German *Volkspartei*, the National Liberal party whip, Rudolf von Bennigsen, objected that 18 March 1848 had been 'no more than a highly embarrassing episode' in the national movement of that year. Preferring to call to mind the Frankfurt National Assembly and the 'finest forces of the entire nation' who had met there, he led into an official letter of thanks to Bismarck for completing the unification of the *Reich*.[9] The Paulskirche was played off against the actual revolution. In contrast, popular Liberal Democratic analyses (Hugo Preuß) and works by the Social Democrats Wilhelm Blos, Eduard Bernstein and Franz Mehring, preferred to focus on barricade battles and uprisings.[10] Blos, for example, sold more than 45,000 copies of his book.

New trends in the academic study of history emerged only slowly. In the context of the anniversary, Hermann Oncken demanded that 'the conflicts between convictions prejudiced by party-politics be resolved and a higher level of understanding be achieved'.[11] In practice, however, this plea was hard to follow. Historians became embroiled in the issue of the role of the Prussian King Frederick William IV, in his feelings and motivations in refusing the imperial crown. Yet, stimulated by Erich Marcks, Friedrich Meinecke and Erich Brandenburg, a number of works were written, dissertations in particular, which re-examined the events of the revolution, for the first time reconstructing it from an historical point of view. Historians of a younger generation, including Veit Valentin and Ludwig Bergsträßer, continued this work, accompanied by countless analyses of personal, local, territorial and cultural history.

With the revolution of 1918, that of 1848 acquired a new currency. And yet the leading German historians of the Weimar period continued to pursue the same lines: foreign policy and nation-state perspectives still overshadowed those of domestic and social politics.

The Paulskirche obscured the events of the revolution as a whole, and the distinction between the *realpolitik* of state power and inadequate idealistic professors' politics persisted.[12]

If, after 1918, historians still reflected on the 'ideas of 1848' with constitutional political aims, the ideas had acquired a new status. Ernst Troeltsch diagnosed a change in function in assessments of the revolution:

> Only the very short sighted could triumph and assert that the aim of 1848 had now been achieved. Indeed, what had been a brave attempt at progress in 1848 was now regarded as a conservative retardation, a way of dealing with the revolution and securing the legal activity of the opponents of the revolution, as well as their increasing influence.[13]

What is still regarded as the standard history of the German revolution of 1848–9 was published by Veit Valentin, who was regarded as an outsider, and who lost his licence to teach in 1917 in a pan-German university conspiracy against him.[14] His work was based on the analysis of vast quantities of source material, but was objected to by Valentin's fellow historians on the grounds that it was biased towards the parliamentarianism of the Weimar constitution.

When the National Socialists seized power, a number of promising perspectives were lost: the change in the way historians treated the revolution initiated by Valentin; the subsequent attempts to integrate intellectual, political and social history and to establish links with the economy, both of which were demonstrated by Hans Rosenberg[15]; and the early socio-historical research into the associations of the *Vormärz* (or pre-March revolution)[16] period.[17] Advocates of such approaches were forced to emigrate, and after 1945 historians initially proceeded as if these approaches had never existed.

This was demonstrated above all in the anniversary celebrations of 1948, which gave rise to a flood of commemorative writings on the subject.[18] The emphasis was now placed on the battle of the 'forty-eighters' for the freedom of the middle classes, with the Frankfurt National Assembly constituting the focus of analyses. Friedrich Meinecke, Otto Vossler and Hans Rothfels concentrated on the development and preservation of political ideas. Only Rudolf Stadelmann focused on the revolution as the culmination of an extensive social and economic process of change, which mobilized all sections of the population[19]: however, initially, this approach was almost completely ignored.

The emergence of two competing political systems on German soil brought about a completely new situation, which also created a split in German historiography. But there was one aspect of the analysis of the revolution in which historians from East and West behaved as one: each side sought positive points of departure on which it could build its own traditions. This gave rise to the 'battle for the legacy' of 1848,[20] in which the GDR secured an early lead, since its efforts were focused on the beginnings of the labour movement, the role of Marx and Engels in revolutionary events and the actions of 'the people'. This early interest in the people, defined here as the lower, sub-middle class orders, was published in the form of a widely disseminated collection of pamphlets.[21] Until 1975, historical studies in the GDR followed a 'central research plan', which exploited the revolution for contemporary politics. The *Illustrated History of the German Revolution of 1848–9*, an edition marking the revolution's 125th anniversary, rehearsed this for a wider public. It ends with the words:

> The revolution of 1848–9 remains an indisputable element in the revolutionary tradition of the German Democratic Republic. The achievements of the socialist German state also have their roots in the battles and endeavours of the revolutionary masses of 1848. Their ideals were translated into action by that class which 125 years ago was taking the first tentative steps in its own movement – the working class – and it is clear to all that this class is the one true heir of 1848.[22]

In the Federal Republic the state does not prescribe guidelines for historical research with which scholars are forced to comply. And yet it would certainly not be true to say that the need to find points of reference for the present day in historical traditions has never existed there. How else would the 'battle for the legacy' of 1848 have been possible? When the then Federal President Gustav Heinemann demanded that the liberation movements in German history be accorded the attention they deserved, he encountered a lively response from the public, although it was mixed with a degree of criticism. He was referring to 1848 in particular, and one of his final acts of office was officially to open the 'Memorial for the Liberation Movements in German History' in Rastatt, a project which he himself had initiated. In his opening address he warned:

> Revolutionary traditions are consciously fostered in the GDR, and many books and numerous events are devoted to them. But these

traditions are steadily changed until they become the oppressive Communist state. It is intolerable that inaction on our part should encourage this to occur, and that we should allow part of our history to be stolen from us. We compete with the other German state for a better ordering of public affairs, of freedom and of justice. Bound into this is the issue of who has the greater right to refer back to the liberation movements in German history, and who has been or will be more successful in achieving their aims.[23]

As is documented by the very choice of Rastatt as the site of this speech, Heinemann was referring in particular to those who were defeated in 1848, and they included those who fought on the barricades and in the volunteer corps: Rastatt was the last bastion of the revolution in July 1849 during the resistance to the victorious Prussian troops. As early as 1931, referring to the end of the revolution, Veit Valentin had written, 'Present-day Germany has stopped mocking the defeated. Yet fairness towards both parties in the sorry civil war for the imperial constitution of 1849 is still no easy task, even today.'[24]

This was not exactly what Heinemann wanted. However, the extent to which the most recent historians have also experienced problems with the issue of 'fairness' is shown even in Karl-Georg Faber's balanced, factual and scholarly analysis of 1979. Difficulties arise in the perspective he adopts, for despite his attempts to remain objective, the value judgements of the governments' to side constantly creep in. He refers, for example, to the 'ring-leaders' of the Palatinate revolution, or describes the Badenese Oberland as being 'purged of units of insurgents'. Elsewhere, the April revolution of 1848, defeated by the army and avenged in more than 3000 trials, is qualified as an 'attempted putsch'. A position deviating from the 'centre' towards anti-constitutionalist royalism is described as 'conservative' or 'highly conservative', yet the adoption of a position in favour of parliamentary democracy and a social republic is characterized as 'extreme' or 'radical'. Elsewhere still, the revolution may be termed a revolution, but soldiers who decided to support the revolution are described as 'mutinous', while coups and infringements of the law on the part of the governments are presented as 'the re-establishment of peace and order'.[25]

Taking social movements as their subject, social historians have brought many new and important ideas to light in their research into the revolution, although of course, as always, social history continues to adhere to detailed analyses of personal, local, territorial and constitutional history.[26] The early 1960s saw a fundamental shift in the direction of social history. Werner Conze and the 'working group for modern social history' took *Vormärz* society as their theme. The circle's first two publications in 1962 pointed the way forward.[27] The intensive analysis of Anglo-Saxon and American historiography, the rediscovery of the works of Hans Rosenberg,[28] and the associated reception of new social scientific issues and methods, all provided the impetus to get to grips with the German revolution once more, both in its own context and in that of Europe. They continue to the present day, as testified by the current lively interest in the 'rebellious century' (C. Tilly), and the socio-historical research into protest movements which has emerged from it. Finally, the focus on the narrowly circumscribed 'world' of historical 'everyday life' has also turned historians' attention to regional revolutionary history.[29]

The research into the revolution which has taken place over the last 25 years has brought so much new knowledge to light that the work of the 'builders of tradition' (D. Langewiesche) has become ever harder.[30] The image of *the* revolution has dissolved, as has the concept of *the* middle classes, *the* workers and *the* liberals. Even GDR historians finally began to differentiate their traditionally neat 'concept of the bourgeoisie'.[31] The politicized society of the mid-century and its, to some extent, conflicting endeavours proved to be unexpectedly complex after all; too complex to allow conclusive identifications to be made.

It is because of this very complexity that social scientific attempts have as yet failed to develop a temporally broadly conceived theory of revolution from which fundamental insights into the European movements of 1848 might be drawn.[32]

On the other hand, the controversies surrounding the features, trends and structures of the 'modernization' of Europe since the end of the eighteenth century have made a major contribution to our understanding of the revolution of 1848-9. They have freed it from the perspective of national isolation and have placed it in the context of a common European process of transformation. At its centre was the transition from the agrarian to the industrial economy, from pauperism to proletariat, from a society based on the *Ständeordnung* or system of estates to one which was based on class. Its integral features were mobilization, political emancipation and participation, the growth of the parliamentary system, increasing bureaucratic activity on the part of the state, and the division of society into political parties and mutually antagonistic pressure groups and associations. What for decades had been constrained by the so-called 'Metternich System' established a strong position in March 1848; the revolution may have broken out spontaneously and in an unplanned fashion, but it was certainly no accident. It affected all sectors of the population, but only very few people – including Gervinus and Marx, though their approaches were very different – succeeded in gaining a deeper insight into the development of 'middle-class society'. 'The mobility of property, equal distribution of inheritance, common schools and improvements in transport all brought the *Stände* closer together.'[33] These were indices of modernization and it was this unavoidable, enforced *rapprochement* that bred new conflicts, which both fostered and split the revolution.

To do justice to all the events of 1848, it is necessary to examine it from many different perspectives. One has to examine the contradictory forms of collective protest, the tensions in the social, agrarian and commercial spheres, the nature of the crisis cycles of the *Vormärz* period, the different stages of development in individual German territories and the regional centres of industrialization and politicization.

It is against this backdrop that the 'failure' of the revolution is put into perspective: it becomes comprehensible as an irreversible process of modernization which continues to the present day. Where and how far this took place is the subject of this analysis; but not at the price of trivially mapping out courses of action or reaffirming our own position, for which history would have to place its own arsenal at our disposal: the time has passed for one-track approaches of that kind. It is not simply that historical methods demand this; it is also necessary because of the fairness referred to above, which calls for impartiality, but also insists that we recognize 'not lessons for today, but above all the problems that caused the revolutionaries to fail at the time'.[34] We will not attempt to identify simplistic points of reference on which we can build traditions.

Part I
Structures and Crises

1 German Society before 1848

The entire population was gripped by the German revolution of 1848–9. To a far greater extent than the Peasant Wars of the early modern age, for example, or the Wars of Liberation of 1813–14, it affected the population on a national scale, from the smallest village community to the heart of the country. Rulers were presented with an image of the March revolution's unity, uniformity and dynamism, and yet the facade of a common oppositional front hid an alliance of profoundly contradictory and sometimes incompatible social conflicts. The following analysis of pre-revolutionary German society attempts to examine in detail the problems and interests peculiar to individual social classes, and investigates the opportunities for political influence and forms of protest open to them.

The Aristocracy

The aristocracy was the privileged, pre-eminent political class and was portrayed as such in critical journalism. The word 'aristocracy' was employed as a polemical term by the German Jacobins of the turn of the century and by the democrats and socialists of the *Vormärz* period. Even exponents of liberalism, such as the Freiburg political scientist Karl von Rotteck, made use of the 'ideological two-party dichotomy':[1] an enlightened revolutionary democratic stance (without the aristocracy) on the one hand, against a restorative alliance of church and aristocracy on the other. The middle class, which itself was far from homogeneous, defined itself in political terms in opposition to the aristocracy. It was not by chance that the Frankfurt National Assembly debate on the 'abolition of the aristocracy' so

13

inflamed the passions and sensibilities of the middle classes: 'aristoc-racy' and 'privilege' were regarded as two facets of the same deplor-able state of affairs in society and represented the most prominent target in the fight for the equality of all citizens.

Although the 'aristocracy' was perceived in this light by political writers, in reality it was made up of a number of different social groups, and was not without inner contradictions. The following classes of aristocrats may be identified:

* the *Hochadel*, the high nobility, with the ruling princes and the *Standesherren* or mediatized princes;
* the aristocracy of the courts and those whose title derived from being in the King's service (*Hof- und Dienstadel*);
* those aristocrats who before 1803 had been self-governing, and the freeholding, landowning aristocracy – the minor aristoc-racy or *Kleinadel*;
* the aristocracy of the towns: the urban patriciate.

The Hochadel

Generally speaking, the ruling princes remained unchallenged in the *Vormärz* discussions, although the conduct of adulterous liaisons, notably by the Hesse Elector William II with Countess Reichen-bach, and above all by the Bavarian King Ludwig I with Countess Landsfeld, the dancer Lola Montez, provoked great criticism. In February 1848 moral outrage came to a head in Munich in a state crisis and outbreaks of rioting, although one should not overlook the importance in these events of the deep-seated 'knife and fork interests' (Valentin) of those inhabitants of Munich who had been deprived of their student boarders following the closure of the univer-sity. Standards of middle-class respectability combined with general condemnation of corruption, maladministration, wastefulness and despotism to form a dangerous mix. Nevertheless, such situations were exceptional before 1848.

The position of the *Standesherren* or mediatized princes was rather more problematic. These were the approximately 80 families of princes and counts who had enjoyed *Reichsstandschaft* in the old Empire before 1806; that is to say, they had been autonomous rulers under the Kaiser, represented in the *Reichstag*. Article 14 of the German Federal Act of 1815 ranked these 'mediatized princes' as the 'most privileged class' in the state.[2] Not only did this entitle them to privileges which, by virtue of their ownership of the manors or estates, were theirs for the taking anyway, but it also accorded them important additional political privileges, such as jurisdiction over the higher and lower courts and a seat and a vote in the Upper Chambers of the provincial diets.

These mediatized princes interposed themselves between the sovereign and the general population of the state as intermediate powers with their own bureaucracy. The social position of their mainly peasant subjects was often worse than that of others, since they owed taxes and services to two masters. The stuff of social conflict accumulated in these areas and was ignited during the March revolution, notably in Hesse-Darmstadt, Baden, Württemberg and Bavaria, where there were large numbers of mediatized princes. The only mediatized principality in central Germany was the Duchy of Schönberg, with Waldenburg castle at Glauchau, which was set alight in 1848.

Two of the most prominent *Standesherren* were Prince Ludwig von Öttingen-Wallerstein, Bavarian Foreign Minister until 1848, and Prince Karl von Leiningen, the first Minister President of the revolutionary Provisional Central Power of 1848. There was also an older group of higher aristocrats which had been subsumed under the category of mediatized princes. For the most part they hailed from Austria, Saxony, Upper and Lower Lausitz and from Silesia. All these areas later contained centres of the agrarian revolutionary movement.

The Hof- und Dienstadel

The aristocrats of the courts, the administrations and the army formed a separate 'caste', which formed a barrier to the middle classes' attempts to gain equal access to public office. It was at the centre of royal power, forming its diplomatic, governmental, bureaucratic and military pillars. This group of aristocrats formed the core of the counter-revolution, of 'the reaction', as it was perceived by the middle classes. In Prussia it gained considerable influence through the trusted circle of advisors and friends surrounding King Frederick William IV, a group which referred to itself as a 'camarilla'. The brothers Leopold and Ernst Ludwig von Gerlach were two of its leading lights, as was the philosopher of the state Friedrich Julius Stahl. This circle formed 'the pinnacle of a political party which was not organized, but was no less aware of itself as such for that'.[3]

The Kleinadel

The broad mass of the aristocracy was made up of the freeholding, landowning aristocracy and the former self-governing aristocrats under the Kaiser: the minor dukes and imperial knights. Of this group the lords of the manor, also known as *Junker* in Prussia, rose to prominence in the manorial estate regions of Mecklenburg, Pomerania, Brandenburg, Saxony, Silesia, Bohemia and Moravia.

The position of the manor- and estate-owning aristocracy was closely linked to the fundamental changes taking place in agriculture; the shift from feudal rule to the capitalist order, with its focus on the market and on cash values. The social consequences of these agrarian reforms will be examined in greater detail below in the context of the position of the peasants. But one thing should be made clear at the outset: there can be no doubt that the real winners of the 'liberation of the peasants' were the aristocrats. When these radical changes were introduced, aristocrats, in contrast to the peasants, were granted credit aid by the state, as occurred in Prussia, for example. What they lost in political control, they gained in economic power.[4] Peasant liberty had to be bought; that is to say, compensation was demanded for the loss of their services and their taxes. Indeed, in many cases it took several generations before these dues were finally paid off. Regardless of the extent to which the agrarian reforms were carried out in reality, and not just on paper, local police power and patrimonial justice remained firmly in the hands of the estate owner or lord of the manor. In almost every German state he remained the decisive authority in the village.

In those regions where particularly oppressive feudal taxes and services remained in force, where the peasants had to pay twice – once to the state and once to the landowner – calls for 'feudal burdens' to be lifted grew particularly insistent during the March revolution.

A small group of aristocrats broke through the isolation more typical of their class, seizing the chance to co-operate with the middle classes in an attempt to carry through or to develop constitutionalism. A number of these aristocratic exponents of constitutionalism became Paulskirche deputies during the revolution. They included the East Prussian landowner, Ernst Friedrich von Saucken-Tarputschen, the Rhenish landowner, Carl von Stedtmann, and the most famous of this group, the Hessian landowner and chairman of the Rhine-Hesse Agricultural Association, Heinrich von Gagern.

As early as 1840, at a diet to pay homage to Frederick William IV, the East Prussian Supreme Administrator (*Oberpräsident*), Theodor von Schön demanded the universal representation which had so often been promised. In 1845 Georg Freiherr von Vincke, son of a Prussian Supreme Administrator, formed a coalition with the middle classes in the Westphalian provincial diet which rejected government proposals.

In the absence of middle-class representation, a constitutionalist aristocratic party had been developing in the Austrian *Ständeversammlungen* since the 1830s, particularly in the Bohemian and in the Lower and Upper Austrian diets. It temporarily took the initiative during the March revolution. Its prominent spokesmen included Freiherr Anton von Doblhoff, a later Austrian *Märzminister* or March minister, and Anton Ritter von Schmerling, the second Minister President of 1848 after von Leiningen, referred to above.

A similar process of *rapprochement*, though in the opposite direction, can be identified amongst those members of the middle classes who bought into manors and attempted to win the same class-based and economic privileges as the aristocracy, though with no intention of forming constitutionalist alliances with them.[5] The assimilation of the standards and interests of the aristocracy was also apparent amongst some members of the *Bildungsbürgertum* or educated middle classes. During the revolution this would become an important factor in the policies of the March ministries and the formation of parliamentary factions.

The Middle Classes

A social history of the German *Bürgertum* or middle classes of the nineteenth century has not yet been written. This is all the more surprising, given that this era is often characterized in terms of the 'breakthrough of the middle classes' (E. Weis). Yet any attempt to analyse the social structure of the middle classes in more detail brings us up against still-unresolved problems regarding the social composition of this class as a whole. The negative demarcation from the nobility, referred to above, remains the easiest course. Taking into account the principal players of 1848–9 and the zones of conflict which emerged during the revolution, we distinguish here between:

- the commercial middle class (the 'bourgeoisie');
- civil servants and the educated middle class employed by the state;
- the freelance intelligentsia;
- and the lower middle classes or *Kleinbürgertum*.

The Commercial Middle Class

In contrast to France and England, the commercial class[6] in Germany was extremely small. Some of its members came from the old manufactories and wholesale trades of the traditional merchant towns; others from the emerging heavy industries. The new 'moneyed patriciate' (Valentin) was comprised of shipping and commission agents, wholesalers, factory owners and bankers. A well-informed contemporary identified 12 centres of commerce and emerging industry:[7] (1) Lower Austria, with Vienna at its centre; (2) Silesia; (3) Bohemia; (4) Lausitz, with Zittau and Görlitz; (5) Upper Saxony, with Chemnitz and Plauen; (6) Franconia, with centres in Nuremberg, Fürth, Bamberg, Bayreuth, Schweinfurt and Würzburg; (7) Southern Thuringia; (8) the south-eastern Harz region; (9) Westphalia and the Lower Rhine, 'where the greatest expansion in German industrial life is to be found in the Wupper and Rhine regions'; (10) the Lower Rhine area around Krefeld and Aachen; (11) the Central Rhine region with Heidelberg and Frankfurt; and, finally, (12) the Swabian Upper Rhine region. Added to these were individual towns such as Augsburg, Munich, Leipzig, Magdeburg, Berlin, Hamburg, Bremen and Stettin. Areas of commercial concentration and early industrialization came to the fore in 1848, since more densely populated regions provided more favourable conditions for the revolution.

The traditional industries had developed from the trades of the towns. They processed agricultural products, expanding as the population grew. They included linen and wool manufacturers, distilleries, breweries, oil mills and tobacco factories. The real modernizing thrust for industrialization came from those areas where coal and iron mining were combined with mechanical engineering. The word to conjure with here was the railway.

It was as a result of its involvement in these industries that the commercial middle class of the Rhineland–Westphalian region became particularly powerful, and this was accomplished on a political level in the provincial diets of the region. This new combination of commerce and politics was practised by the textile merchant, David Hansemann, a future Prussian March minister. As a partner in the Rhenish Railway Company, founded in 1837, he worked with its president, the industrialist's son, Gustav von Mevissen. Von Mevissen later took a seat in the Paulskirche. The banker, Ludolf Camphausen, President of the Cologne Chamber of Commerce, was involved in the development of the Rhenish rail network and in steam navigation: in March 1848 he became Prussian Minister President. Friedrich Harkort, the owner of iron and copper rolling mills in the Duchy of Mark, became the spokesman of the faction of the Berlin National Assembly named after him. The Krefeld merchant and banker, Hermann von Beckerath, joined the Provisional Central Power of 1848 as Finance Minister, and von Mevissen became Under-Secretary of State in the Trade Ministry, while the South German publisher Friedrich Bassermann, became Under-Secretary of State in the Ministry of the Interior.

These examples highlight the way in which the commercial middle class was pressing to gain political power. In doing so it established relations with officials in the upper echelons of the state bureaucracy and with the constitutionalist aristocratic opposition. Its sociopolitical model demanded the unleashing and mobilization of commercial vitality through free trade, freedom of enterprise and of residence.

Increasing economic expansion also had an impact on state organization. Prussia, economically the strongest state in the *Zollverein* or German Customs Union and in the German Confederation, remained without a comprehensive state constitution until 1848. By the 1840s the pressure to dismantle trade restrictions had become a constitutional issue, as is revealed in the events surrounding the planned rail link between Berlin and Königsberg. The Prussian state was not in a position to finance the project without borrowing money. Under the state debt law of 17 January 1820, however, new loans could only be raised by the state if a co-guarantee was obtained from the *Reichsstände* or General Estates. Rigorous fiscal savings policies had helped avoid this until now, but by the 1840s it had become clear that such policies were hampering the economic development of the state. Finally, on 3 February 1847, Frederick William IV was forced to convene the United Diet. This comprised all 613 members of the eight provincial diets, half of whom were knights and lords of the manor (307) and the other half deputies from the '*bürgerlich* class' of the local towns and the country (306). In contrast to the chambers of the medium-sized states, deputies from the educated middle classes were poorly represented here, although the commercial middle class was represented by spokesmen such as von Beckerath, Camphausen, Hansemann and von Mevissen. The United Diet was officially opened by Frederick William IV on 11 April 1847. The Rhenish commercial middle class and the constitutionalist East Prussian aristocracy, with its interests in grain export, formed a coalition for the purpose of the railway project. At the same time they attempted to push through the Diet as a permanent institution. When it encountered government resistance to the idea of regular meetings, the Diet rejected the *Ostbahn* loan by a two-thirds majority. The King responded by halting work on the railway, laying off some 8000 railway workers. This intensified social tensions in the crisis year of 1847. On the other hand, the fact that Prussia was on the path to a constitutional state raised hopes that a new era in the history of Germany as a whole was in sight.

The Civil Servants and Educated Middle Classes Employed by the State

The civil servants and educated middle classes employed by the state profited from the attempts made in most German states at the beginning of the nineteenth century to modernize and to reform.[8] The majority of states ruled by princes or monarchs accomplished the transition from an association of subjects to a society of citizens with the help of bureaucrats. Territorial gains made as a result of the dissolution of the Old Empire meant that most central and southern states now contained a politically, denominationally and socially heterogeneous population within their new borders. In its attempts to modernize, the state typically made less use of the aristocracy to integrate these people, and instead opened to the emerging middle classes a sphere of activity and professional opportunity in the growing, rationalized regional bureaucracies. Organized judicial systems, a growth in administrative tasks and the expansion of the military, university and education sectors increased the weight of the middle classes in the administrations, driving back the aristocracy, and forcing it into a position of competitor and object of middle-class criticism.

Since the 1820s an 'aristocratic rebuttal' (W. Conze) had hampered middle-class attempts to penetrate the state administration.[9] In Prussia in particular, the proportion of aristocrats in central authorities, in the provinces, in regional administrations and in the districts had risen. In 1820, for example, the aristocracy had held 40 per cent of all posts in Prussian provincial administration (including the *Landräte*). By the mid-1840s this figure had risen to half. The same applied to Austria, though not to the southern German states. This aristocratic restoration in the sphere of employment coincided both with cuts in public sector posts, which had begun in the 1820s, and the larger numbers of candidates for posts overall, which came as a result of population growth. Combined with the numbers of fully qualified trainees still waiting for official posts, they formed a dangerous potential for protest. *Privatdozente* such as Arnold Ruge or Karl Nauwerck became radical critics of the system. *Privatdozente* had been leading members of the revolutionary uprising in 1830 in Göttingen too. Owing to limited state funding, trainees in Austria had been obliged since 1814 to serve at least 2 to 3 years without remuneration, and as many as 5 to 7 years in those posts which led to the so-called *Konzeptsfach*. In the period between 1814 and 1848, the numbers of trainees increased three- or fourfold, while the numbers of posts remained unchanged. Candidates for official posts would soon have to wait for between 10 and 12 years after completion of their legal studies. There were even cases of trainees waiting for 17 years for a paid position.[10] In Bavaria in 1841 there were more than 200 aspiring officials still waiting for a position after an 11-year period of preparation.[11] Not surprisingly, this situation had a disciplining effect on established post-holders.

The expansion of early constitutionalism gave the educated middle classes and civil servants the opportunity to become politically active in the chambers of the *Landstände*. By 1841 a total of 25 federal states had become constitutional states. The chambers were clearly dominated by local government officers and civil servants, who comprised more than half of their representatives. In Württemberg, for example, during all six electoral periods between 1820 and 1848, civil servants (including senior teachers and professors) made up at least two-thirds of all representatives. During one period this figure rose as high as 85 per cent (see Table 1).

Unlike the self-confident, independent commercial middle class, most of the representatives in these chambers were dependent on the state for their employment, and so would hardly have been in a position to form 'an avant-garde in the struggle for a socially mobile meritocracy and political self-government'.[12]

And yet these chambers were not entirely submissive tools of the governments. Indeed, they frequently fought for the extension of

Table 1 Composition of the Württemberg second chamber, 1820–49

Professions	Election periods (figures in percentages)						
	1 *1820–4*	*2* *1826–30*	*3* *1833*	*4* *1833–38*	*5* *1839–43*	*6* *1845–8*	*7* *1848–9*
Civil servants	42.5	56	32.4	38.8	55.3	48.2	28.1
Local govt officers	25.3	21.2	24.3	27.8	29.4	20.6	17
Merchants, manufacturers, bankers	12.6	9.2	5.4	4.7	4.7	8.4	12.7
Lawyers, notaries	5.7	6.6	9.4	7.1	2.3	8.4	17
Other academics, without state posts	–	1.4	6	5.9	2.3	1.2	5.6
Clergy	–	–	2.6	–	–	2.4	4.2
Senior primary teachers, professors	1.2	–	9.4	7.1	3.6	6	8.4
Landowners, tenant farmers	3.5	–	1.3	2.3	1.2	1.2	2.8
Middle Classes	**90.8**	**94.4**	**90.8**	**93.7**	**98.8**	**96.4**	**95.8**
Peasants	2.3	1.4	1.3	1	–	1.2	–
Innkeepers, coaching inn keepers	4.5	1.4	4	2.3	–	1.2	2.8
Craftsmen	–	1.4	2.6	1	–	–	1.4
Elementary teachers	1.2	–	–	–	–	–	–
Lower middle classes	**8**	**4.2**	**7.9**	**4.3**	**–**	**2.4**	**4.2**
Officers (retd)	1.2	1.4	1.3	1	1.2	–	–
No profession given	–	–	–	1	–	1.2	–
Total	**100**	**100**	**100**	**100**	**100**	**100**	**100**

Source: D. Langewiesche, *Liberalismus und Demokratie in Württemberg zwischen Revolution und Reichsgründung* (Düsseldorf, 1974), p. 73.

suffrage and for the power to approve taxes and to formulate legislation. The administrative and legal civil servants represented on them often became the most dangerous critics of the business of government, since their positions allowed them profound insight into the way the states operated as they modernized themselves.

In criticizing the governments, however, they risked their jobs, and those that lost them were generally exponents of constitutionalist, not to say parliamentary and democratic liberalism. Prominent victims of oppositional 'chamber liberalism' of this kind, who either lost their posts or had their licences to teach revoked, included the Würzburg professor of constitutional law Wilhelm Joseph Behr, and the Freiburg professors Karl Theodor Welcker and Karl von Rotteck. Others were forced to resign by the threat of a disciplinary transfer. They included the Tübingen professor of constitutional law Robert (von) Mohl, whose licence to teach was withdrawn, or the Mannheim *Hofgerichtsrat* Johann Adam von Itzstein. The Tübingen Professor of German Literature Ludwig Uhland left state employment when the government denied him leave to take up his seat as deputy. With the exception of Rotteck, who died in 1840, all these men were later elected to the Frankfurt National Assembly.

Their work in the chambers taught the middle-class representatives how to deal with the governments on a political level. After years of being ready to make concessions and compromises, many of them gave rapid consent to 'the conclusion of the revolution' in 1848. Proximity to state power had taught the deputies all about its disciplinary methods: the denial of leave to elected officials; the influencing of elections; the dissolution of insubordinate chambers; threats of removal from office or early retirement. They became adept at treading the fine line between constitutionally decreed compromise and fundamental opposition.

This was the technical side of the learning process of life as a chamber official. But there was a substantive side too. All the central demands made by the March revolutionaries (the *Märzforderungen*), had been heard in the chambers since their establishment: freedom of the press, trial by jury, public administration of justice, and the freedom to form associations were some of the recurring themes. In these matters, and in the personal contact between deputies from various states, the chambers bridged political and regional divides. This pre-revolutionary activity culminated in two events: the foundation on 1 July 1847 of the Heidelberg *Deutsche Zeitung*, which later became the central organ of the constitutionalist liberals of the revolutionary period; and the first *Heppenheim Meeting* on 10 October 1847, where deputies from the chambers of the southern German states and the Rhineland met and agreed a national programme: the creation of a German federal state; the guarantee of liberal principles based on the rule of law; and 'measures to combat impoverishment and need'.[13] The liberal middle classes had a programme of demands ready and waiting, even before the revolution broke out.

The Freelance Middle-Class Intelligentsia

Long before 1848, during the July revolution of 1830, a clear split had developed within the politically active middle class. Senior state civil servants, usually educated to university level, had begun to distance themselves from those academics who were not employed by the state: the freelance intelligentsia.[14] The latter group included writers and poets, such as Heinrich Heine, Ludwig Börne, Ferdinand Freiligrath, Georg Herwegh and August Heinrich Hoffmann von Fallersleben, journalists and editors, including Johann Georg August Wirth, Philipp Jakob Siebenpfeiffer, Julius Fröbel and Karl Marx, and lawyers, the most prominent of whom were Friedrich Hecker and Gustav von Struve. It also included doctors such as the Königsberg democrat, Johann Jacoby, the Cologne members of the 'Communist League', Andreas Gottschalk and Karl d'Ester, and the socialist, Otto Lüning, from Rheda in Westphalia. And finally, it included pharmacists and jobless and would-be academics, from the student to the *Privatdozent*.

The professional life of this middle-class intelligentsia was insecure, its ability to earn a living to some degree dependent on the growing literary market and the publishing industry. Riehl dubbed this group 'proletarians of intellectual activity', and also included among them candidates for the clergy, subaltern officials and above all teachers from the *Volksschulen* or elementary schools, who, unlike their higher-ranking colleagues in grammar schools and universities, had little to lose, but a great deal to gain.[15] Local government officers and *Volksschule* teachers did not enjoy security of tenure.

These political activists were acutely sensitive to the social plight of the 'manual working classes'. In the 1840s 'pauperism' and 'the proletariat' seemed to them to be the major issues of the day. In some cases their work as physicians, lawyers or pharmacists to the poor had given them direct experience of the deprivations suffered by the people. They joined extra-parliamentary political organizations in large numbers, maintaining a distance from the chambers. Following the Hambach Festival of 1832, for example, they had formed 'Press and Fatherland Associations'.[16] Rigorously enforced bans then compelled many groups to continue their political activity underground, including the circle around Georg Büchner and the clergyman Friedrich Ludwig Weidig, from Butzbach in Hesse. Others operated from political exile, principally from Switzerland, Brussels or, to take the example of Heine and Börne, members of 'Junges Deutschland', from Paris.

Wherever possible, this social group expressed itself in oppositional publications. Arnold Ruge first published his *Hallische Jahrbücher für deutsche Wissenschaft und Kunst* in 1838. Karl Marx wrote for the *Rheinische Zeitung für Handel und Gewerbe* from 1842 onwards. Journals and newspapers of this kind were always subject to censorship at short notice. To a far greater extent than the established civil servant and commercial middle class, this group sought links and unity of action with the lower orders, with shop assistants, journeymen, peasants and the lower middle classes.

The democrats proclaimed their programme of action at the *Offenburg Meeting* on 12 September 1847. Like the Heppenheim constitutionalists, they demanded the revocation of the repressive Federal Decrees of 1819 and 1831 to 1834, freedom of the press, of conscience and of association. They also called for equal suffrage, people's armies and 'the levelling out of the disparity between work and capital. Society is charged with the improvement and the protection of work.'[17] It was here that one section of the middle classes mapped out the revolutionary and democratic path, and already in the pre-revolutionary period exposed the tensions inherent in the constitutionalist liberals' programme. But it also showed its readiness consciously to regard the lower middle classes and the rural population as a mass base which might be mobilized in the future.

The Lower Middle Classes

The lower middle classes appeared even to contemporaries as a large, indistinct, shimmering mass. Marx and Engels also included members of the freelance intelligentsia in this group, as did the democratic minorities in the parliaments of 1848–9.[18] Given the socio-economic reality of the 1840s, we should include in this social category those 'who work on their own account with their own relatively modest means of production, and who employ no, or only very limited, paid labour':[19] that is to say, self-employed master craftsmen and shopkeepers. They formed the core of the traditional urban (lower) middle classes. They rarely looked beyond the walls of their own towns, and were barely represented in the legislatures. They were not 'available', for, unlike civil servants, they could not take leave of absence from their small businesses. But they did participate in politics at a local level; on the local district council,[20] where they defended traditional guild regulations and were reluctant to award newcomers domiciliary rights, which also included welfare provision in times of need. As a group they were concerned with protecting the municipality from the influx of impoverished journeymen, day labourers, rural workers: the lower orders, in other words.

Actions of this kind caused them to be regarded by critical, though ill-informed writers as *Biedermeier* 'philistines'. Yet one should not overlook the fact that this lower middle class group had been engaged in a basic struggle for survival during the two decades before the outbreak of the revolution, a struggle which had become increasingly bitter since the 1840s. Its earnings base was small, even at the best of times. It is possible to analyse in detail the economic position of the lower middle class in Baden, which became a focal point of the revolution on several occasions. The Badenese *Kontrollbüro der Zolldirektion* reported that in 1844 approximately 80 per cent of *self-employed people* subject to trade tax – the core of the lower middle class – operated without working capital. A further 11 per cent was exempt from trade tax, so that only 9 per cent overall had working capital to declare. Of these only 2.4 per cent paid tax on more than 1000 *Gulden*; roughly equal to the annual salary of a senior civil servant. Of the 60,560 self-employed *master craftsmen* whose details are recorded, 89 per cent had no working capital, and a further 5.9 per cent were exempt from trade tax altogether.[21]

In reality this meant that far in excess of half of all masters had to work without assistance. Technically their self-employment scarcely differed from that of a day labourer. Contemporary sources saw it in the same way. Because these craftsmen required part-time agricultural employment in order to make a living, they had strong links with the countryside. They were one-sidedly dependent on the local market, and their economic fate was directly linked to the agricultural economy. Food price rises and decreases in purchasing power had an immediate impact on their social position.

Population increases, which in Germany amounted to more than 50 per cent between 1815 and 1849, brought these craftsmen to the brink of catastrophe. Measured against the total population, there were above-average increases in the numbers of craftsmen, and the figures were higher amongst assistants than masters. The most detailed statistics for this period and, therefore, the example which must always be cited in preference to others, come from Prussia, where master craftsman positions increased by 53 per cent between 1816 and 1840 (rising from 259,000 to 396,000). Assistant's positions – journeymen and apprentices – increased by 93 per cent (from 145,000 to 280,000) against a population growth of only around 40 per cent.

Since the 1830s, the numbers of craftsmen in the towns and the countryside who were forced to live an overwhelmingly proletarian existence had also been gradually growing. Many craftsmen found themselves slipping into the proletariat, without consciously identifying with that class. This created a psychological potential for protest. By 1845 this pattern of decline had assumed almost crisis proportions.

The crisis was not linked to emerging industrialization, however. As the Marburg economist and future Paulskirche deputy, Bruno Hildebrand, observed to Friedrich Engels, poverty in Germany was, in fact, greatest in those areas which had no industry. Most commercial businesses in Upper Hesse around 1840, for example, had one journeyman for every two masters, and most master craftsmen there were to be regarded as proletarians.

The situation was aggravated by the liberalization of trade laws.[22] Freedom of enterprise made it easier to become a self-employed craftsman. Of course, this was a miserable existence, made worse by population growth and competition: as existing craftsmen found less work, individual jobs were devalued. Given the large numbers of journeymen who could no longer count on becoming masters, the division of masters and journeymen into two distinct classes was already apparent by 1848.

The socio-political expectations of this lower middle class were conservative. It was against freedom of enterprise, freedom of movement and industrial competition, but in favour of guild restrictions. Its model was a society of property-owners with moderate livelihoods. In terms of constitutional politics, it might be anything from democratic to radical, and could be activated as a revolutionary mass base. It seems reasonable to assume that, during the March revolution, the archetypal revolutionary, excluding the peasants for a moment, was not the poorest person, or the one who had come down in the world socially, but rather the member of the 'middle class' under threat of social demotion.

The Peasants

Before 1848 Germany was overwhelmingly a land of peasants. If we take the three major professional spheres, 60 per cent of the population of the territory covered by the German Confederation worked in agriculture, as against 25 per cent in commerce (in industry, mining or transport, or as craftsmen) and 15 per cent in the service sector (this also includes others, such as pensioners or the supported poor).[23] Small-town life was almost always closely linked to the countryside: small businesses were drawn to rural areas, since townsmen were forced to earn extra money from their smallholdings.

It is hard to define *the* peasantry, because of the countless regional and legal differences between them, and the fact that the extremely complex process of the 'liberation of the peasants' had reached different chronological and territorial stages, sometimes even within a single state. Indeed, as a rule, it had halted altogether, except in Prussia.[24] Nevertheless, we will attempt to define this population group according to regions of peace and conflict. In general it is true to say that the better the property rights, the larger the farms, the further the abolition of feudal and seigneurial relations or defeudalization had progressed, the less potential for conflict existed. Wherever intermediary powers such as mediatized princes or lords of the manor demanded services and levies alongside the sovereign, there was a good chance of agrarian uprisings. This is not simply deduced from our knowledge of the peasant uprisings which did occur in 1848, for certain regions had long traditions of peasant revolts. To some extent memories and patterns of behaviour dated back to the Peasant Wars of 1524–5.

We should look first at the *'Prussian model'*. Defeudalization was furthest advanced in the manorial estate regions of the Prussian East, although even here it varied from province to province. The agrarian edicts of 1807, 1811, 1816 and 1821 freed the agricultural world from its ties with the natural economy, placing it on the same footing as the moneyed economy with free work contracts. Following the discontinuation of peasant services, the manorial estates now offered permanent posts for waged workers. There had been waged labourers in the countryside since long before 1800; it was not that the reforms reintroduced them, but rather that they considerably increased their number. The *rural working class* was partly made up of small tenants who had to perform labour services, whose position had been weakened by the reforms. These people were now forced on to poorer land and were not entitled to credit aid. In the redistribution of common land they forfeited the usufruct which had often been vital for their survival, and, since they had no capital, they were forced to pay for their liberation with part of their land. At the end of the day, they could no longer compete economically and slipped into the lower class, dependent on wages. As K.-G. Faber has pointed out, there was a separation of 'an agricultural proletariat from the peasant middle class'.

There was a desire on the part of some day labourers and former small farmers to profit from the distribution of the demesnes and parish lands, or to secure a reappraisal of the distribution of common land, from which they had gone away empty-handed. This was seen in Pomerania and the Altmark, for example, where village mayors, peasants and even day labourers were elected to the Berlin National Assembly in 1848. In Regenwalde 52 day labourers elected a journeyman miller as their deputy when he promised to acquire ten *Morgen* of land for each of them.[25]

For the most part, however, rural workers remained royalist and peaceful. Their basic ethos was loyal and conservative. Even in the worst years of poverty and famine, they held on to their hard but secure livelihoods. They provided areas of calm against the storms of the revolution.

The *peasants of average means*, who were '*spannfähig*' (who had access to their own team of horses) had suffered some losses in the agrarian reforms. Yet in the areas east of the Elbe they found new opportunities to earn money in the cultivation of wasteland, more intensive farming and the clearing of meadows, and in the gains they made from the distribution of common land. Increasing productivity created an additional demand for workers. Indeed, the possibility of finding work drew many people to the east from the over-populated west. It was not bad harvests so much as excessively good ones that created problems for these farmers, for they could result in overproduction and sharp drops in the prices of agricultural produce. Price increases and speculation on the part of some farmers also created a social gulf between them and the agricultural working class.

Silesia held a special position. Because compensations had not been fully paid, *Latifundium*-like manors still demanded numerous feudal services. But here it was not the poorest, not the small farmers or the settlers with small properties, not the Silesian weavers who had risen up in 1844, but the better-off who became restless. 'Of all peasants, it was those who were rising both politically and socially'[26] who became active. Legal and psychological matters were more significant to them than economic issues. These peasants were capable of forming associations and co-operated with the urban middle-class democratic intelligentsia.

In the other German rural areas land was largely fully developed, and in some cases over-populated. Despite continuous rises, harvest production was unable to keep up with population growth in many areas. When the basis for survival was very small, harvest crises always had an immediate impact. The land could no longer feed younger sons and unmarried daughters. Here, what Marx described as the proletarianized 'industrial reserve army' grew. It was a reserve, it is true, but as yet there was no industry.

Large- and medium-sized farming concerns were able to withstand the crises. Wherever laws of inheritance insisted on property being passed on without division, conditions remained stable, as in Schleswig-Holstein, in north-west Germany from the Lower Rhine to Hanover, and in the Münsterland. In 1848 these regions sent to Frankfurt deputies whose own experience had convinced them of the blessings of property which could not be divided, and who fought passionately against the liberal doctrine of the right to divide property as one wished.

However, continuing obligations to the local lord of the manor in areas with such laws of inheritance could feed the readiness to revolt, as occurred in parts of Bavaria or Austria, where peasants still had to pay levies made up of tithes and manorial land obligations. Although feudal dues had almost always been exchanged for cash, it was this very issue that the peasants perceived as unjust. They demanded social reforms, by which they would be taxed by the sovereign, but not by the lord of the manor, the mediatized prince or the church.

This double rule assumed catastrophic proportions where continuing rule by a mediatized prince coincided with a *Realteilungsgebiet*, where a farmer's property was divided upon inheritance. These structurally weak areas were characterized by large numbers of small tenants obliged to perform labour services, a high density of rural population and an increase in members of the sub-peasant classes.

Realteilungsgebiete were concentrated in south-west Germany, in the Upper Rhine region, the Hohenlohe areas, in Franconia, the Eifel, Hunsrück and the Odenwald. They were also found in central Germany, most notably in Thuringia and Saxony. A weak subsistence base, high susceptibility to crises and, above all, feudal relics prepared the ground for a social and agrarian revolutionary mass movement, which emerged in 1848.

The 'Fourth Class'

The aristocracy, the middle classes, and the peasants – the three pillars of the traditional system of estates or *Ständeordnung* – were distinguished from the broad mass of the so-called underclass, which could in turn be subdivided into a number of different groups. This category included the *poor* of all descriptions: 'paupers', the '*ordo plebeius*' or 'rabble class', which had always existed, and which was regarded as a God-given, to some extent natural, group on the margins of the *Ständeordnung*.[27] It was the target of the church, of municipal welfare provision and of the sovereign's welfare police; it was made up of beggars, the sick, those incapable of working, vagrants and former serfs.

Included in this group were the 'manual working classes', who were bound into employee–employer relationships; one might call them 'workers' in the pre-industrial sense. Their common feature was a 'lack of independence'; a characteristic which would exclude them from the elections to the Frankfurt National Assembly in the spring of 1848. Lacking their own agricultural or commercial subsistence base, their survival depended on wages[28] and, since these were frequently inadequate, they also relied upon the extra income which women and children were forced to earn through occasional work. They were the major victims of 'mass poverty and famines' (W. Abel). Prussian statistics divided them into the groups shown in Table 2.

Many of these workers were angry at their loss of social status, which they perceived as unfair. Six broad groups may be defined, many of whom had just cause for social discontent.[29]

1. *Journeymen* worked in the overstaffed small craft businesses and had only limited prospects of rising to become independent masters themselves. They lived under threat of demotion to the proletariat, yet they belonged to the most highly politicized group of

Table 2 Men of the 'manual working classes' as a percentage of male inhabitants over 14 years of age, 1822–46

	1822	*1846*
Miners and salt workers	0.6	1.1
Factory workers	2.5	4.2
Commercial assistants and apprentices	8.8	11.6
Commercial and industrial professions	**11.9**	**16.9**
Servants, farmhands (of which 85% in agriculture)	12.6	11.4
Day labourers and manual workers (half of whom worked in agriculture, including railway and road workers, overwhelmingly rural underclass)	16.5	17.2
Primarily rural underclass in agriculture and unskilled day-labouring work	**29.1**	**28.6**
Total 'workers'	41.0	45.5

Source: W. Conze, 'Vom "Pöbel" zum "Proletariat"', in *VSWG*, 41 (1954), p. 348.

the underclasses. Their journeying, undertaken in accordance with the requirements of their guild, broadened their horizons far beyond the regions and small towns they came from. In France (Paris) and Switzerland they were introduced to early socialist theory. For years one of their number, the Magdeburg journeyman tailor, Wilhelm Weitling, was responsible for 'education and organization in the German journeyman and worker associations' in Paris and Switzerland.[30] These early workers' societies and strikes and protests were dominated by printers and typesetters, cigar workers, tailors and cobblers, joiners, cabinet-makers and bricklayers. The traditions of their profession had taught them solidarity and the power of common action. The freelance intelligentsia in exile outside Germany often joined these associations, providing them with conceptual support in the formulation of their programmes.

2. *Miners and iron and steel workers* still enjoyed special corporate rights, and their positions were not dissimilar to those of civil servants. The miner's guild provided them with social security and they seemed astonishingly immune to the onslaught of the revolution, as has been documented in the case of the miners of the Ruhr.[31]

3. *Wage earners and outworkers* worked on their own account, yet were dependent on an employer: the distributor and merchant. In terms of formal status, however, they were usually defined as masters (*Lohnmeister*). Most were employed in the textile and ironware industries and in hand-weaving. They, too, faced social relegation, population pressures having forced too many of them into increasingly unprofitable work. This resulted in a process typical of the *Vormärz* period: the surplus in workers was not translated into unemployment, but instead led to the devaluation of all jobs. More hands had to work for the same wage. Wages fell, working days lengthened, and child labour increased.

The growing pre-industrial crisis in the industries employing outworkers reached a bloody climax in the Silesian weavers' uprising against their factory and commercial bosses in June 1844. And yet in this of all industries, manual labour was replaced by machinery only very gradually, owing to the complex technical problems associated with mechanized weaving. In 1846 the cotton industry in the area covered by the German *Zollverein* had at its disposal a mere 2628 mechanical looms, as against 116,832 manual looms.

4. *Factory workers* were qualified workers. Frequently recruited from the ranks of former journeymen, outworkers or masters, they corresponded most closely to the modern image of the 'worker',[32] and might be compared to the French '*ouvrier*'. Their material existence seemed relatively secure, yet they had to work under legally uncertain industrial regulations, without provision for sickness or invalidity. They represented only a small proportion of workers. In 1846 in Prussia, as Table 2 indicates, they were estimated at only 4.2 per cent.

5. *Manual workers* or *day labourers* formed the bulk of the 'manual working class'; in total an army of occasional workers with no security. Without particular qualifications, they lived in the town or the countryside, entered the service of the wealthy middle classes, or were employed by councils or the state to work on roads, fortresses or the railways. They included former small tenants forced to give up their agricultural work, or to leave the parental farm as superfluous boarders. Their livelihood could not be guaranteed by their work alone. Wherever possible they tried to grow enough produce to feed themselves on their own plots of land, or the women had to earn extra income as washerwomen or day labourers in the sewing industry. Here, too, surplus workers led to the devaluation of jobs.

6. Finally, *servants* traditionally belonged to the underclass of the town and the country. They were members of a household, were given board and lodging, and were subject to specific servants' regulations, which allowed their 'master' to use corporal punishment, but also obliged him to provide welfare in the event of illness. Domestic servants and maids were part of any self-respecting middle-class household. However, they only accounted for a small proportion of servants overall (between 10 and 20 per cent): the majority worked as maids and farm labourers in agriculture. In 1848, issues surrounding their day-to-day duties, working conditions and servants' regulations gave rise to separate petitions, protests and meetings.[33]

The middle classes and the aristocracy regarded the fate of this 'fourth class' as a 'social question', which exposed the crisis in employment, but also revealed the existence of a social crisis. Family structures amongst this class were weak and wretched, with large numbers of illegitimate births and long working hours outside the home. Family ties were further weakened by high mobility. These people were among the 'oppressed and suffering' referred to by Gervinus, and yet their numbers grew disproportionately after marriage restrictions had been eased, and opportunities to acquire food improved, so that a family could feed itself after a fashion.

All in all, a potential for protest developed amongst these people which has been included in the 'social undercurrents' of the revolution (R. Stadelmann). Contemporaries also referred to them as the 'proletariat'. They were moved, not by the sophisticated political programmes culminating in the March demands, but by 'knife-and-fork interests', and from time to time by the anxiety created by the loss of their social position and security. Politically difficult to predict, they instilled in the middle classes the fear of 'anarchy' and a 'red republic', not only by their presence, but more still by their 'insubordination, excesses, riots, disturbances and scandals'.[34]

2 Middle-Class Organization and Social Protest

Social and political tensions culminated to form a unique constellation in the March revolution of 1848. From the petition to the barricade, however, no form of protest or political expression was new, as constitutional historical studies and recent socio-historical protest research have shown. On one side of the spectrum of action we find non-violent forms of the representation of interests: the forum of the chambers, the accompanying election campaigns, the middle-class pre-political associations, and the press, as far as censorship allowed. But each formally tolerated expression ran the risk of entering the grey area between legality and illegality. On the other side of the spectrum lay the illegal form of protest: socially motivated collective outbreaks of violence.

State Secret Justice: A Barrier to Middle-Class Resistance

Wherever an autonomous public group formed a political opposition, the state intervened to suppress it. In doing so it employed its police forces and all the legislative and administrative means at its disposal. Significant milestones in this respect are the Karlsbad Federal Decrees (1819) and the intensification of these decrees following the July revolution of 1830 (Decrees of 1832 to 1834). They gagged the press, placed a total ban on the formation of political associations (5 July 1832) and disciplined the legislative bodies and the universities. Individual states frequently imposed laws far more rigorous than the guideline laws themselves. Prussia, Hanover and Austria, for example, ordered general preliminary censorship, which included books of more than 20 *Bogen* (320 pages), despite the fact that the decree of 1819 had provided for the exemption of books of that kind. New findings on the *Vormärz* secret police leave no doubt as to how intensively social life was officially probed whenever it came to the attention of the authorities.[1] Yet these policies had a mixed effect, on the one hand paralysing the opposition, but on the other hand radicalizing it and forcing it underground or into exile. Spectacular examples of political secret justice were seen in Prussia and Austria, and in constitutional states too. As far as they lived to see it, the victims were celebrated as martyrs of freedom in 1848 and elected to the parliaments.

'Turnvater' Friedrich Ludwig Jahn was imprisoned for five years in Prussia, on charges of demagogic activities. Austria attracted unwelcome publicity when it arrested more than 40 people, including the Italian poet, Silvio Pellico, who was held as a member of the Carbonaria secret society. He was sentenced to imprisonment in the Spielberg fortress in Brünn from 1820 to 1830. Pellico subsequently published an unemotional account of this period in his memoirs, *Le mie prigioni*.

In Bavaria King Ludwig I imprisoned the Würzburg doctor and journalist, Gottfried Eisenmann, from 1836 to 1847, following a period of strict detention awaiting trial. He was sentenced to 'prison for an indeterminate period of time and to make an apology before the portrait of the monarch'.[2] Eisenmann had refused to convert his *Bayerisches Volksblatt* into an official state newspaper.

In the Electorate of Hesse the Marburg professor of constitutional law, Sylvester Jordan, penned the liberal Kurhesse constitution of 1831. Constitutional reality was such that in 1839 Jordan was arrested on suspicion of revolutionary activities and was not cleared until 1845, having served six years in prison.

In the Grand Duchy of Hesse, the Butzbach clergyman, Weidig, who had conspired with Büchner, took his own life in 1837 following brutal physical abuse in prison. A few days before, Büchner had succumbed in Zurich exile to typhoid fever.

In Berlin the authorities imprisoned the dialect poet and Jena *Burschenschafter*, Fritz Reuter, in 1833 on charges of demagogic activities. With no evidence against him, and despite the fact that the Prussian Court had no jurisdiction over a subject of Mecklenburg, he was sentenced to death. He was subsequently reprieved and his sentence commuted to 30 years imprisonment. Finally, with his health severely impaired, he was deported to Mecklenburg, where he did not see freedom again until 1840. Later Reuter admitted: 'When they first locked us up none of us were democrats. By the time we got out all of us were.' His words articulate the basic paradox of repression. The many unknown cases of repression outweighed the spectacular ones cited here, but these alone made clear to the oppositional political intelligentsia the risks they were taking. It was no coincidence that public hearings and trial by jury were among the March demands of 1848.

Middle-Class Associations

The middle-class desire to participate in politics developed within the associations they formed. This placed them in that grey area between activity tolerated by the state, and that which was illegal. For although *political* associations had been banned in the *Vormärz* period, it would be wrong to assume that the ban encompassed all forms of association. The political background of many was hard to establish. Others managed to evade justice: they included the religious revival movements of the 'German Catholics' and the '*Lichtfreunde*' or Friends of the Light, the *Burschenschaft* associations which continued in secret, the reading circles, gymnastic, singing and rifle clubs.

Only recently have regional studies systematically unearthed the many types of association formed in the individual nerve centres of the revolution.[3] Records from the town of Elberfeld identify around 90 associations between 1775 and 1848, ranging from social, religious, patriotic and national, cultural and academic associations, to economic organizations and those dedicated to social welfare.[4]

Despite the ban on parties, these pre- or crypto-political associations had an indirectly politicizing effect on their members. Admissions procedures, the implementation of rules and regulations, the formulation of programmes, decision-making by ballot and the internal democratic development of informed opinion by means of votes trained them to act in a manner which, in practice, was the prerequisite for the formation of political parties. There is no other explanation for the fact that, during the course of the election movement in the spring of 1848, competing associations were able to emerge within a few short weeks, and to act politically.

Pre-political associations were concentrated in the towns. Craftsmen had their associations abroad, referred to above, but in Germany commercial laws forbad such undertakings by the 'workers' themselves. The middle classes dominated the associations. The overriding purpose of such organizations was after all that they 'were part of that social field of relations on which the leading urban class based its standing'[5] – in other words: it was important to belong, and to that end hurdles such as admission procedures and membership subscriptions had to be cleared. Dignitaries meeting in this way had a head start over organized education or training. In March 1848 the experience they had gained in their associations meant that they were in an ideal position to seize the initiative and to stamp the initial revolutionary movement with their own demands. This had a significant influence on the elections and the composition of the parliaments.

Social Protest and Collective Violence

In contrast to the middle classes, who preferred their interests to be represented in a non-violent manner, the 'manual working classes' typically opted for 'social protest': popular unrest in which collective violence was brought to bear in riots. Wide-scale actions of this kind were first witnessed during the July revolution of 1830. Between then and 1848 there was an uninterrupted series of similar regional collective protests.

Failed harvests in 1828 and 1830, dramatic rises in the price of food, a decrease in orders for craftsmen and commercial businesses, together with long-term political dissatisfaction, culminated in a wave of socially motivated local expressions of outrage, with demonstrations in front of town halls and royal residences, attacks on police stations and customs offices, and raids on bakeries and the homes of factory owners and the aristocracy. They were centred on the Hesse states, Brunswick, Hanover, Saxony, the Prussian province of Silesia and the Bavarian Palatinate. Where the official forces of order were inadequate, civil guards intervened to restrain them. An examination of 165 cases between 1830 and 1832 shows journeymen, workers, the rural population and the urban lower classes to be the leading actors and activists.[6]

To some degree, these events are comparable to those of March 1848, especially since from 1830–2 the revolutionary movement had also developed a European dynamic through the involvement of France, Belgium, Poland, Northern Italy and Switzerland. One might even refer to the period as a 'trial run' for 1848, which was only restrained in its scope and impact by the stability of the Prussian and Austrian rulers, and by the fact that nationalism in Germany was still largely undeveloped.

In the small and medium states, federal laws stifled the short-lived opportunities for a free press and the formation of associations. Traditional protests, however, continued, albeit with waning intensity. They increased once more in the 'hungry forties' (T.S. Hamerow). If one takes these socially motivated and collective outbreaks of

Table 3   Popular unrest in Germany, 1816–75 (classified according to type of unrest)

	Students[1] Universities	Religion[2]	Politics[3]	Socio- economic[4]	Others	Total
1816–29	13	9	4	3	–	29
1830–9	13	20	72	28	3	136
1840–7	5	17	33	103	–	158
1850–9	5	15	61	21	5	107
1860–75	1	21	77	32	2	133
Total	**37**	**82**	**247**	**187**	**10**	**563**

[1]   Students were either the main actors, or else student or university matters were the main subject of the conflict.

[2]   Religion was, at least allegedly, the main subject of the conflict.

[3]   The protest was directed at the state and its organs in order to bring about political change (replacement of a specific civil servant, implementation of a new law, etc.).

[4]   Violent strikes, bread riots, machine-storming (Luddism), illegal mass trespass on woods and fields, tax riots and uprisings which were clearly linked to a specific socio-economic group, e.g., attacks on the rich by the poor.

Source: Richard Tilly, 'Unruhen und Proteste in Deutschland im 19. Jahrhundert', in Richard Tilly, *Kapital, Staat und sozialer Protest in der deutschen Industrialisierung* (Göttingen, 1980) p. 154. Tilly bases his findings on selected newspapers, and in particular on the *Augsburger Allgemeine*. He defines 'unrest' as 'collective disturbances of the peace with the use of physical violence' (ibid., p. 145)

From: W. Fischer *et al.*, *Sozialgeschichtliches Arbeitsbuch*, vol. I (Munich, 1982) p. 184.

violence as indicators of tension, in fact the 1840s stand out as unique, as is highlighted in Richard Tilly's analysis (see Table 3). Note that he does not include the years 1848–9.

Since the mid-1840s, the position of those groups living on the margins of minimum subsistence levels had worsened considerably. 1845 and 1846 in particular had seen extremely poor harvests. Potato blight was also rampant, and had shrunk the yields of this food to far below average levels. The last economic crisis of a pre-industrial nature was based on the adversity of nature, to which people were still unconsciously subject, like the biblical plagues of Egypt. In the 1840s, poverty spread from the agricultural to the commercial sector. Food prices rose, intensified by speculation and profiteering, while in real terms wages continuously fell. An analysis of fluctuations in the price of rye, potatoes, pork and butter in Prussia highlights the extreme rises seen between 1845 and 1847 (see Figure 1).

The crisis was not concentrated primarily in Prussia, as has recently been suggested, and it is certainly not true to say that Württemberg for example 'experienced above-average harvests from 1845 onwards'.[7] An examination of the fluctuations in prices and purchasing power alongside the birth rate (Figure 2) clearly demonstrates

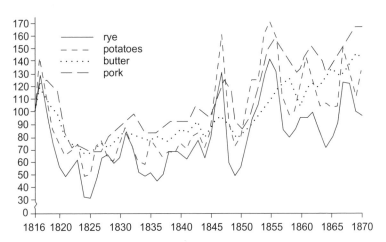

Source: W. Fischer *et al.*, *Sozialgeschichtliches Arbeitsbuch*, vol. I (Munich, 1982), p. 182.

Figure 1 Changes in the price of rye, potatoes, butter and pork in Prussia, 1816–70 (1816 = 100)

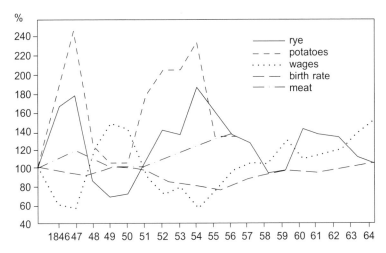

Source: D. Langewiesche, *Liberalismus und Demokratie in Württemberg zwischen Revolution und Reichsgründung* (Düsseldorf, 1974), p. 62.

Figure 2 Fluctuations in prices, purchasing power and birth rates in Württemberg, 1840/5–64 (1840–5 = 100%, factory workers'/journeymen's wages translated into rye prices)

that from 1846 to 1847 there was a wide gulf between prices and purchasing power, and that the birth rate fell as a result of the food crisis.

Increases in the price of food meant that less money was available for industrial and commercial products: bread was more important than textiles or the carrying out of repairs. Food price rises also intensified the modern industrial economic crisis cycles, which spread to the continent from Britain in 1847. German industry, which was still in its infancy, suffered a number of setbacks: production in the textile and mechanical engineering sectors decreased; railway share prices dropped; and in Hamburg alone 128 firms were forced to declare themselves bankrupt. This depression in the industrial economy followed an initial cyclical recovery between 1845 and 1847, but then became fully manifest again in 1848, to some extent worsened by the effects of the revolution. Interruption of business also had a major impact on early factory workers.

Werner Conze describes the situation as a whole between 1845 and 1848 as 'of unique significance', because in these years a new and an old type of economic crisis coincided, 'independently, not simultaneously, but overlapping chronologically'.[8] But, with the exception of the commercial middle class, contemporaries regarded the industrial economic collapse as far less significant than the old-style famines and price rises which followed the failed harvests of 1845 and 1846. Price rises provoked a wave of social protest. In Austria the peasants of western Galicia rose up as early as 1846. Rebellions in Germany peaked in the spring of 1847. In February armed groups in Silesia set off for the manor houses in order to help themselves to potatoes. On 21–2 April 1847 the population in Berlin stormed and plundered market stalls and shops, and attacked potato merchants. At the beginning of May food riots broke out in Ulm, Stuttgart and Tübingen. Here, too, anger was directed at profiteers and grain speculators. Order was re-established by hastily formed civil guards and the army. An analysis of 102 incidents of protest between February and July highlights the extent of this social unrest in Germany, the significance of which has not previously been fully appreciated (see Figure 3).

Regional centres of action were located in Pomerania, East and West Prussia, in the Prussian province of Saxony and in Württemberg. But we should not overlook areas of calm. Primarily situated in northern Germany, in the states of Hamburg, Brunswick, Hanover and Oldenburg, these regions remained calm because they continued to be self-sufficient. For inadequate infrastructures meant that an area of crisis might exist directly alongside an area where there was enough food to go round: there was no question of a nationally integrated corn market. This may sound abstract, but it had a highly concrete background, for provision requires communication. This was seen in northern Silesia,

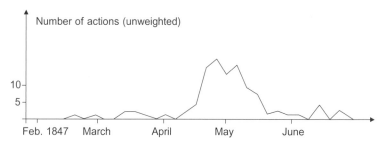

Source: M. Gailus, 'Soziale Protestbewegungen in Deutschland 1847–9', in H. Volkmann and J. Bergmann (eds), *Sozialer Protest: Studien zu tradioneller Resistenz und kollektiver Gewalt in Deutschland vom Vormärz bis zur Reichsgründung* (Opladen, 1984), p. 78.

Figure 3   Food riots, February–July 1847 (at 5-day intervals)

where the population suffered indescribable hardship. Censorship simply suppressed the truth about the conditions there, for 'Frederick William IV's Prussia should be regarded as a blessed and fortunate land'. Publicity would also have drawn attention to grotesque miscalculations made by the 'Prussian civil service, whose art of government was highly praised'.[9] Even contemporaries said that, had a free press existed, the famine in northern Silesia would not have been possible. If the truth had been known in time, the authorities would simply have been forced to take remedial action.

All statistical analyses show that the excellent harvest of the summer of 1847 brought the period of insufficiency to an end. Grain prices fell sharply, even before the outbreak of the March revolution in which the socio-revolutionary undercurrents played a major role. On this basis, it seems reasonable to ask how far economic cycles in general might be regarded as a cause of the revolution. Yet at the same time the question should be qualified: living people are hidden behind figures, graphs and statistics, and living people do not act as economically determined automata. The psychological environment which accompanied the crisis was particularly significant, and this represented a potential which could be activated at a later stage. So who took part in the uprisings of 1847? It is important to know their identities if their actions are to be properly judged. The leading Württemberg opposition newspaper, the *Beobachter*, printed a leading article on the riots associated with price rises which took place on 19 May 1847. In an astute analysis it warned against misunderstanding the unrest simply in terms of food riots:

> In all areas it is not the genuinely starving who have initiated them and carried them through. Throughout Germany the participants are down-at-heel small craftsmen, journeymen, apprentices, women from the large towns (involved in clashes at the weekly markets) etc. – in a word, people whose profession, work, surroundings and educational career makes them more accessible to the secret currents of the times than peasants, day labourers and so on.[10]

It was here that the urban campaigners of March 1848 emerged. Food riots had a politicizing effect on the major participants, as well as on broad sections of the middle classes, who became aware of the existence of the rebellious 'proletariat' and the 'social question' for the first time during this period. The issue had moved from learned treatises into the concrete world of experience.

The events of 1847 had an even more profound effect. The authorities were restrained in their use of force, and this led people to believe that more could be ventured. As the numbers of protest actions grew, inhibition levels decreased, even amongst the peasants, who had not previously taken part. Frequently, however, even the authorities were unable to deny that social discontent was justified. The monthly reports of the Prussian district administrator on the state of the population, for example, made no secret of the misery suffered by broad sections of the people.[11]

The protests of 1847 revealed the incompetence and helplessness of the government, and at the same time strengthened the belief that only profound social and political change could pave the way for improvements. But for many this meant simply a return to the old peasant rights and a resurrection of the traditional guild system.

3   The European Point of Departure, 1847–8

It may be surprising to find a section devoted to events in neighbouring European countries in an analysis of the German Revolution of 1848. However, the European character of the movements of 1848 makes it impossible to regard the German individual states in isolation. 'The European revolutions of 1848'[1] were far more than the simple sum of regional movements, each with their own weight and particular features. They were born of a deeper social and economic structural crisis, and only when we understand this can we comprehend the extent to which their outbreak, course and failure in France, Italy, Hungary, Bohemia, Poland and Germany were interwoven. If they are regarded as mutually interdependent, the image of *the* German revolution is relativized: it loses its inner cohesion; the weight of individual actors, and with it the 'blame' frequently attributed to them, is reduced and bound into constellations in western, eastern and southern Europe. Indeed, this interdependence was as real to the European statesmen of the *Vormärz* period in the days of the movement as it was to the revolutionaries themselves, who observed every intensification of 'the reaction' in a European capital with the concern that their own position might in turn be weakened. This raises questions regarding the international structures and conditions which underlay these synchronous revolutions.

A *European* political system was shattered in 1847–8. Based on the Vienna Treaties of 1815, it had often intervened in other nations' affairs and taken repressive measures in order to safeguard its own survival, albeit consistently only during the early 1820s. But even in 1847 the major European powers of 1815, Russia, Austria and France in particular, were in favour of military intervention in the *Sonderbundskrieg* in Switzerland, although in the event the conventional procedures of the ministerial congresses proved too cumbersome to allow this to occur.

The 1815 system had given rise to four fundamental factors which affected people throughout Europe: first, the unfulfilled middle-class demands for political participation in the states of the monarchically legitimized restoration since 1815; secondly, the striving for national self-determination and independence, embodied in the German, Polish, Czech, Hungarian and Italian national movements; thirdly, the crisis in the pre-industrial craft trades, the effects of over-population and the proletarianization of the cities and large tracts of the countryside; and finally, the failed harvests, famines and the crises associated with the price rises of 1845 and 1846, which peaked in 1847. This crisis had a profound social impact. It led Friedrich Engels, to look back and form the (albeit somewhat exaggerated) conclusion 'that the world trade crisis of 1847 was the true mother of the February and March revolution'.[2]

This combination of increasing democratization, the growth of the national movements and a build-up of socio-economic conflict was expressed in parallel courses of events. The beginning was astonishingly similar: a brief climax in the spring was followed by a lull in the summer and autumn of 1848, with a decline in the first half of the following year.

There also appear to be parallels in the significance of the capitals and cities, where the revolutions largely originated and were formed. They did not remain an event of the capital cities, however, but required the support of proletarian and agrarian revolts.

Of key importance was the stability of the political systems in France, in the Habsburg monarchy and in Prussia. The Netherlands, Belgium, England, Scandinavia (except Denmark) and Russia remained untouched by the revolution, although these countries did experience an increase in political agitation. Schleswig, under Danish rule, and Switzerland and Italy provided the impetus for the politicization taking place within Germany, which also grew in intensity in the states of the German Confederation after the outbreak of the February revolution in France.

Denmark and Schleswig

The Schleswig crisis forms an integral part of the prehistory of the revolution. It is distinguished by the fact that it united all political camps in Germany, arousing national passions on all sides. The causes of the conflict date back to the pre-national Early Modern Age, and so were only fully comprehensible to scholars educated in legal history. The Duchies of Schleswig and Holstein were bound into four separate but overlapping historical legal districts, making a division according to nationalities impossible.

Firstly, the duchies were united with the Kingdom of Denmark by a personal union in the form of the rule of the Danish King Christian VIII. Secondly, the Schleswig and Holstein *Stände* referred back to the Ripen Charter of 1460, which guaranteed that they would remain '*up ewig ungedeelt*' (eternally undivided). Thirdly, the Duchy of Holstein, though not Schleswig, had been part of the old German Empire before 1806, and since then had been a member of the German Confederation. And finally, there was the issue of the different laws of succession: in Denmark both Christian VIII and the heir to the throne, his brother Frederick, were childless; female succession applied in the State of Denmark, but not in the Duchy of Holstein. In the event of succession, Holstein, with enforced primogeniture, would therefore fall to the collateral line of Duke Christian August von Augustenburg. The law of inheritance for Schleswig was controversial.[3]

In this latter case we are dealing, typically enough, with an initially hypothetical scenario. This highlights the force of the national passions created by the unresolved situation in Schleswig during the 1840s. The issue of succession was but the starting point for the national political conflict which was expressed in a confrontation between the 'Eider-Danish' and the 'German patriotic' parties. In the newspapers of the day the complex legal situation, guaranteed under international law, was reduced to the simple question of whether Schleswig should belong to Denmark or Germany.

Open conflict erupted in 1844 when the Eider-Danes in the Danish representative chamber petitioned the King to declare the property of his house as a whole to be indivisible. In an 'open letter' of 8 July 1846, Christian VIII announced his intention to integrate Schleswig fully into Denmark.[4]

The significance of this border dispute for the course of the revolution of 1848 has never been in doubt, but its widespread politicizing impact *before* March 1848 has only recently been fully appreciated. Apparently apolitical organizations, in particular associations of singers and gymnasts, focused on the national pathos surrounding Schleswig-Holstein. This national issue transcended local systems of communication.

The first significant instance of this was the national song festival held in Würzburg from 4 to 6 August 1845, in which 1626 organized singers from all over Germany took part. The small Schleswig-Holstein delegation lent the festival a unifying note with the song '*Schleswig-Holstein meerumschlungen*'. An editor who was there described what happened afterwards: 'Cannons thundered, an incredible storm of applause broke out, hats were waved and it was clear that every heart was filled with sympathy for our dear brothers in the north.'[5]

A similar situation was repeated at the song festivals in Cologne in 1846 and in Lübeck in 1847, which was attended by 1127 singers. If one also includes the audience which had travelled to hear the singers, it is clear that such festivals were national events on a mass scale. The Schleswig-Holstein issue united all social groups of the middle-class national movement. Some German courts even allowed themselves to be drawn in: princes, chambers, universities, popular rallies and politicians, and even the *Bundesversammlung*, voiced their support for the national rights of the duchies, creating greater scope for political action. In contrast to 1830, in 1848 the national element, carried by the middle class in its widest sense, was completely activated and responsive. It operated as a dynamic force, which also drove the revolution forward. This fact makes clear the inadequacy of monodimensional crisis analyses for an explanation of the constellation of events in 1848.

Switzerland

In contrast to the Schleswig-Holstein issue, it was primarily the democratic wing of liberalism and the republicans in Germany who concerned themselves with the domestic crisis in Switzerland. Its repercussions had a politicizing effect mainly in south-west Germany. But it had a wider impact too, for it shook the European system of the Vienna Congress of 1815 to its very foundations.

Since 1815 the old patricians had been able to consolidate their positions of supremacy in the constitutions of the Swiss cantons. The landowning and educated classes had cut themselves off from the rest of the population by means of a strict property franchise. Already during the July revolution of 1830, in conflicts verging on civil war, ten of the most important cantons had attacked the supremacy of aristocratic rule. The '*Bewegungspartei*' had demanded a representative democracy, with a separation of powers and equality under the law, civil rights and universal suffrage.

Although it had still been possible to suppress this movement, the liberal revision of the federal constitution became a political issue, which led to the formation of parties, splitting the cantons into liberals and conservatives, paralysing the country, and inhibiting attempts to modernize and bring about economic unity and freedom.

An acute conflict then erupted during the 1840s in the sphere of religion and politics, when the traditional cantons won ground through the increased support of the rural population. The liberal government of the canton of Aargau blamed the monasteries for the vanishing restraint, and moved to dissolve them. In doing so, it contravened the monastery guarantee enshrined in the *Bundesvertrag* of 1815. This denominational issue led to the formation of parties, and platoons of volunteer corps organized to bring down conservative governments.

Seven Catholic cantons subsequently formed the *Sonderbund*, a special military defence union. On 4 November 1847, the *Tagsatzung*, the national assembly of all cantonal envoys, declared this to be in contravention of federal law and dispatched the federal army to put an end to it. Within 25 days the conservative cantons had been defeated. Hitherto a confederation of states, Switzerland now became a federal state, with a fixed central power and a federal capital in Berne.

In the autumn of 1847 the political opposition in south-west Germany saw the platoons of volunteer corps and the fall of the conservative governments as a model for the German politics of freedom and unity, and as proof that the system of 1815 could be checked. The Swiss were supported with financial donations, in newspaper articles and in calls to form volunteer corps.

Italy

Switzerland had hit upon a favourable period in history to bring about a change in its constitution autonomously, without the intervention of the major powers, for the military forces of the Habsburg monarchy, the prime restorative power alongside Russia, were tied up in Galicia and, above all, in Italy. This, too, is an example of the interdependency of events in Europe at the time.

In Italy the actions of the liberals during the 1840s had brought the 'Metternich system' and Austrian rule over northern and central

Italy into disrepute. Yet of all things, it was the change in pontiff in 1846 in the backward church state run on authoritarian lines which fostered the growth of nationalism. For the new Pope, Pius IX, granted a political amnesty, introduced policies of reform, granted freedom of the press and freedom of assembly, raising hopes that further reforms would follow in the rest of Italy.

This politicization activated the *moderati*, the liberal, democratic and Mazzinian movements, which had grown up underground, and spread to neighbouring Lombardo-Venetia under Austrian rule. Metternich acted swiftly. In August 1847 Austrian troops moved into the town of Ferrara.

This weakened his policies in the German Confederation, however, particularly in relation to south-west Germany, where, under the influence of the *Sonderbund* war, the opposition had begun to organize, as seen in the meetings at Heppenheim and Offenburg in September and October 1847. Here and elsewhere the synchronous parallel course of the preliminary phase of the revolution created room for manoeuvre, which in turn had a stimulating effect on the political movements. Domestic and foreign policies were closely interwoven.

The Pope's vehement protest against the invasion by Austrian troops heightened his standing as a figure of national integration. In September 1847 protest rallies were held in Milan, and a war of pamphlets began. The movement gained additional impetus through the advances of the Swiss *Sonderbund* war on the one hand, and the easing of censorship in the kingdom of Sardinia-Piedmont on the other. December 1847 saw the first publication of *Il Risorgimento*, the most important newspaper of the Italian national movement, and from which it took its name.

Under the circumstances, the continuing absolutist policies of individual Italian states, and above all King Ferdinand II's policies in Naples–Sicily, were seen as provocative. It was still possible to put down an uprising in Messina in September 1847. But on 12 January 1848 the revolution won its first victory in Palermo. As in other European arenas, the social undercurrents were also now clear: liberals and democrats were joined by urban proletarians and rural workers. *Moderati* from the middle classes and the aristocracy also joined the oppositional front. In Naples on 27 January 1848, the King, as the first sovereign of Italy, promised 'both Sicilies' a constitution: it was granted as early as 16 February 1848. This accelerated developments in the rest of the country; before February was over, Florence and Sardinia–Piedmont followed with their own constitutions.

As the events in Italy show, the image of a chain reaction following the French February revolution is inadequate. Switzerland and large parts of Italy were already revolutionized when the Paris coup triggered the unrest in Vienna, and led to the complete collapse of Austrian rule in Lombardo-Venetia. On 17 March 1848 Venice rose up, supported by officers and soldiers of Italian nationality, and by workers from the armoury. A day later, on 18 March, five-day street battles erupted in Milan. The insurgents forced the Austrian Governor, Field Marshal Johann Graf Radetzky, and his garrison to leave the city. Radetzky withdrew his troops to the square of fortresses between Etsch and Mincio, where Austrian soldiers from other rebelling towns were also gathering. These troops would form the basis of the subsequent reaction in northern Italy. Provisional governments in Venice and Milan successfully put an end to the revolution in March 1848.

France

To the amazement of contemporaries, the July monarchy collapsed within the space of a few hours in February 1848. The ground had

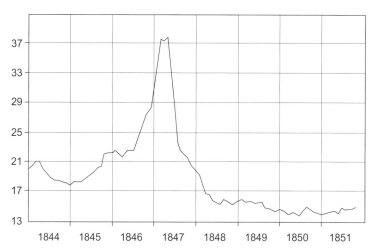

Source: E. Labrousse, 'Panorama der Krise', in H. Stuke and W. Forstmann (eds), *Die europäischen Revolutionen von 1848* (Königstein, 1979), p. 73.

Figure 4 Average monthly prices per hectolitre of wheat in France, January 1844–December 1851

been prepared by intensifying economic, social and state crises. The extent to which the European agrarian crises of the old order had taken hold in France is made clear in Figure 4. The economic crisis[6] which began in 1846 finally led to an alliance between the petty bourgeoisie, workers and journeymen and the Parisian intelligentsia. Their journalistic spokesmen, who included V. Hugo, H. de Balzac, Stendhal and L. Blanc, propagated oppositional ideologies ranging from democratic socialism to philanthropic liberalism. Louis Philippe's system lost support and legitimacy as a result of the wide social gulf between the itinerant unemployed, who attacked grain merchants and landowners, and the rich ruling class of the financial and banking bourgeoisie. Theories on the 'organization of work' forced apart previous social frameworks.

The indistinct opposition found a concrete point of attack in the reform of suffrage regulations, which increasingly became a focus of demands in the growing extraparliamentary agitation. A systematically organized '*campagne de banquets*' publicized the opposition's cause. Students and the National Guard were also mobilized. Events culminated in a call to a demonstration for electoral reform on 22 February 1848 in Paris. In the face of bans, mass meetings were held and barricades built. As would later occur in Vienna and Berlin too, the uprising was ignited when the army opened fire on the crowd: 50 participants lost their lives. On 24 February King Louis Philippe abdicated in favour of his grandson, but pressure from the masses brought down the monarchy. One of the spokesmen of what had been the opposition, the lawyer Alexandre Ledru-Rollin, proclaimed the republic and formed a provisional government. In the other European states this was perceived as the end of the system of 1815. It also triggered the revolution in the German Confederation, in Poland and in Hungary.

Part II
The Revolution:
Action and Reaction

4 The March and April Revolutions of 1848

Our examination of the areas of conflict in German society has shown that only a single trigger was required to provide revolutionary thrust to the widely held conviction that things could not go on as they were. Although its motivations were complex and conflicting, the opposition presented a united front. Its unity rested on the commonly held view that the ruling princes and aristocrats would no longer be able to master modern crises. At the same time, the experience of widespread, sometimes decade-long poverty and hardship became concentrated in one great hope for the future: that everything would change for the better overnight if fundamental reforms were carried out by new men, with modern political institutions and policies more in tune with the people. This hope – a vain one under any circumstances – united people on barricades who would never normally have joined together for the purposes of common political action.

The barricade battles of 22–24 February 1848 in Paris provided the German situation with the impetus which had been lacking until now. News of the abdication of the 'bourgeois king' and the words 'revolution in Paris' acted like a signal, triggering a chain of revolutionary events in Germany, which then went on to develop their own dynamic, independent of the French example. That is to say, they went according to plan, without there ever having been a plan.

The rapid sequence of events and the spontaneity alone surprised contemporaries, alarmed the governments and led to early capitulations. Unity of action and similarity of demands made a profound impression. The slogans for the speeches, articles and associations were ready and waiting, having been rehearsed for years. But even with the coincidence of many individual factors, the outbreak of the revolution cannot be explained without the readiness to believe in the dawn of a new era referred to above. But hope for the future soon gave way to sobriety, as it became clear how riven, how shot through with conflicting interests this newly liberated German society was.

This could hardly be foreseen in the early days of March. Yet already in this initial phase it is possible to define five spheres of action in which the revolution took place. Only when they are distinguished and examined in terms of their reciprocal influences do we gain access to the complex dynamics of this German revolution. In principle, the other four spheres of action should always be borne in mind when we turn our attention to any single one of them.

The first sphere was that of the, for the most part, spontaneous popular movements, the street barricades, the protest meetings in front of town halls and royal residences, the rallies where all classes of the population participated in the formulation of resolutions, where calls for a social revolution were heard, and where the lower orders' long-accumulated potential for protest was proclaimed, initially united with the educated and craftsmen middle classes. Entire village communities sometimes set off for the residence of the mediatized prince. We might call this sphere of action the grass roots revolution. It was a broad mass movement and played a vital part in the accomplishment of the policies of 1848. When the revolution of 1848 is described as a 'revolution of the middle classes', it is easy to overlook this aspect of it, and all too tempting to reach hasty decisions as to who the most important actors were.

The revolution paved the way for the long-suppressed freedom of the press and of political association. This created a second sphere of action: that of the extraparliamentary and journalistic public. Journalists and those forming associations set their sights beyond spontaneity, on permanent organization. But although they were aiming for continuity, for long-term members, subscribers and readers, their prominent spokesmen, pamphlets and placards linked them inextricably with the grass roots movement.

The third sphere emerged as the revolution became institutionalized and legitimized. It sought to create new legitimacy in constituent assemblies: the sphere of the legislatures of the individual states and the National Assembly in Frankfurt, where opportunities arose for action on the part of the factions dependent on parliament. Through their deputies they were closely linked to each of the previously mentioned spheres of action. This sphere was dominated by the middle classes.

The fourth sphere was that of the authorities in the narrowest sense: the newly appointed 'March ministries' and the municipal authorities in the larger towns, which are still largely overlooked by researchers. The Imperial ministries of the Provisional Central Power belong here too.

We should not forget the fifth sphere: that of the old powers of the princes and the aristocrats; the three monarchic privileges which remained almost untouched during the revolution and were therefore almost completely accessible during the counter-revolution. We refer here to the state bureaucracy – the entire internal administration, including the police – the army, and finally those representatives of state sovereignty who worked externally; the diplomats. The fifth sphere of action was in a permanent position of tension with all the others, with the so-called March ministries acquiring the function of a catalyst.

Strictly speaking, one should also take into account a further sphere, which emerged as a result of inaction: the regions whose populations remained almost entirely peaceful during the revolution. None the less, these regions of calm were politically significant, since they offered the old powers uninterrupted support even before energies in the other spheres of action began to flag and crumble. Whilst Vienna was in the throes of revolt, for example, the Imperial Court found a safe haven in peaceful Innsbruck.

The 'Third Germany'

It is not simply that the revolution fanned out into these five spheres of action; it also lacked the kind of central political arena that France had, for example, where decisions for the whole country were fought out. As in Italy, Germany's division into states created a number of individual, interdependent points of action. The German revolution presented an image of a chain of local rebellions, all rapidly following and coinciding with one another. They followed two major courses: starting in Baden, the revolution initially spread to the north and the east, gripping all medium and small German states, the so-called 'Third Germany', as it went. Only then was it able to take hold in Vienna and Berlin, where its inherent power was demonstrated.

The signal was given at the *Mannheim Rally* on 27 February 1848. Its course and thrust were typical of the rallies, gatherings, demonstrations, petition and address movements emanating from the urban centres. The Mannheim petition to the government in Karls-ruhe was penned by the Republican Gustav von Struve:

> The shape of France has been changed by a massive revolution. In a few days French armies might well be standing on our borders, while Russia assembles its own armies to the north. One thought flashes through Europe. The old system is faltering and collapsing in ruins. Everywhere the strong hands of the people have seized the rights which their rulers have long denied them. Germany can no longer stand by patiently and allow itself to be kicked. The German people has the right to demand wealth, education and freedom for all classes of society, without distinction according to birth or rank.[1]

The perspective was European, the petition claimed to speak for the whole of Germany. Four demands were made: (1) a people's army with freely elected officers; (2) unconditional freedom of the press; (3) trial by jury according to the English model; and (4) the immediate creation of a German parliament. This list circulated throughout Germany and became known as the *Märzforderungen*, or March demands. Their realization would imply a change in the system which went far beyond even the constitutionalism practised hitherto.

The movement gripped the entire country. Petitions from the Badenese towns were to be submitted to the chamber meeting in Karlsruhe. Hundreds of delegates, respected law-abiding citizens, set off for the capital in person to underline the seriousness of their demands. They were accompanied by journeymen, unemployed agricultural workers, workers from Strasbourg and members of gymnasts' associations. The railway brought further demonstrators from Mannheim and Heidelberg. Their destination was the meeting room of the chamber, which, with the government, suddenly found itself subjected to the unwonted physical presence of the population.

The popular revolutionary movement broke ground in other medium and small states as well as here in Baden: in Hesse-Darmstadt, Kurhesse, Nassau, Hanover, Württemberg, Bavaria, Saxony, Olden-burg and Brunswick, and also in individual Prussian provinces, such as the Rhineland and Silesia.[2] In Munich the armoury was stormed, and in Mannheim, Mainz, Hanau, Schmalkaden and Salzungen, workers rose up against their employers, destroying machinery, industrial plant, steam ships and trains. But such violence was rare. More typically, petitions were submitted and the ruler asked or urged to guarantee political rights. After all, this movement had its sights on political organization.

Simultaneous, though barely coordinated agrarian revolts[3] had been occurring since the beginning of March. They modelled themselves on the traditional patterns of peasant protest; spontaneous unrest, based on local issues, without political direction, triggered by a current crisis. Although these revolts often ended in violence, they did not constitute a revolution. In the eyes of the rulers, however, they lent support to the urban movements.

The revolts started in the overpopulated rural areas of the Badenese Odenwald and the Black Forest, where the liberation of the peasants had been carried out inadequately, and where the peasants were anxious to wrest free of their twofold dependency on both the ruler of the state and the mediatized prince. The movement spilled over into the Hessian Odenwald and to Bavaria to the Hohenlohe area. Armed with scythes, hatchets and axes, whole village communities rose up in an attempt to force the aristocracy to renounce the rights it had been granted by charter. Thousands were drawn to the peasant meetings where memories of the 12 Articles of the Peasant War of 1525 were revived. The uprising reached its climax in the principality of the mediatized Prince Karl von Leiningen in Amorbach – paradoxically, since of all princes, von Leiningen had constitutionalist leanings and was more prepared than most to make concessions.

The Badenese peasants' revolt took with it large tracts of Württemberg. Prince Hohenlohe-Bartenstein's castle was burned down, and records of outstanding tithe debts destroyed. In Weinsberg, arena of the old Peasant War, the peasants protected the coffers of the *Amtsschloß*, but burned its records. After cheering the King – they wished to serve only one ruler – they left. Thousands of peasants moved on the prince's residence at Hechingen, armed with cudgels, and forced the ruler to waive all levies due to him. Similar events occurred in upper Hesse.

The social undercurrents were particularly pronounced in Nassau, following the dissemination of the March demands from 1 March onwards and the arrival of messengers calling the peasantry to Wiesbaden. They came by train! Approximately 30,000 of them made their way there on 4 March, expecting the distribution of the demesnes. Leaflets calling for a 'per capita division of property' were circulated, and the Duke's Palace was almost set alight. But when the hitherto rather unpopular Duke Adolf moved through the crowd with unassailable composure, the excitement died down. From the balcony he declared, 'I will grant you everything. Disperse now, and have the same faith in me as I have in you.'[4] The peasants went home, trusting him. There was another large peasant meeting in Michelstadt in the Odenwald on 31 March, at which the dissolution of the rights of the mediatized princes was discussed. Republicans attempted to steer the movement, yet in April the numbers of agrarian revolts began to wane and the social base of the early revolutionary March days melted away.

One arena should be examined in detail here, because it remained the focus of the most lively national emotions throughout the entire revolution, and was therefore increasingly seen as a handicap to the movement of 1848 as a whole: Schleswig-Holstein. Immediately before the outbreak of the revolution, the conflict between the Eider-Danish and German patriotic factions had been rekindled following the death of the Danish King Christian VIII on 20 January 1848 and the energetic preparations of his successor, Frederick VII, for a pan-Danish constitution, which would include Schleswig. Resistance on the part of the duchies to this separation came right in the middle of the March revolution. A mass meeting was held in Rendsburg, and a petition was submitted to the Danish King on 18 March. The monarch's response was unambiguous and heralded the annexation of Schleswig. The middle-class leaders of the German movement in Schleswig-Holstein then declared a state of emergency, alleging that the King had been robbed of his freedom of action by the Eider-Danes in his ministry. Calling on their right to resist, on 24 March 1848 they formed a provisional state government led by the lawyer Wilhelm Hartwig Beseler.[5]

This was a direct attack on the representatives of a monarchy. The revolution did not 'halt before the thrones' as was more usual elsewhere in March. Its particular explosive political force lay in the fact that a movement which was reformist and constitutionalist by nature acted in an openly revolutionary manner, motivated purely by issues of national politics. From the outside it appeared to have united with the democratic republican front. If nowhere else, here, in the national conflict surrounding Schleswig-Holstein, it was possible to overcome the divisions amongst the middle classes. The 'democratization' of Prussian troops, unattainable anywhere else, also seemed a possibility, through their contact with the volunteer corps as they streamed into the German north after Danish troops had entered Schleswig. There was always the risk that events might escalate and turn into a European war, in which case the vision which von Struve declared in Mannheim would have become reality. Indeed, this course of events remained an option for the next six months, until it was decided in September 1848.

Austria

The Habsburg monarchy had already seen heralds of the revolution in northern Italy in January 1848. In Hungary the Imperial Diet had been steering an increasingly open oppositional course since the beginning of the year, even before the news from Paris reached the 400,000 inhabitants of Vienna. No other city in the German Confederation suffered such an extreme combination of rigorously suppressed middle-class opposition and the social privations of an impoverished suburban proletariat. This lent the outbreak of the revolution an ambiguous character from the very start.

Since news of the Paris overthrow had become known, the middle-class social and cultural associations of Vienna had emerged as cells of the revolutionary movement. The first petitions containing the March demands came from the Book-sellers' and Trade Association. The decisive impetus was provided by a petition from the Juridical Political Reading Society, whose authors, the writer Eduard von Bauernfeld and the advocate Alexander Bach, formed a union with the constitutionalist aristocracy of the Lower Austrian *Ständeversammlung*.

The convening of this diet in the capital on 13 March provided a focus for all political activity: students, members of the upper middle classes and representatives of the lower middle class craftsman and working classes gathered before the *Ständehaus*. Ludwig Kossuth's speech of 3 March was read out, in which the Magyar People's Tribune in the Hungarian Imperial Diet in Preßburg had condemned the absolutist system and demanded constitutional reforms for all provinces of the monarchy. Calls for Metternich's resignation grew ever more vociferous as the speech was read.

The *Stände* stalled for time, events overtook themselves, and the crowd stormed the *Landhaus*. As in Berlin a few days later, clashes with the advancing army triggered the construction of barricades. The revolution took place in two arenas: in the centre of the city, which saw a middle-class uprising; and in the suburbs of Vienna, where a social revolution took place, accompanied by the storming of machines and the plunder of merchants', bakers' and landlords' property.[6] From here attempts were made to penetrate the centre of the city, and the candelabras were torn from their anchors in the glacis dividing the city. The escaping gas was ignited and as night fell the town was surrounded by a halo of fire which could be seen from the Hofburg. This terrifying, visible sign of the mass uprising played a significant role in Metternich's resignation; from now on the *Staatskonferenz* (the assembly of all heads of the highest court authorities, together with the archdukes) deliberated on the demands of the united middle-class and student forces. Metternich was unable to pursue the unrestricted military course of action he desired. The *Staatskonferenz* forced him to resign, and permitted the formation of a student legion and a general civil guard (a national guard). Government troops were ordered to retreat. Student legions and citizens' associations stormed the armoury, and now held the capital in their hands.

Fresh demonstrations on 15 March forced an Imperial Manifesto, which included the unconditional promise of a constitution and the lifting of censorship. A citizens' committee formed an executive body, and without authorization took over the administration of the city. With the aid of the National Guard, the unrest in the suburbs was brought under control.

Already in this initial phase a gulf opened between the constitutionalist middle classes and the emerging democratic party organization, which was centred on the 'Democratic Club', and which retained its links with the lower classes. To some extent the dynamics

Table 4 Survey of those who died in March 1848 in Vienna

	Middle classes		*Lower orders*
1	professor's wife (non-participant)	34	journeyman, day labourers, apprentice boys
1	vinegar maker	1	maid
1	milliner	1	washerwoman
1	master shoemaker	1	female prebendary
1	joiner		
1	caretaker		
1	teacher		
2	students		Identity unknown: 2

Source: W. Häusler, *Von der Massenarmut zur Arbeiterbewegung, Demokratie und soziale Frage in der Wiener Revolution von 1848* (Munich, 1979).

of the revolution are reflected in the composition of its victims: four-fifths of the 48 dead listed in the *Wiener Zeitung* on 4 May were journeymen, day labourers and apprentices (cf. Table 4).

Prussia

The revolution in Prussia first took hold in the Rhine province. Although the petitions submitted to the rulers suggested that there was a unified oppositional front, an examination of the accent and aims of the opposition's demands reveals three distinct currents. *Großbürgerlich* commercial liberals such as von Beckerath, Harkort and other members of the Rhenish Provincial Diet were in favour of popular reform and continued liberal developments based on the United Diet. Their motto was legal continuity and cooperation with the constitutionalist aristocracy. Liberal democratic circles on the other hand, petitioned the King for a Prussian representative constitution, universal suffrage and a national parliament.

Events almost took a social-revolutionary turn at a rally in Cologne on 3 March – a veritable publicity coup at which approximately 5000 participants submitted a petition in an attempt to put pressure on the city council. Under the leadership of Andreas Gottschalk, doctor to the poor and member of the local community of communists, they demanded the dissolution of the standing armies, the arming of the populace, the protection of employment, a guarantee of the basic requirements for survival and state-funded education for children.[7] An alliance of the freelance intelligentsia and the lower middle classes with the lower orders made its voice heard. The army managed to disperse the demonstrators and temporarily arrest the spokesmen.

The events in Cologne were repeated only in the movements in the larger towns, and a few days later in Berlin and Vienna too. In other Prussian provinces, however, petitions were almost invariably submitted which called for the further development of the United Diet.

As in other towns, the revolution in Berlin grew from a series of rallies which took place from 6 March onwards. Again and again, large numbers of people streamed into the Tiergarten, declaring their support for the March demands. As in Cologne, the urban lower classes had also become restless. When the Borsig machine factory sacked 400 workers at the beginning of March, they began to express their hatred of 'capital' in a series of actions led by a group of democratic literary figures from the *Berliner Zeitungshalle*. Unlike the 'Third Germany', Berlin, as the capital and political centre of Prussia, intensified the dynamics of the revolution. Soldiers had moved in and had been stationed at strategically important points since 13 March. They had a profound impact on the situation, transforming the initially non-violent demonstrations into emotionally charged arenas of tension between civilians and the army. Individual incidents and the first deaths whipped up the atmosphere dangerously. On 15 March Metternich's resignation became known. On 17 and 18 March Frederick William made several political concessions; censorship was lifted and the United Diet convened for 2 April.[8] The announcements were made in a situation which had already acquired its own psychological dynamic through the presence of the army and the masses of people who felt under threat.

The consequences of this were revealed on 18 March, when a large crowd of people gathered on the palace square was preparing to cheer the King for the two announcements made earlier that day. Two shots – perhaps intentional, perhaps fired in error – were enough to give a signal for bloody street battles and barricade fighting which took place after the King had ordered that the army be used to force the people to leave the palace square. Like wildfire the call spread through the streets: 'To arms! To arms! The citizens defending us in front of the palace are being beaten up and shot to pieces!' These words also reached the ears of the writer Varnhagen von Ense, who witnessed events and recognized the barricade-builders in his neighbourhood:

> Some well-dressed young people who looked like students were giving instructions and orders. A mixed crowd – domestic servant lads, citizens old and young – were hard at work; . . . And yet the enterprise could easily have been prevented; had a civil guard already existed, it would not have permitted barricades to have been built. But now everyone helped, even down to the most respectable men and women.[9]

Although almost all social classes were united in their condemnation of the actions of the army, the social origins of the main fighters should be defined in greater detail. The authorities later discovered the personal details of 303 people who fell in the fighting or who died of their wounds soon afterwards (see Table 5). Journeymen and

Table 5   Survey of the 303 people who were killed in March 1848 in Berlin, or who subsequently died of their wounds

'Workers and proletarians'	52
working men, book printers, railway workers, dyers, calico	
printers, machine workers, silk knitters, weavers and wool sorters)	
Apprentices	13
Journeymen	115
(including 27 joiners, 15 tailors, 11 shoemakers, 10 locksmiths,	
8 blacksmiths, 8 silk knitters, 7 book-binders, 5 carpenters,	
4 bricklayers, 20 others)	
Masters	29
Servants, small traders	34
(domestic servant boys, postmen, grooms, shop assistants,	
waiters, victuallers)	
'Educated classes'	15
(1 government trainee, 1 artist, 1 merchant, 1 manufacturer,	
1 private secretary, 2 subaltern civil servants, 2 students,	
1 pensioner, 5 others)	
Non-working women	7
(in all, 11 women were killed: 2 workers, 2 maids, 1 manual	
worker, 1 basket maker's wife, 1 seamstress, 1 silk knitter's wife,	
1 journeyman joiner's widow, 1 master weaver's wife, 1 senior	
tax inspector's daughter (non-participant))	
Non-working youths	4
Unidentified	33
Identified, no profession given	1
Total	**303**

Source: Compiled from R. Hoppe and J. Kuczynski, 'Eine Beruf-bzw. auch Klassen- u. Schichtenanalyse der Märzgefallenen 1848 in Berlin', in *Jahrbuch für Wirtschaftsgeschichte*, IV (1964), pp. 200–76.

workers made up the bulk of them; for the most part they came from Berlin. None of those identified had 'previous criminal records'.

The outcome of the Berlin barricade battles led to two misunderstandings which influenced the political judgement of the middle classes and were, therefore, of prime importance for the further course of the revolution, particularly with regard to the aims and strategies adopted.

Firstly, the King ordered the unconditional retreat of the army from the palace on 19 March, and then from the city altogether. He conveyed his deepest sympathy for all those who had died, whose bodies were laid out on the palace square. Convinced that they had scored a victory over the princes and the army, the revolutionaries started to believe that they were stronger than they actually were. In reality, however, they had only forced the army to retreat; they did not have it under their control. The troops did not join the revolution, but remained loyal to the King, providing uninterrupted support for the increased reaction which would soon follow. Indeed, this reaction began in March itself, secretly at that stage. For the King was acting against the intentions of the leading military and court circles, against the 'military party' (Valentin) and 'the conservative faction' (Huber). On 19 March these groups, and above all Prince William, advised him not to withdraw the army. Between 20 and 25 March the United Diet deputy Otto von Bismarck, held conspiratorial discussions with the commanding generals in which he tried to persuade them to take counter-action. The mood amongst the Prussian officer corps was revealed in the Guard's reaction to the King's famous address of 25 March in the Palace's Marble Hall: 'At the words: "Never have I felt freer and safer than under the protection of my *Bürger*", a mumbling and scraping of sword sheathes arose, such as a Prussian King has never heard amidst his officers, and, it is hoped, never will hear again.' This eye-witness account was given by Bismarck.[10]

Before March was even over, an ultra-royalist group from the 'camarilla' circle under the leadership of Leopold von Gerlach, had already set about forming a shadow government to prepare the counter-revolution in secret.

A second misunderstanding arose when the King announced his belief in a constitution and in German unity. In his Potsdam speech he declared (in front of his soldiers, no less) that all his promises had been 'made freely and in complete conviction, and have been pre-pared for a long time'. No power, he said, could move him to go back on his word. It was 'necessary for the salvation of Germany to place me at the helm of the movement'.[11] On a ceremonial ride through Berlin he wore armbands of black, red and gold, the colours previously banned by a Federal Decree. In a proclamation 'to my people and to the German nation' on 21 March, he evoked the appeal made by Frederick William III on 17 March 1813 at the beginning of the War of Liberation, swearing an oath to 'the

Fatherland' and to 'the German nation'. 'Germany', he said, was in the gravest danger. The 'deepest union of German princes and people under one leader' was necessary. To this end he promised:

> I will today assume the leadership for the period of danger. My people, who do not fear danger, will not abandon me, and Germany will place its trust in me. I have today adopted the old German colours, and placed myself under the venerable banner of the German Empire. Prussia will henceforth merge into Germany.[12]

No German monarch appeared more suited to lead a united German constitutional monarchy. Frederick William IV seemed to be able to redeem hopes of Prussia's German 'calling' to be the hegemonic power of German unity. Indeed, some political journalists had been propagating this for decades. His words fed the mistaken belief that he would offer himself as a support for the unification of the nation on the basis of a written constitution. Draped in national pathos, he acted no differently than most of the other princes: he made political concessions and concessions to public vocabulary; he won time; and he avoided further bloodshed, the consequences of which he found shocking and uncertain.

By capitulating – and not only verbally – the King appeared to be confirming the new constitutionalist course. After a ten-day transitional cabinet (the ministry of von Arnim-Boitzenburg), on 29 March he appointed a union of constitutionalist aristocrats and *großbürgerlich* commercial liberals as March ministers; that is to say, the *Vormärz* 'protest parties' of the provincial chambers assumed power.

The new leaders were Ludolf Camphausen (Minister President), David Hansemann (Finance Minister), Graf Alfred von Auerswald (Interior Minister) and Freiherr von Arnim-Suckow (Foreign Minister). The appointments of Camphausen and Hansemann were intended to re-establish confidence in the creditworthiness of the Prussian state and its leading banks, a faith which had been shattered at the beginning of March.

People speak of the 'victory of the liberal middle classes' (Faber); but it was a Pyrrhic victory, in that in reality the middle classes had played a lesser part in carrying the revolution. The monarch had appointed new ministers; but he shuffled the cabinet a total of six times between March and December, each time taking a further step in the direction of counter-revolution. The army, the diplomats and the administration remained unchanged, and were still subject to his right of disposal.

The April Revolution in Baden

The victories in Vienna and Berlin were followed, not by a further grass roots revolution, but by a process of legitimization, which involved institutions such as the March ministries, election committees and parliaments. While this process was taking place in March, the Hecker uprising took place in southern Baden, and the grass roots revolution made further advances. The events can be quickly outlined. But it is their consequences and significance for the revolution which require detailed attention.

Following years of agitation on the part of the democratic middle-class intelligentsia, a republican movement had formed in southern Baden. Its traditional spokesman was the lawyer, Friedrich Hecker, supported by the less popular Gustav von Struve, who was also a lawyer. The republicans' newspaper, the *Seeblätter*, was edited in Constance by Joseph Fickler. The movement found social support in rural areas; in the southern Black Forest and Baar region, above all amongst the peasant subjects of the *Standesherr* Prince zu Fürstenberg, who held sway over more than 70 000 subjects. All in all, lands belonging to mediatized princes and former imperial knights, burdened by the typical feudal relics, comprised a third of the Badenese area: a quarter of the Badenese population (300 000 inhabitants) lived here.[13]

At the beginning of April the southern German republicans united around Hecker and von Struve had failed in their attempts to turn the *Vorparlament* or Pre-Parliament meeting in Frankfurt into a permanent revolutionary body. Convinced that the revolution should be forced on to the point of the republicanization of Germany, at this time the fate of the revolution seemed to be swinging in their favour. They were just waiting for the most favourable time for a violent *coup d'état*.

The opportunity seemed to be presented by the illegal and unauthorized intervention of the chamber deputy, Karl Mathy. On 8 April 1848 Mathy 'ordered' some non-commissioned officers, who happened to be at Karlsruhe station, to arrest Fickler on suspicion of conspiring with the provisional French government. It was this act which provoked the uprising, for Hecker feared that the police might take similar measures against himself and his closest supporters. Following Fickler's arrest, workers and apprentice craftsmen gathered in the inns of Constance and then took to the streets in demonstrations. Aldermen and the Committee of People's Associations organized a large rally in Constance on 12 April, where Hecker proclaimed the republic and called for the general arming of the populace.

But how many men did he have at his disposal who were genuinely prepared to fight? His troops reflect the diversity of his supporters: Johann Philipp Becker, a brush maker from Frankenthal, and active fighter in the Swiss *Sonderbund* war, collected together a German legion of volunteer corps near Basle. The young officer Franz Sigel was able to recruit over 3000 men. The writer Georg Herwegh, organizer of the 'German Democratic Club' in Paris, moved on Strasbourg with his legion of around a thousand craftsmen, workers and students. Hecker himself was able to recruit some 6000 men in a campaign starting from Constance.[14] All these troops cannot be added together, however. Some of them were armed only with scythes. They were not deployed in any planned fashion and united action was never undertaken.

The behaviour of the Badenese government was decisive. Turning down Prussia's offer of support, it instead requested military intervention from the *Bundesversammlung*, and this was granted in the Federal Decree of 15 April. The Eighth Federal Corps, made up of troops from Hesse and Nassau and supported by soldiers from Baden and Württemberg, comprised a force of some 30,000 men. The decisive clash at Kandern on 20 April 1848 led to the miserable defeat of Hecker's campaign. With the defeat at Niederdossenbach on 27 April, all campaigns collapsed. The commander-in-chief of the federal troops, Friedrich Freiherr von Gagern, brother of Heinrich von Gagern, was killed at Kandern. This lent a dramatic note to the entire April revolution in the eyes of the constitutionalist middle classes, who began to fear 'anarchy' and the 'red republic'.

It has become customary to describe the first of the three Badenese revolutions as a 'putsch' (Faber, Real). But this is to misjudge events by their outcome. Hecker's campaign brought to light four aspects of the revolution which had not previously been recognized.

1. Hecker attempted the first violent campaign using platoons of volunteers, organized by arming the populace, and aimed at overthrowing the monarchical system. Until now outbreaks of violence had always been either spontaneous in individual campaigns or on the barricades – and then only selectively. Yet two issues remained uncertain: how prepared for revolution was the population; and could the standing army be won over? Given the central ·March demand for a people's army, a demand made by all sides, the testing of these issues was unavoidable if the arming of the populace called for in the revolution was going to make political sense at all.

Hecker was popular, dissatisfaction amongst the population was great, and the government unsure of its troops. Hecker himself calculated that he had 60,000 men at his disposal. On the other hand, on 24 March the Prussian envoy in Karlsruhe, Siegmund von Arnim, said of Hecker's campaign forces, 'With one word, which might already have been given, he could unite under his command an army of more than 20,000 desperate and rabid proletarians from south Germany and the Alsace, where, according to the latest news, countless German factory workers have been sacked.'[15]

2.   Hecker may have been deluding himself as to the extent of the numbers expected to join him, but he was not wrong about the composition of his forces or his social base. His followers included journeymen, workers, day labourers, peasants and students, though few members of the civil guard or independent traders. The campaign bore the hallmarks of an agrarian revolt, albeit with remarkable 'confusion of terminology' amongst its democratic spokesmen and the rebelling peasants. We will return to this issue of the confusion of terminology in the context of the dynamics of the revolution below.

3.   The *Bundestag*'s power and readiness for action was also unclear. It subsequently became apparent, however, that it was entirely capable of acting from a military point of view. Furthermore, its possession of military resources enabled it to prove its internal executive might. The availability and the role of the federal forces have always been underestimated by scholars, least of all in Valentin's analysis of the revolution. The federal army was made up of contingents, with each individual state providing a proportion of the total of ten army corps commensurate with its population: Austria and Prussia each provided three corps; Bavaria supplied one. The remaining three were a combination of military units from the other federal states, from Hanover to Liechtenstein. In total the army comprised 300,000 men.

These troops were ready for deployment here in Baden, later in Schleswig-Holstein, in numerous other individual campaigns, and finally in the campaign for the Imperial Constitution. With the establishment of the Provisional Central Power, they became 'Imperial

Troops', with their command transferred to the Imperial War Minister. Individual states were happy to comply with his request to place their troops at his disposal for military contingents which varied from situation to situation, since on each occasion they were used to defeat revolutionary outbreaks.

The strategic significance of the Federal or Imperial Army lay in the fact that part of it could always be called upon, as and when occasion demanded. It was stationed as a standing army in the federal fortresses: in Mainz, the largest, in Luxembourg, Landau, Germersheim, Rastatt and Ulm; that is to say, with the emphasis on the Rhine-Palatinate-Baden area, which was particularly turbulent from a political point of view. Troops from the Federal Fortress in Mainz were often deployed during the revolution.

In the fight against the revolution, the reliability of the standing armies, which Hecker and von Struve wanted to dissolve, was proved for the first time in Baden in April. This strengthened the democratic republicans' resolve to win over the troops as a matter of necessity, to force them to swear to uphold the constitutions, and to use a people's army, however it might be defined, to compete against them or to paralyse them. The Kandern experience taught the liberal constitutionalist supporters of the monarchy that their efforts to legitimize the revolution would have to be stepped up if it was ever going to be tamed.

4.   Wherever the constitutionalists faced the democrats in opposing 'camps', the constitutionalists showed that they were prepared to counter the democrats' revolutionary force with military force. Mathy's involvement in the Fickler case assumed an exemplary function, and was perceived as such. Indeed the former political refugee and comrade-in-arms of Mazzini owed his appointment to the Badenese March ministry to his actions at Karlsruhe. The Badenese government avenged the attempted uprising by placing numerous towns and areas under siege, by trying more than 3000 insurgents for high treason, by imposing the most severe sentences, incarcerating them in prisons and in the casemates of the Rastatt fortress, and by dissolving the 'People's Committees' (4 May 1848) and the democratic associations (22 July 1848).[16]

All in all, the Badenese revolution represented an important stage in the assessment of the chances of the revolutionaries. The evidence suggests that already in April 1848 their room for manoeuvre was actually far more restricted than is usually assumed.

5 The Legitimization of the Revolution

The March Ministries

The princes' political response to the revolutionary movements was to appoint new ministries; this represented a degree of legitimization, since the March demands could serve as the basis of legal policy. The cabinet reshuffles appeared to herald the long-awaited 'breakthrough of the middle classes' (E. Weis). In Prussia the first middle-class government authority took over, headed by Ludolf Camphausen. Confidence was inspired by the fact that the princes almost invariably appointed constitutionalist liberal spokesmen from the former oppositions in the legislatures of the individual states. They included the deputies Friedrich Römer and Gustav Duvernoy in Württemberg, August Hergenhahn in Nassau, and Carl Bertram Stüve in Hanover. Constitutionalist aristocrats proved themselves in coalitions with the middle classes. They included the experienced oppositionist Heinrich von Gagern in Hesse-Darmstadt, Freiherr Gottlieb von Thon-Dittmer in Bavaria, and the professor of law Ludwig von der Pfordten in Saxony. To some extent the pressure of the revolutionary grass roots movement led to the parliamentarization of the system: to the outside observer it seemed that the chambers had exercised the change in government and had brought the opposition to power.

This must have had a calming effect on wide circles of the middle classes. It was seen as a kind of 'handshake' from the prince, guaranteeing that he would henceforth practise constitutional parliamentary policies. So much seemed to have been won that people began to say that it was time to 'conclude the revolution'. Further steps were required to safeguard the political changes from a legal point of view: new electoral laws had to be enacted, the constitutions had to be brought up to date and the newly appointed chambers had to frame the overdue political and social reforms into laws.

Yet two major considerations influenced the actions of the March ministries in the tasks they had been set. Since they themselves came from the representative legislative bodies, they regarded these bodies as the legitimate representatives of the people, and were reluctant to reform them. In the medium states, in particular, they neglected to increase the power of the chambers sufficiently, and to extend the parliamentary base of legislation. The March ministers' actions were also circumscribed by considerations as to future laws which might be enacted by the Frankfurt National Assembly in the context of the *Grundrechte* or Basic Rights. Here too it seemed appropriate to wait and see what happened.

The new governments channelled their energies not into legislation, but into the exercise of executive power. In establishing 'peace, law and order' in the face of continuing revolutionary agitation, they fulfilled the real function which the princes had intended for them.

This was particularly evident in Baden after the unsuccessful Hecker revolution. The Württemberg government put the Württemberg activists on trial for high treason, and tightened criminal law. Political associations throughout the state were subject to attack. In Württemberg the central democratic district association in Stuttgart was banned on 12 July 1848. Bavaria banned the democratic associations on 12 August 1848.[1] The Hesse-Darmstadt March ministry under Heinrich von Gagern suppressed continuing local unrest with the aid of the army and the police, and on 21 March announced that the full force of the law would be applied in the event of further rioting. Von Gagern's successors enacted new legislation 'relating to the maintenance of law and order' (6 July 1848) and against the 'improper use of the press and of public rallies' (18 October 1848).

At this point the policies of the March ministries ran parallel to those of the Provisional Central Power, provoking the dilemma that they might be attacking 'the soil of the revolution' to which they owed their existence. The issues of how seriously the enforced concessions made by the reshuffled governments were meant, and whether they could ever be permanent, remained unresolved. There is no doubt that the princes were shrewd in their calculations. King William of Württemberg was frank in his discussion of such matters. He justified the appointment of the March ministry to the Russian envoy Gorčakov with the words: 'The appointment of the new ministry wins me time and avoids bloodshed.'[2] This made various concessions possible.

King William made the following declaration before a delegation on 21 April 1849, with a Hohenzollern in mind as an elected Kaiser. His words were generally significant, and also applied in the princes' dealings with the March ministries:

> It may be possible to use declarations or riots in the land to force my hand. If you stand on the ground of the revolution and force me to give my word, then it is not a free word. You can see this for yourselves, and you cannot possibly want that: for a word forced out of me would not be binding. I could simply go back on it as soon as my will was free again.[3]

The short lives of the March ministries confirmed this frank view. Only very few of them survived 1849. The last to be sacked was Stüve's ministry in Hanover on 27 October 1850.

The Autonomous Middle-Class Movement for National Elections

The March ministries aspired to legitimize the revolution 'from above'. The opposite course of action was chosen by deputies from south-west German chambers, who met in Heidelberg on 5 March 1848 under the influence of the emerging March movement. Without legitimization from the state, but entirely in the tradition of the autonomous middle-class assemblies of the *Vormärz* period, 51 leading liberals and democrats debated the steps that needed to be taken to form a German national parliament. On the face of it, constitutionalist liberals such as Bassermann, Welcker, H. von Gagern and Hansemann were united with democrats such as von Itzstein, Hecker and von Struve.

Yet the resolutions they formulated together hid profound contradictions. The most controversial, though still hypothetical alternatives at this early stage were between a German Empire under Frederick William IV (von Gagern) or a German republic (Hecker, von Struve), between the sovereignty of the people and cooperation with the government. Yet the 51 agreed on one resolution, which declared as urgent the 'meeting of a national body of representatives elected in all German states in proportion to their population'.[4]

These self-appointed representatives of the nation did not only make proclamations. They also set up a *Committee of Seven*, which in turn was to appoint 'a more complete assembly of trusted men from all German peoples'. Newspapers were used to address all former and current members of the *Ständeversammlungen*, as well as 'publicly respected' personalities who had not been represented there, including Robert Blum. They were to present themselves in Frankfurt on 30 March for what would later become known as a 'Vorparlament' or Pre-Parliament.[5]

Already in Heidelberg the democrats were forced to make concessions for the sake of unity, not least in the formulation of the task of a future National Assembly: 'to surround the entire German Fatherland and the thrones with this strong protective wall.'[6] In contrast to the simultaneous popular movement, the Heidelberg Assembly exhibited 'a predominantly antirevolutionary character' (Botzenhart). Von Gagern later acknowledged that he had regarded the measures adopted in Heidelberg as a move towards 'the pacification of the general unrest'.[7] The conflict which would later emerge in the parliaments was already quite clear at the heart of the Pre-Parliament stage: pacification or an appeal to 'the people'.

The 'Pre-Parliament' met in the Paulskirche between 31 March and 3 April 1848. Since it had not been commissioned by the state, it was still on a revolutionary footing. Regarding itself as the leading voice of the nation, it undertook the task of devising Germany's reorganization. The German states were disproportionately represented by its 574 members: Austria had only two deputies; Prussia 141; Baden 72 and Hesse-Darmstadt 84. On the other hand, the most famous liberals and democrats were present.

Four areas of controversy emerged during the debates: the attitude towards the revolution; the programmes to be adopted by the future National Assembly; the manner in which it would be constituted by means of national elections; and finally, the movement's position on the *Bundestag*.

1.   It is generally true to say that the politically active middle classes decided on their future course here in the Paulskirche. Von Struve's famous motion forced the members to address all the major problems at once.[8] Had the motion been accepted, the Assembly would have set itself up as the revolutionary centre of action. It would have laid claim to legislative power, transferring executive power to an executive committee. For many this came too close to the Jacobin rule of the convention, on the French model of 1793. The

Pre-Parliament would also have had to declare itself a permanent institution. The revolutionary path was rejected by 356 votes to 142. This made the balance of power in the Assembly abundantly clear.

2.   Von Struve's motion proposed a federal constitution on the model of the North American free states, with an elected president at the helm: the republican form of state. Against the grain of modern state organization, he demanded the dissolution of the standing armies and the abolition of the professional civil service. Although utopian in terms of its chances of success, the motion attacked the very heart of state power.

The democrats around Hecker and von Struve had their roots in the south-west German lower middle classes. Naturally, then, the 'social question' formed an integral part of the motion, which proposed 'the elimination of the poverty of the working classes and the middle class, the commercial class and in agriculture', 'the levelling out of the disparity between capital and work, by means of a special ministry of work', protection of employment and profit-sharing for workers. It was a programme of social reform, not of socialist principles nor of a communist expropriation of property.

At the end of the day a vote was not taken on von Struve's motion, ostensibly because members of the Pre-Parliament did not wish to restrict the sovereignty of the future National Assembly in any way. On a formal level this sounded convincing enough, but the polite formulations surrounding the issue masked the fact that the programme as a whole was unacceptable to the majority. The links with the social undercurrents of the revolution were already broken here.

3.   The desire to hold national elections to form the future National Assembly was unanimous. The elections would be held according to universal and equal suffrage. Yet at this point a remarkable 'blunder' occurred, quite possibly a deliberate one. Inexplicably, the demand found its way into the published resolutions of the Pre-Parliament that entitlement to vote would be determined by the issue of 'independence'. The assembly had never voted on this point, and yet the passage later became binding.[9]

4.   The position adopted on the *Bundestag* or *Bundesversammlung* represented a crucial test. The Mainz lawyer, Franz Zitz, submitted a motion demanding that all extraordinary resolutions made since 1819 be lifted, and that the men who had worked on them be 'removed'. This was to be done '*before* the *Bundesversammlung* set about founding a constituent assembly'.[10] Had it complied with the ultimatum and passed a resolution purging these men, the *Bundestag*

would have compromised itself. When Bassermann replaced 'before' with 'while', the motion was toned down, and it was possible to win the support of the majority. But in doing so, a condition which could not be postponed was transformed into a mere inference from the changed situation. This second defeat led some of the democrats around Hecker and von Struve to attempt to break up the Pre-Parliament. The withdrawal of their minority of about 40 men did not elicit the desired response, however, for the group around Blum submitted to the majority resolution, remaining firmly on the parliamentary path. Hecker and his supporters later returned to the plenum when on 2 April the *Bundestag* lifted all the extraordinary resolutions of its own accord. All mention of a purge ceased.

With the passing of the resolutions regarding preparations for an election, the work of the Pre-Parliament came to an end. Future action was not ruled out, however. A *Committee of Fifty* was formed to advise the *Bundesversammlung* on further procedure. It was also charged with immediately reconvening the Pre-Parliament 'if ever the Fatherland appears to be in danger'. At the end of the day, the Pre-Parliament debates had helped to crystallize the different political camps: liberals, parliamentary and revolutionary democrats had become more conscious of their political identities. Autonomously they had highlighted the middle classes' demand for national representation. Yet at the same time, the majority had decisively rejected revolutionary methods of achieving this representation: they had handed the responsibility for preparing the elections to the *Bundestag*, thereby confirming it as a legitimate organ, and pursuing the course of legal continuity and evolution.

The Policies of the Bundestag: Adaptation and Concession

The Frankfurt *Bundestag*, also referred to as the *Bundesversammlung*, had received a number of appeals for the constitutionalist reform of Germany since 1815. Yet this permanent congress of envoys from 38 German states had always acted completely passively on such matters. Contrary to its federal structure, until 1840, however, under the united supremacy of Austria and Prussia, it had always pursued solidly repressive domestic policies.

Yet under the impact of the revolution it showed itself to be unexpectedly adaptable. By making concessions it attempted to check the movement and to steer it on to the path of legal continuity. The appointment of the March ministries also had an effect on the *Bundestag*, in that the envoys from individual state governments were replaced. Their successors belonged overwhelmingly to the middle-class movement, and now received their instructions from middle-class cabinets. The prestige of the *Bundestag* was therefore enhanced by the *Vormärz* oppositional aura surrounding such prominent envoys as Welcker (for Baden), or Jordan (for Kurhesse).

Even before the reorganizations, the *Bundestag* had found itself subject to public pressure. As early as 12 February 1848, the Badenese deputy, Bassermann, had submitted a motion to the Second Chamber of the state, calling for the formation of a national body of representatives in the confederation, indirectly elected by the individual legislatures. On 28 February 1848, Heinrich von Gagern submitted a motion to the Hesse-Darmstadt Second Chamber which took Bassermann's motion as a starting-point, but was also directly influenced by the February revolution. Von Gagern proposed the election of a national parliament and the appointment of a national government with a central leader and accountable ministry. This motion, too, was aimed primarily at the *Bundestag*.

On 29 February the *Bundestag* attempted to take the initiative on the issue of a constitution, adopting its tried-and-tested method of problem-solving: the appointment of committees. The 'Political Committee', which was appointed on 29 February, formulated a number of decisive, almost revolutionary measures when compared to previous policies. These later became federal decrees and included the granting of press freedom (3 March), the acceptance of the need for a 'revision of the federal constitution on a truly contemporary and national basis' (8 March), the recognition of the hitherto unconstitutional colours, black, red and gold, as federal colours (9 March), and the appointment of a committee of 17 'men trusted by the public' to draft the constitution (10 March).

The structure of the Committee of Seventeen was based on that of the Select Council or *Engere Rat*, the real organ of action of the *Bundestag*, which represented 17 of the leading individual states. Middle-class constitutionalist liberalism was well represented on the committee. Indeed, it contained some of its most prominent representatives: Dahlmann (for Prussia), Bassermann (for Baden), Jordan (for Kurhesse) and Gervinus, von Schmerling and Droysen. This highlights the key position held by individual constitutionalists at this time.

At the end of the day, however, despite the efforts of the Committee of Seventeen, the *Bundestag* gave away its claim to reform 'from above', when on 30 March it asked individual states to call national elections to a constituent assembly, and hastily adopted the suffrage resolutions formulated by the Pre-Parliament (7 April). The way was now clear for the revolution to form a constitution under the mantle of legal continuity. With the repeal of all exceptional laws passed since 1819 (2 April), it finally freed itself completely from the past.

The readiness of the *Bundestag* to take action and the fundamental reform of federal law which now got underway should not be overestimated. Federal laws may have been rapidly adopted in March and April 1848, but they were revoked just as quickly in 1851. Nowhere was the instrumental nature of the law expressed more clearly than in the governments' actions on the federal decrees and state constitutions they sanctioned.

The particularist weight which opposed the middle-class national movement was revealed when on 8 May the draft constitution was put before the Committee of Seventeen. Even before the first meeting of the Frankfurt National Assembly on 18 May a clear programme was evident. Its key features were formulated after long battles in the Paulskirche in the spring of 1849. They were: a bicameral system with universal suffrage for the Lower Chamber; a 'German Kaiser' with imperial ministries and central imperial power; a list of basic rights and an imperial court. A hereditary monarchy on a democratic basis was not without precedent in Europe: Germany was preceded in this respect by Sweden in the Kingdom of the Bernadottes and Belgium in that of the Coburgs.

From time to time questions are raised as to whether they should have taken advantage of the fortune of the hour in this draft, whether they should have acted swiftly already in the spring. Excluding hypothetical speculation, one should not forget that even in May 1848 the German governments of the major powers and medium states were in a position to reject the draft decisively, which they saw as too centralist. The foundation of the *Reich* 'from above' turned out to be 'a still-born child' (Botzenhart) after all. Already in May 1848, when Dahlmann, vice-president of the committee, offered Frederick William IV the imperial crown without Austria, the King refused it in no uncertain terms. Dahlmann received four letters to this effect. As a leading constitutionalist in the Paulskirche, he should perhaps have been more sceptical towards renewed calls for a hereditary monarchy with the Prussian King as the future Kaiser.

The Elections to the Constituent Parliaments

The March ministries, the *Bundesversammlung* and the autonomous assembly movement were based on an extremely small stratum of the politically active middle classes; it was constitutionalist in political leaning and loyal to the monarchy. Through the elections to the constituent parliaments, its policy of legitimizing the revolution acquired the dimensions of a mass movement. For a short time it appeared to all that the politics of their local environment was becoming 'popular'. Energy was released and then channelled and bound into election campaigns, committees, assemblies and resolutions.

The Elections to the Frankfurt National Assembly

If people are allowed to vote they do not build barricades. They do, however, protest when the numbers of those entitled to vote are restricted. Problems surrounding the issue of suffrage were revealed at every turn, for the definitive federal decrees of 30 March and 7 April had left a great many issues unresolved. The election was to be general and equal, albeit limited to the mature, *independent* male members of the states. Yet the term 'independent' was not defined, nor was the question resolved as to whether the elections should be open or secret, direct or indirect (with primary and delegate elections). Open elections might make it possible to pressurize the electorate, whereas indirect elections would give local dignitary delegates a disproportionate influence. How the elections were actually carried out was left to the discretion of each individual state. In the event, therefore, voting practice varied considerably from state to state.

Only in Württemberg, Kurhesse, Schleswig-Holstein and the city republics were direct elections held. As a rule, primary elections were held in which those entitled to vote chose the delegates, who in turn elected the deputies in a second round.

The issue of independence posed the greatest problem. In Bavaria protests halted the attempt to make entitlement to vote dependent on direct taxation: only those who paid such taxes had citizenship and were defined as independent. As a rule, the election laws of most states defined dependent as someone who received welfare support, who did not maintain his own household, or who was in receipt of wages or board in a dependent or servile position; this accounted for the majority of the 'manual working classes'. Where these regulations were strictly enforced, as in Saxony, Hanover and Baden, for example, rural and urban servants and journeymen who lived in the household of their master were excluded. In total they comprised up to 25 per cent of all adult males. The fewest restrictions were applied in Prussia, where it is estimated that only around five to ten per cent were excluded. Obstacles were sometimes imposed to make voting more difficult: entering one's name in the electoral roll, for example, or collecting the voting slip and personally handing it in on the day of election, as was required in Saxony.

Even when all the restrictions are taken into account, at least 75 per cent of adult male Germans were able to vote in the elections of the spring of 1848.[11] As Botzenhart has shown, this figure is far higher than previous research has suggested, and in the European context of the time it was a broad democratic base without precedent. The election turn-out was also remarkable: it fluctuated between 40 per cent (in Holstein and Saxony) and 75 per cent (in Württemberg, for example).

Rash conclusions cannot be drawn from the election results on the consequences of the restrictions, however. In Prussia, the territory with the widest entitlement to vote, a majority of conservative and constitutionalist deputies were elected, while in those areas with many restrictions, such as Saxony and Baden, the democrats managed to win through despite the election regulations. For the most part, the authoritative local dignitary delegates in Saxony and Baden distanced themselves from the constitutionalism embodied by von Gagern, the March ministries and the Pre-Parliament. Old-style liberalism, as represented by senior civil servants, manufacturers, large merchants and professors,[12] had lost the support of the small-town lower middle classes during the crisis years between 1845 and 1847. The democrats' chances lay in this rejection of liberalism.

Elections took place in all 'modern' forms, although truly modern elections were only held in the city constituencies, in Munich, Leipzig and Berlin, for example, and in those places where direct elections demanded that candidates address the electorate with their 'political manifesto'.

Considerable advances in political organization were made during the elections. Committees or associations fielded candidates and arrangements were reached between delegates. In some places, Munich for instance, the election campaign began with large-scale meetings, pamphlets and agitation in the press. In Saxony democratic 'Fatherland associations' and constitutionalist 'German associations' became politically polarized. Yet such developments were by and large limited to the traditional centres of the political movement. Different party groupings only began to emerge properly during the summer, when the lines adopted by the parliamentary deputies were analysed in depth.

One should not lose sight of the fact that the Germany of 1848 was still primarily agricultural. Local 'greats', in particular the mayor and priest delegates, were still the most influential people in the small towns and the countryside.[13] The traditional social order had a far greater influence on the outcome of the election that the theoretical entitlement to vote. Workers, journeymen, day labourers and members of the lower middle classes found themselves unable to compete with the knowledge, political experience and connections, or indeed the financial resources of the upper classes. Even where they were allowed to compete, it was only in rare cases that they managed to 'pass through the sieve of the indirect elections', with their associations nominating election committees and other committees.[14] This helps explain the social make-up of the parliaments in 1848.

The Elections to the Berlin 'National Assembly'

On that memorable 18 March, Frederick William IV had agreed to reconvene the United Diet for 2 April. In doing so he pursued the path of legal continuity, to which this feudal legislature also subsequently subjected itself: it in turn passed the election law for a new National Assembly to '*agree* the Prussian constitution'. This bound the future body to make the constitution they drafted entirely dependent on the agreement of the monarch. The election law of 18 April prescribed a general, equal and indirect election. All men who had been resident for six months or more, and who were not in receipt of welfare support were awarded the active right to vote from their twenty-fourth year of age. No other major German state allowed elections on such a broad basis. Primary elections for both Berlin and Frankfurt were held on 1 May 1848. The elections for deputies were held on 8 and 10 May respectively.

The Path to the Vienna Reichstag

The Kaiser's promise of 15 March in Austria by no means guaranteed a constituent assembly based on national elections, as further developments testify. Reactivating the *Stände* representatives of the individual provincial diets, the Austrian cabinet appointed a *ständisch* central committee to discuss the constitution. This was comparable to the Prussian United Diet. The representatives from Lombardo-Venetia and Bohemia refused to participate from the start, but even the so-called rump committee made only slow progress in its work.

Under the overall control of Interior Minister von Pillersdorf, the government now drafted a constitution. It epitomized the modern constitutionalism of the time, as embodied in the Belgian constitution of 1831. Unilaterally on 25 April 1848 the Kaiser enacted what has gone down in history as the 'Pillersdorf constitution'. This imposition was nothing short of an open break of the constitutional promise of 15 March, which had allowed for agreement. It was purely and simply a *coup d'état*.[15]

This was provocative enough in itself, but when it was combined with the intended appointment of large landowners to the 'senate' and the proposal that suffrage for the planned '*Volkshaus*' elections would be dependent on the payment of taxes, rioting broke out. Starting from the 'Democratic Club', led by the language teacher Karl Tausenau, the protests were initially carried by the Academic Legion, the workers' societies and the largely middle-class National Guard, which had excluded those defined as 'dependent' from its ranks.

The opposition proved its strength when students and the National Guard broke into the house of Minister President von Ficquelmont, forcing him to resign (3–4 May 1848). Minister of State, *Konferenz-minister* and rival of Metternich since 1840, von Ficquelmont was regarded as an exponent of absolutism. Following this victory, the Academic Legion and National Guard formed a *Political Central Com-mittee* (9 May 1848), which organized the fight against the Pillersdorf constitution. A rift in the National Guard was immediately exposed when its commandant tried to use an order of the day to prevent its members participating in the Central Committee. This led to the out-break of the so-called May revolution. Armed students, workers' societies and members of the National Guard marched on the Hof-burg, forcing an Imperial Manifesto (16 May 1848) which would finally pave the way for the democratic legitimization of the revolu-tion: the order of the day was withdrawn and a constituent Reichstag was conceded. It would be represented by a chamber elected accord-ing to the principle of universal and equal suffrage, including 'inde-pendent workers'.

The extent to which the balance of power had shifted is revealed in the court's decision to flee from Vienna to Innsbruck on 17 May 1848. In response to vehement protests from some sections of the Vienna population, the Kaiser demanded the dissolution of the Academic Legion before he would agree to return. Under the leadership of Pillersdorf, the ministry tried to enforce the dissolution and close the university. The building of barricades and resistance on the part of the National Guard prevented that too. The ministry was forced to capitulate and withdraw the dissolution decree (26 May). The revolution would have won all along the line had it simply been confined to Vienna, where it had armed forces at its disposal, and where it could ensure that its forces were effectively organized. 'A committee of citizens, students and guards for security, order and the protection of the people's rights' or *Security Committee* replaced the 'Central Committee'. Led by the doctor, Adolf Fischhof, it acted as a parallel revolutionary government; as judiciary, police force and administration in one. The ministry was at its mercy. When Pillersdorf refused to recall the military commander, Prince Alfred zu Windischgrätz, following his Prague counter-revolution, the Security Committee was able to bring about the downfall of the minister and force a cabinet reshuffle.

At this point there were three political centres of action in Austria: the revolutionary Security Committee in Vienna, and in Innsbruck both the ministry and the imperial-archducal group, which was preparing the counter-revolution together with the leading military

Table 6   Social composition of delegates in 16 constituencies in Lower Austria (districts of Krems, Korneuburg and St Pölten)

Number of inhabitants	773,026
Number of those entitled to vote	129,721
Election turnout	55,371
Number of *delegates*	1,674
of which: farmers and landowners	1,297
tradesmen (craftsmen, master craftsmen, small tradesmen)	221
Bürger (propertied classes: manufacturers, merchants, landlords of houses or inns)	121
civil servants	21
clergymen	7
aristocrats	2
doctors	5

Source: Compiled from K. Obermann, 'Die österreichischen Reichstagswahlen 1848. Eine Studie zu Fragen der sozialen Struktur und Wahlbeteiligung auf der Grundlage der Wahlakten', in *MÖStA*, 26 (1973), p. 366.

commanders. The summer, however, saw political matters hanging in the balance, and the initiative seemed to lie in the hands of the revolutionaries. The fact that their ranks were less closed than they appeared to be from the outside would only become apparent after the elections to the Vienna *Reichstag*.

The election regulations which had been at the centre of domestic political conflicts since April were regarded as the measure of the degree of democratization. The rule that only those people who had lived at the site of the election for six months were entitled to vote was strictly enforced. 'Independent workers' were supposed to be allowed to vote. But this could be interpreted narrowly or loosely: in many places the election committees regarded journeymen, wage earners in general and landless *Einlieger* and other agricultural workers in rural areas as 'dependent'. Peasants on the other hand experienced no problem in acquiring the right to vote. Above all in Galicia, but also in Silesia, Lower and Upper Austria, landowners and large and medium-scale farmers elected *Reichstag* deputies who would vigorously defend their interests.[16]

Indirect elections were held with primary elections in the first round and a second round in which delegates voted for the deputies. The most politically committed members of the Austrian election movement thus came to the attention of the public. Landowning farmers dominated, followed by local officials, judges, lawyers doctors and clergymen. Small businessmen were elected in those regions where small-scale commercial production was important. Analyses of the social composition of the delegate committees (cf. Table 6) show clearly that the future *Reichstag* would have to concern itself with the main subject of agrarian issues (feudal obligations and peasants' duties). Where class-specific interests dominated so heavily, the revolution was bound to lose support as soon as these interests seemed to have been satisfied.

6 Political Associations and Middle-Class Pressure Groups

The revolution had begun with massive demonstrations by different social groups. In rallies, marches and programmatic proclamations the revolutionaries had seized the right which they had been consistently denied throughout the *Vormärz* period: the right to assemble for political purposes and to organize. The political energy which was suddenly unleashed was expressed in a variety of forms: in associations, societies, clubs, committees, reading circles, in spontaneous gatherings and planned meetings.[1]

Although the constitutionalist liberal middle classes took part in these events, they regarded them with growing scepticism. 'Party', and to a greater extent 'party spirit', had always had a bad reputation in the constitutionalist political science of the *Vormärz* period, which taught that each chamber deputy should speak for the good of all the people, and not simply for a 'party'. Moreover, the formation of political organizations before 1848 had always been linked with subversion and conspiracy by officialdom. In the Federal Decree of 5 July 1832, a rigorous ban on all political association had been formally enacted.

1848, however, and in particular the almost free elections in the spring, brought home to everyone that the establishment of parties and parliaments went hand in hand in an open society. The new experience of the formation of parties, on the other hand, split the population into competing groups, which had to learn to tolerate each other as a matter of principle. 'Parties' no longer referred to the organization of thought, formulated in scholarly prose, but to socially organized political groupings. As a result, the connotations of being a 'party man' also changed. Even the leading supporter of constitutionalism, Heinrich von Gagern, discovered that, 'An isolated position is always a weak one; one can only have or gain political influence at the top of a political party.'[2]

The creation of these various different parties had a threefold effect: it mobilized, channelled and structured the political development of informed opinion to an extent that has only recently become clear in the numerous regional studies that have been carried out. The desire to organize political activity was proclaimed not only in the nerve centres of Vienna, Berlin and Frankfurt, but in small communities too. The widely held belief that the population was politically 'immature' is thus shown to be outdated in many respects. After all, immaturity would lead us to expect lethargy or spontaneous, aimless outbreaks of violence, at least amongst the urban classes, but certainly not the formation of organized political associations, which required rationality, practice, training and the observation of commonly agreed rules and regulations. This experience had developed and matured in the associations of the *Vormärz* period.

The modernizing thrust of 1848 changed the dignitary parties into parties with mass-membership, changed party clubs, effective only at parliamentary level, into political associations of like-minded people, active at a social level, whether or not they are regarded as parties. Where we place the beginning of the history of the German 'parties' depends, of course, on the features we are looking at. It is usually said to come somewhere between the end of the eighteenth century and the foundation of the Reich in 1871, that is to say, between the foundation of the first middle-class associations in Germany and the establishment of the German *Reichstag* on the principle of universal suffrage.

The revolution of 1848–9 holds a key position in this debate, because for the first time the nation as a whole enjoyed the freedom to assemble and form associations. This created excellent conditions for the formation of parties. To some extent the argument about the beginnings of the political parties is only a war of words, and we should leave it as such. More important for our purposes are those features in the formation of political associations in 1848–9 which may be regarded as 'modern', and which, therefore, had a formative influence on the establishment of parties far beyond the historical events of the time.

Regardless of their political direction, the associations formed in this period shared a number of basic features. First and foremost, the typical fully fledged political association of 1848 worked internally, within the association: it called its members to attend meetings at regular intervals; it adopted a constitution, which contained a political programme and standing orders; it offered lectures, discussions and readings at its meetings; it elected a committee and delegates; it voted on resolutions, petitions, declarations and protests. Secondly, it was hoped that these things would have an effect outside the association, that they would attract publicity and increase its sphere of influence. To this end, as far as resources permitted, the association published a periodical publication, perhaps even a newspaper. In keeping with the political agitation throughout the country, it sought to find a place in the hierarchy of district and regional committees under a national umbrella organization. Regional and national congresses extended its public platform, and might allow an association to grow to a position of influence in advising parliaments.

This typical association served political purposes. It was established on a long-term basis. It had a fixed programme and a recognizable organizational framework. It was open to new members. It thrived on competing opinions, strove for participation in parliamentary elections, and saw a chance to control the political development of informed opinion. It is rightly regarded as the nucleus of the modern political party, even if, once initiated, its further development was delayed by the decade of reaction which followed the revolution. The basic pattern had at any rate been set. It stuck in people's minds and could be rekindled as soon as circumstances allowed.

The structure of associations characterized according to this ideal type will become clear in the following description of the political lines adopted by various parties. But we must not be misled as to how much of it was transformed by the events of 1848–9. In reality, associations came in a wide variety of shapes and sizes. Answers to the following questions would have varied considerably from one association to another. What was the relationship between central office and local association in the development of informed opinion? How taut was the organization, how homogeneous its programme? Which social groups were the mainstay of the association? To what extent did it participate in the events of the revolution? What was its relationship with parliamentary factions?

The formation of associations was not a continuous process, but took place in phases. Momentum was provided by five key events, starting with the election movements of the spring of 1848, which were concentrated in the towns. Further momentum came from the negotiations of the Frankfurt National Assembly, beginning with the conflicts surrounding the Provisional Central Power and the ideal type of state, and continuing through a succession of important themes in the Basic Rights debates. A third key event was the autumn victory of the counter-revolution in Frankfurt, Vienna and Berlin, whose successes gave rise to movements which sought to defend what had been achieved, including the so-called '*Zentralmärz-verein*' or Central March Association. Then came the elections to the individual state legislatures in the winter of 1848–9, when decisions were made on the modernization and reform of the state constitutions. The final important event was the conclusion of the Frankfurt debates on the constitution, culminating in the election of the Kaiser, which marked the beginning of the revolutionary fight for the Imperial Constitution from April to July 1849.

Despite all the variations, there were five basic types of political association in 1848–9. In organizational terms they were still indistinct, but ideologically they were more clearly differentiated, particularly from the 1840s onwards. They were the workers' societies, the democratic and republican associations, the associations of constitutionalist liberals, the political Catholic associations and finally the conservative associations. This structure has rightly been referred to as 'a kind of multi-party system'.[3]

The Workers' Societies

In 1848 the worker emerged together with the *Bürger* as a political actor in the public sphere: this statement is true, and yet at the same time it is too simple. The social position and the interests of the lower orders dependent on wages were too contradictory to allow us to speak of *the* worker in the revolution. Some were backward-looking, making their animosity to industry clear by storming machines. Others were in favour of social policies and autonomous self-help associations. Others still supported programmes calling for a revolutionary change in the system. The working class was by no means homogeneous. A shared class consciousness emerged only gradually under the influence of revolutionary events. Although contemporaries were familiar with the term 'proletariat', they also spoke of the '*handarbeitenden Klassen*' or 'manual working classes'. But a modern proletariat, conscious of a common class position, such as Karl Marx had postulated before the outbreak of the March revolution in the *Communist Manifesto*, did not exist. Marx offered 'not a diagnosis, but a prognosis' for Germany.[4] The broad mass of workers in 1848 did not work in the factories or build railways. For the most part they were manual workers employed in small businesses. It was above all craftsmen whose existence was threatened, and journeymen in particular, who embodied *the* worker of 1848.

Craftsmen emerged for the first time as a movement intent on organizing at the general *Congress of Craftsmen and Tradesmen* of 15 July 1848 in Frankfurt. It was here that master craftsmen and journeymen formulated their protest against capitalism, against the emerging industries and against free competition and freedom of enterprise. The elimination of guild restrictions had caused a crisis in the craftsmen's small businesses. The congress acted as a lobby to the National Assembly meeting in Frankfurt, and attempted at the same time to harness socio-conservative forces. Its spokesman was the Kassel trade school teacher, Karl Georg Winkelblech, who called himself Marlo. In a remarkable union of retrogressive precapitalistic opinion and modern socialist aims, it was proposed that the guilds be resurrected and enforced to guide and monitor production, which would be ultimately controlled by the state.[5]

Yet the social base and the field of interests of this group were fragile: refusing to debate matters with the journeymen, the master craftsmen organized a counter-conference in Frankfurt (20 July to 20 September 1848). The journeymen later joined a 'General Workers' Congress'. They developed a degree of class consciousness which the newly established Central Workers' Organization in Berlin had already articulated: their founding congress proclaimed its refusal to accept 'the antithesis between masters and journeymen' which the medieval guild system had retained. They were prepared only to accept 'the modern social antithesis between capitalists and workers'. This was formulated by the *Allgemeine deutsche Arbeiterverbrüderung*, the General German Workers' Fraternity,[6] which the journeymen joined in large numbers, making it by far the largest organization of German workers' societies during and after the revolution. As its name implies, it became active at a national level.

The General German Workers' Fraternity had emerged from the debates of the Workers' Congress, which met in Berlin from 23 August to 3 September 1848. Led by a Workers' Committee from Berlin, committees from Hamburg, Leipzig and Chemnitz, and delegates from 31 workers' societies took part in its foundation. They came primarily from Saxony, the old Prussian provinces and northern Germany. To a large degree the Workers' Fraternity owed its success to the superb organizational talents of the typesetter Stephan Born. District and local committees throughout Germany came under the central committee formed in Berlin, which subsequently moved permanently to Leipzig.[7] In the spring of 1849 this organization counted among its members more than 15,000 workers from approximately 170 local workers' societies.[8] It extended its sphere of influence with its own newspaper, *Die Verbrüderung*, which became the most widely read newspaper amongst organized journeymen and workers.

Its unusual success testified to the underlying need of its members to bring their own poverty to the attention of the public. But it was not only economic pressures which provided the impetus for organized self-help; a wave of local wages strikes in April 1848 had stirred up the textile, metal, building and book printing trades. The Frankfurt National Assembly, which had been meeting since May, demonstrated disappointingly scant understanding of the workers' problems. As the circular issued by the founding congress declared, 'We workers must help ourselves.'

But these workers did not pursue an anti-parliamentary course. On the contrary, the Workers' Fraternity presented its Berlin resolutions to the Frankfurt National Assembly in the form of a manifesto, with the request that its organization be protected 'for all time' by future legislation and favoured by the state.[9] This reflects its desire to remain firmly within the middle-class constitution. Where the National Assembly neglected the social issue in the Basic Rights, the Workers' Fraternity pursued a kind of 'social parallel policy' (W. Schieder): it sought to expand the policies of the middle classes by means of socio-political activities, production and consumer co-operatives, by support for journeymen and health insurance schemes. It also focused on workers' education, for it had become clear during the elections that the higher standards of education enjoyed by the middle classes had been instrumental in keeping the workers out of the parliaments. The long-term aim was the integration of the workers into the political democracy.

The Workers' Fraternity concerned itself with more than education, unions and social policy, however: it also saw itself as a political force. This was shown in May 1849 in its appeals to take up arms in the campaign for the Imperial Constitution. This too was a battle *for* constitutional law.

These workers' organizations favoured socio-conservative policies or social reform. There was a third variant too, embodied by the

Communist League, which favoured social revolution. The League had its origins in the secret journeyman associations of the *Vormärz* period in Paris, Switzerland and Germany, and had emerged from the '*Bund der Gerechten*', whose members included Born and Marx (after 1847). At a League conference in June 1847 in London, it had changed its name to the 'Communist League' under Marx's influence.[10] From then on the motto: '*Proletarier aller Länder vereinigt Euch*' (workers of the world unite) had appeared in the statutes. Marx formulated the statutes (8 December 1847) on behalf of the League, and in them its aims: 'the overthrow of the bourgeoisie, rule by the proletariat, the abolition of the old bourgeois society based on class conflicts, and the establishment of a new society, without classes and without private property.'[11]

Even before the outbreak of the revolution at the end of February Marx wrote these principles in the *Communist Manifesto*. The Cologne branch soon became the most important branch of the League in Germany. Marx moved to Cologne during the revolution.

The 'Communist League' presents us with a number of problems, not least because it represented a focus of historical research in the GDR, and was constantly used to 'secure communist evidence' (D. Langewiesche) on the subject of its membership and its sphere of influence. For a long time it was underestimated or misjudged. A great deal of further research was necessary before the facets of its real political significance could be recognized.

There was a huge gulf between its demands and reality. At the end of March the central office of the League in Paris published the seventeen *Demands of the Communist Party in Germany* in a pamphlet signed by Marx, Engels and others.[12] Aimed at the 'interests of the German proletariat, the lower middle-classes and the peasant class', the Demands did not propose the unrestricted nationalization of all private property, as stated in the statutes. Together with the abolition of all feudal burdens without compensation, it was proposed that the following should become 'state property': princes' and feudal estates, banks, means of transport and the postal service.

But it was impossible to act in a politically effective manner on a mass basis with a programme such as this. At the beginning of April the League failed in its attempt to unite the emerging workers' societies in a national framework organization with a base in Mainz. In terms of numbers, the small League and its emissaries were not up to the task; local organizations and the central office in Mainz were uncoordinated. Locally based special efforts and diverging aims contributed as much to the failure as the fact that the large associations in Cologne and Berlin rejected the centralization efforts concentrated on Mainz.[13] These facts were not denied by GDR researchers either.

In this light it is irrelevant whether or not Marx had wished to dissolve the League in May and June 1848, because there was no longer a need for secret organizations, such as the League had originally been. All the same, at the end of 1849 he attempted to reorganize it anyway from exile in London. But it is also a fact that in 1848 Marx and Engels channelled their political energies not into the League, but into the middle-class democratic movement, above all through the propaganda of their *Neue Rheinische Zeitung*, which defined itself as an 'organ of democracy'. By contrast, they neglected the organization of an independent workers' party, the core of which had developed in the Workers' Fraternity.

The pages of the *Neue Rheinische Zeitung* reflect several changes of tack undertaken by Marx. First he moved away from the German 'bourgeoisie', whose Frankfurt Parliament he had initially welcomed. At the end of 1848 he turned towards the 'lower middle-class masses'. Finally, he changed tack again, moving away from them, and from April 1849 onwards set his sights on the independent organization of workers. None the less, it can be demonstrated that he remained convinced throughout that the emancipation of the proletariat could only be expected after a middle-class revolution had been completed.

Without Marx's knowledge, however, and against his wishes, small cadres of the Communist League had continued to work since the spring of 1848. They made significant advances in the organization of workers' societies. But it is not possible to draw conclusions on the loyalty to the party line of the League's membership. Double membership was by no means uncommon. So far, it has been shown that 48 leading 'functionaries' of the Workers' Fraternity also belonged to the Communist League, more than three-quarters of whom were workers.[14]

In these turbulent times programmes were often only concomitant forms of political expression. In fact, it was frequently irrelevant whether someone was a confirmed democrat, a social democrat, a socialist, a communist supporter of 'Marx's Party' or a member of the Communist League, as the example of Lassalle shows: he was in close contact with Marx, was not a member of the League, yet rightly saw himself as 'of the party'.[15] Many societies also pursued independent actions and autonomous aims at local level. This was documented by the largest German workers' society in its *Zeitung des Arbeiter-Vereins zu Köln*, the columns of which recorded areas of conflict and cooperation between the middle classes and the workers.[16]

The Democratic Associations

A split between democrats and constitutionalists had already formed during the *Vormärz* period. This was not just an ideological division, reflected in political writings. It was also manifested in separate actions: a leading democratic republican stratum first emerged with the Hambachers in 1832; the constitutionalists had made their presence felt in the protests of the Göttingen Seven in 1837. Tangible evidence of these separate paths of development was revealed in the autumn of 1847, when the democrats sought an organizational platform in Offenburg and the constitutionalists in Heppenheim.

For the most part, the democrats called their organizations 'people's associations' or 'democratic (people's) associations'. Only in some regions, Saxony for example, were they called 'fatherland associations'.[17]

Since the term 'liberalism' is a category taken from later processes in the formation of parties, it is difficult to define '*the* liberalism' of 1848 from an organizational point of view. Like the division of the Paulskirche centre into 'left' and 'centre-right', the 'liberals' of 1848 belonged to both constitutionalist and democratic organizations. Their constitutionalist wing shared a number of features with the later National Liberals (1866), whilst their parliamentary-democratic wing had more in common with the future *Fortschrittspartei* (1861). There too the organizational division was continued.

In the democrats' programmes the origins and driving forces of state power lay with the people: they were steadfast in their commitment to the principle of the sovereignty of the people. They called for a single chamber system, universal, equal and direct elections, usually with an accountable president as head of state. Only amongst the parliamentary liberal supporters was the tactical toleration of a constitutional monarchy observed, and even then it was 'on the broadest democratic basis'. Their revolutionary wing, on the other hand, favoured direct action and was prepared even to contemplate violence. This had already become clear in the Pre-Parliament. Similarly, on several occasions during the revolution, republican democrats attempted to form counter-parliaments or to break up the Frankfurt National Assembly.[18] The social question was addressed in demands for a ministry of work, the right to work and for a progressive income tax, and now and then in calls for the socialist organization of society and national workshop projects.

Some of the democratic associations developed as autonomous organizations. Others emerged as a result of rifts, as was seen in Württemberg. A call issued by the Göppingen Fatherland Association on 26 March 1848 had still managed to unite constitutionalists and democrats.[19] Its aim was to establish a nationwide organization with district groupings and a head association in Stuttgart. Approximately 50 associations answered the call for members. Apparently as a result of the Frankfurt Central Power debates, the Stuttgart head association experienced a leadership controversy of its own. On 8 July a minority rejected the existing constitutional monarchy as a political programmatic aim and split from the main group. The remaining constitutionalist '*fatherland* associations' now found themselves in opposition to the new democratic '*people's* associations'. The rift soon spread to the other local associations in the state.

Parties were also formed as a result of independent programmatic attempts to which the constitutionalists could only respond by founding counter-organizations. This happened in Saxony, where in Leipzig on 28 March 1848 the democrats called for the foundation of 'fatherland associations' throughout the state. The response was good: the first General Assembly of 23–4 April was attended by 116 delegates representing 43 associations with a total of 11,463 members.[20] Shortly afterwards there were said to be as many as 75 associations. It was a mass phenomenon, repeated throughout Germany, which grew in intensity by a process of action and reaction. 6 April saw the formation of the constitutionalist 'German associations' in Saxony. Within a short time they were in a position to activate at least 30 branch associations with approximately 10,000 members. At the same time, the foundation of these early associations testifies to the fact that in 1848 the formation of parties took place independently, and did not go hand in hand with the formation of parliamentary parties, as was believed for a long time.

This applies in particular to the earliest attempt to establish a party organization for the whole of Germany with affiliated municipal, regional, district and state associations. Here, too, the initiative lay with the democrats, who resolved to organize in this way at the Offenburg Meeting on 19 March 1848.[21]

The democratic wing of the Pre-Parliament also attempted to form a national organization. On 4 April 1848 Hecker, von Struve, the Cologne communist, d'Ester, Zitz and Mohr from Rheinhesse and others formed a democratic central committee in Frankfurt, with the intention of influencing the elections to the National Assembly. Subsequent events, however, showed the democrats to be in the minority. This strengthened the resolve to use as great an extra-parliamentary force as possible to oppose the policies of the Frankfurt National Assembly, which were aimed at pacifying the revolution. To this end, the Democratic Association and the Workers' Society of Marburg organized a *First Democratic Congress* in Frankfurt (14–17 June), at which 234 delegates from 89 associations in 66 towns drafted a programme for the emerging democratic party.[22]

Under the chairmanship of Julius Fröbel,[23] debates were held by such prominent members as the materialist philosopher Ludwig Feuerbach, the leading German Catholic Johannes Ronge, the Communist and leader of the Cologne Workers' Society, Andreas Gottschalk, Ferdinand Freiligrath and Ludwig Bamberger – in short, a spectrum far broader than anything seen in the Paulskirche. Representatives of the Silesian 'rustic associations' were also present. This sole peasant mass organization of the revolutionary period worked closely with the democratic associations and in its heyday was said to have included 200 associations, representing some 200,000 members.

The Congress set about the task of forming a party very seriously. It appointed a five-man central committee in Berlin, the first central party office in Germany to support itself, though only after a fashion, from subscriptions raised and to appoint full-time functionaries. At the same time, the transfer to Berlin clearly implied that the democrats expected the political focus of future developments to be in the Prussian capital. Indeed, the lively activity surrounding the formation of parties in Prussia justified this prognosis. Conservative estimates suggest that in October there were approximately 700 political associations in the monarchy as a whole, of which some 300 were constitutionalist, approximately 250 democratic, and around 50 conservative (Prussian and patriotic associations, associations for the safeguarding of property). Twelve were workers' societies and six 'Pius associations'.[24]

In October Prussia suddenly found itself in the throes of the counter-revolution. In response to this crisis a *Second Democratic Congress* met in Berlin from 26 to 31 October. The central committee which issued the invitation favoured revolutionary action, calling in a manifesto of 3 October 1848 for the overthrow of the Frankfurt National Assembly, so that 'the true will of the nation can be expressed'. Only new elections, it was claimed, would be able to 'prevent the necessity of a new and bloody revolution'. Two hundred and thirty-four delegates representing 260 associations in 140 towns converged on Berlin.[25] Eighty-seven associations declared their support for 'democracy' in their titles, with a further 50 identifying themselves as 'peoples' parties' (*Volksverein, Verein für Volksrechte, für Volksfreunde, für Volksfreiheit*).[26] These terms were used to distinguish themselves from the 'constitutionalist' associations.

A range of political opinion was represented, including speakers from the Workers' Fraternity (Born) and the 'Communist League'. The Congress's position on the Vienna October revolution and to the social question provoked profound disagreements. The Congress refused to give its consent to Born's motion to adopt the resolutions of the Berlin Workers' Fraternity. The convening of a new German National Assembly was regarded as vital.

Scholars often criticize the Congress for the controversies between the 'political' and 'social' democrats, and even that such intense arguments took place at all. But in doing so they overlook the fact that this party, which was still in the process of being formed, was allowed precious little testing time by the Prussian reactionary policies. Given the energies expended in suppressing the political associations, its chances of development were probably not so unfavourable after all. A state of siege and a ban on associations (12 November 1848) put an abrupt end to the centralization efforts of the democrats in Prussia.

The days immediately preceding the coup are characterized by the frantic search for the right political strategy on the part of the democrats who were prepared to take action. A *Counter-Parliament* met in Berlin on 27 October. Deputies from the individual German chambers and six members of the Paulskirche 'Donnersberg' faction agreed resolutions to support the revolutionaries in Vienna with donations and volunteer corps. But this too failed and only served as an additional pretext for further military action.

Suppression in Prussia, the crisis within their own organization, together with the general advance of the counter-revolution, led the democrats to reorganize their central office on a more homogeneous basis after Berlin was abandoned as the centre of action. It was based on the democratic factions of the Frankfurt National Assembly. On 21 November 1848 deputies from three factions ('Donnersberg',

'Deutscher Hof' and 'Westendhall') united for the purpose of defending the '*Märzerrungenschaften*' or March achievements. Forming a loose umbrella organization, they now called themselves the '*Zentralmärzverein*' or Central March Association, which took over the task of informing affiliated associations by means of manifestos and circulars. They issued press releases, organized rallies and co-ordinated demonstrations. For the Central March Association the main issues were the imposition of the Prussian constitution, the proclamation of the list of Basic Rights and above all the campaign to push through the Imperial Constitution of 28 March 1849. During this period at least 950 local associations with a total of 500,000 members joined the Central March Association in Frankfurt.[27] The constitutionalist associations remained aloof and continued to pursue independent organization.

On 6 May 1849, under the leadership of Fröbel, the Central March Association held a General Assembly in Frankfurt, at which it went as far as to prepare the revolutionary battle. German soldiers were asked to uphold the Imperial Constitution, and calls were made to form civil defence associations.

When looking at the social composition of the democratic people's associations, it is important to distinguish between leadership and general membership. Accurate statistics from these associations are

Table 7 Social composition of the Democratic People's Association, Nördlingen (430 members)

Members	%	Leading group
Craftsmen and tradesmen	65.1	
Merchants	6.7	5 teachers
Brewers and innkeepers	6.7	2 innkeepers
Ordinary employees	3.7	2 doctors
Primary school teachers	2.1	1 merchant
Doctors	0.9	1 bookseller
Junior civil servants	0.9	1 editor
Peasants	0.9	1 lithographer
Other middle-class professions	4.8	
No profession given	8.2	

Source: M. Botzenhart, *Deutscher Parlamentarismus in der Revolutionszeit 1848–1850* (Düsseldorf, 1977), p. 376.

rare, but it is possible to collate a number of different statistics to gain an impression of the structure of the 'People's Association' in Nördlingen. It is probably not untypical of the democratic associations in smaller towns (see Table 7).[28]

The structure of the Nördlingen association reflects the following trends: the spokesmen tended to come from the freelance intelligentsia – that is, lawyers, doctors, pharmacists, legal trainees, candidates for state service, editors and, surprisingly frequently, *Volksschule* teachers. The majority of members were craftsmen and journeymen. Strong links were maintained with the lower orders. This was seen in the most extreme terms in the Dresden democratic 'Fatherland Association': at the end of 1848, 1691 journeymen, 570 workers, 391 soldiers and 30 servants comprised more than 50 per cent of its 4346 members.[29]

The Constitutionalist Associations

As a rule the constitutionalists understood their attempts to unify as a response to 'the tireless activities of the opponents, the so-called democratic clubs, which do everything they can to bring about a social republic', as a correspondent from the *Deutsche Zeitung* put it on 21 July 1848.[30] The constitutionalist associations, as they were overwhelmingly called, also used the terms Fatherland, German, constitutional-monarchical, national or simply 'Bürger' in their titles; rarely employing the term 'liberal'. In the language of the time, 'constitutionalist' meant reconciling the idea of a monarchy with a written constitution.

For this reason their programme included the maintenance of the monarchy, the bicameral system, protection of the interests of the middle class, of landowners and of property in general, suffrage based on the payment of taxes, to the exclusion of those who were not 'independent', the absolute veto of the monarch on the chambers as 'the right to perform an act of rescue' (Dahlmann). The constitutionalists were most frequently represented in the Paulskirche by the 'centre-right' and the 'right'; by the 'Casino', 'Landsberg' and 'Augsburger Hof' factions. Those of an emphatically royalist persuasion were represented by the 'Café Milani'. As a general rule, they favoured the course adopted by the majority factions of the Paulskirche, and a number of their proclamations were designed to voice public support for the National Assembly.

In some towns their local associations were not far behind the democrats in terms of membership numbers. The 1100-strong constitutionalist '*Bürgerverein*' in Kassel was even able to match the democratic '*Volksverein*' in Hildesheim. On average they had between 300 and 700 members. The majority of the local associations formed parties in the typical fashion. However, in terms of their efforts to form centralized organizations, the constitutionalists were clearly behind the democrats. In various different towns, including Cologne, Berlin, Halle, Leipzig and Kassel, simultaneous independent efforts were made to establish a national umbrella organization. The attempts in Kassel proved most successful. In general, the leading constitutionalist Paulskirche deputies remained largely passive in this.

The resolutions of the First Democratic Congress in June 1848 strengthened the resolve of the 'constitutionalist club' in Berlin to convene a general congress in order to build up a party organization which might be pitted against the democrats. A hundred and fifty-eight delegates from 90 associations met in Berlin from 22 to 24 July 1848, two-thirds of whom were academics and civil servants. The rest were merchants, senior employees and landowners.[31] Despite the best beginnings, however, these attempts soon foundered.

The call to found a 'National Association' issued by the '*Bürgerverein*' in Kassel on 7 September 1848 came during the heated debates surrounding the Schleswig–Holstein issue. Sixty-six delegates met there from 3 to 5 November 1848. They represented 28 associations, some of which were state-wide organizations; the Leipzig 'German Association' for example represented 40 local groups. Deputies came from Saxony, Hesse, Kurhesse, Brunswick, Hamburg, Bremen and Oldenburg.[32] The Prussian constitutionalists were absent, probably because they could already foresee the imminent coup in Berlin. This time the attempt to form a national organization was more successful and lasting. During the period of its greatest expansion in April 1849, some 160 associations belonged to the 'National Association'. Most came from northern, central and south-western Germany. There were very few indeed in Prussia, Bavaria and Württemberg. In the case of the last two this might be explained by the fact that the central office was in favour of a Prussian hereditary *Kaisertum*.

The 'National Association' maintained a strict distance from the 'Central March Association'. Only during the campaign for the Imperial Constitution did it venture a degree of *rapprochement*. The main association in Kassel invited members to attend a 'national congress' in Frankfurt on 14 May 1849. Under the chairmanship of the historian, Heinrich von Sybel, later exponent of *kleindeutsch*-Prussian historiography, 78 delegates met at the *erbkaiserlich* 'Weiden-busch' restaurant. Hopes for an alliance with Paulskirche deputies were dashed when only eight of them turned up. The 'National Asso-ciation' saw itself as 'the expression of the will of the moderate, mainly conservative, but honest and freedom-loving party of the German people'.[33] Attempts to form an alliance with the 'Central March Association' foundered, and the National Association fell silent in June 1849, when the National Assembly was also broken up. Initia-tives to form a national party organization were taken up again by the Paulskirche *Erbkaiserlichen* who were meeting in Gotha; but these efforts form part of the concluding phase of the revolution.

In terms of social composition, the constitutionalist associations represented the middle and upper middle classes: civil servants, pro-fessors, manufacturers and master craftsmen who were conscious of their rank as they organized themselves at the Frankfurt Craftsmen's Congress. Members of the lower orders did join the associations, but their numbers were small and the associations' own regulations forced them to take a back seat (see Table 8).

The social structure of the constitutionalist associations reflected the main social tasks which they had set themselves:

> To form enlightened, law-abiding, moderate, peace-keeping citizens of the state. The lower classes, namely the workers, will learn that it is only when the law is respected . . . only when fair, moderate demands are made, when they are well and truly willing to be *active*, that they will be able to achieve their reasonable aim of assuming a more respected and equal position amongst other citizens of the state.

This is how a leading member of the Leipzig 'German Association' put it.[34] In so doing, he described the model of a classless society of citizens of moderate livelihoods, to which the dependent man should aspire.

The Political Catholic Associations

Catholics had already become politicized during the *Vormärz* period, when disagreements between the Prussian state and the Catholic

Table 8 Social composition of constitutionalist associations (percentages in brackets refer to members 'with no details' who are proportionately added to the other groups)

	German Assoc., Leipzig (%)	Fatherland Association, Brunswick (%)	Constitutionalist–monarchical Assoc., Darmstadt (%)	Civic Assoc., Kassel (%)	Fatherland Association, Hanover (%)	Fatherland Association, Stuttgart (%)	Constitutionalist Congress, Berlin 1848 (%)	Congress of the National Association, Frankfurt a.M. 1849 (%)
Academic and teaching professions	20 (24)	21 (22)	3 (3)	8 (8)	16 (18)	8 (11)	35	50
Merchants, traders, bankers, factory owners	29 (34)	21 (22)	6 (7)	21 (23)	22 (26)	28 (37)	8	
Civil servants	5 (6)	26 (27)	16 (19)	26 (28)	20 (23)	15 (20)	33	17
Members of the army	4 (5)	9 (10)	20 (24)	5 (6)	2 (2)	2 (2)	2	
Senior employees[1]	7 (8)	2 (2)	13 (15)	4 (4)	7 (8)	3 (4)	4	
Junior employees[2]	7 (8)		7 (9)	6 (6)		2 (2)		
Master craftsmen		6 (6)	7 (8)	15 (16)	4 (5)	6 (8)		
Journeymen, workers	10 (12)	7 (7)		6 (7)	16 (18)	11 (16)		
Others[3]	3 (3)	4 (4)	13 (15)	2 (2)			6	13
No details	15 (−)	4 (−)	15 (−)	7 (−)	13 (−)	25 (−)	12	20

[1] Directors, engineers, and similar.

[2] Assistants, coachmen, servants and similar.

[3] Landowners, demesne tenants, pensioners, etc. Includes members of the above professional groups if they represent less than 2 per cent.

Source: H. Gebhardt, *Revolution und nationale Bewegung* (Bremen, 1974), p. 165.

Church on the mixed marriage conflict threatened to turn into a *Kulturkampf*. In 1848, memories of the conflict gained expression in demands for religious freedom from the state and the retention of the Church's influence in society. The new freedoms regarding the press, the formation of associations and the right to assemble gave rise to a highly influential extra-parliamentary mass movement. The Frankfurt parliament was bombarded by a well-organized petition movement, aimed at influencing the debates on the list of Basic Rights. It was steered by newly formed Catholic associations, with the '*Pius-Vereine*' or 'Pius associations' playing the most important role. They took their name from Pope Pius IX, who had assumed the position of Pope as a liberal in 1846, until the revolution turned him into a bitter opponent of liberalism, paving the way for the *Kulturkampf*.

The first 'Pius association' was formed at a public meeting on 28 March in Mainz. This was followed by a wave of further Pius associations, founded in the Rhineland, in Nassau, Silesia, Bavaria, Württemberg and above all in Baden, home of the movement's leading propagandist, the tailor's son and Freiburg professor of canon law, Franz Joseph Buß. The political leanings of the Catholics were by no means clear-cut. Some were close to the March movement, but most of them inclined towards the conservative stance represented by Buß. In the Paulskirche he belonged to the 'right' ('Café Milani'), and, by the nature of things, found himself in opposition to the democrats, whose demands included the democratic election of priests; a profound attack on the heart of the Church structure. The democrats also sought to reduce the Church's influence in society, to nationalize schools and to eliminate existing denominational schools.

By the end of October 1848, the 'Pius association' movement in Baden alone was based on approximately 400 local associations, with a total of 100,000 members.[35] The success of the movement here may be attributed to the efforts of Buß, who once maintained that he had held nine or ten meetings before 150,000 voters in the space of three days. Like other association movements with a broad organizational base, the 'Pius associations' also aspired to form a national umbrella organization. This was duly founded by a 'General Assembly', presided over by Buß, which met between 3 and 6 October 1848 in Mainz. Bishops and deputies from state parliaments and the Paulskirche figured prominently at the Assembly. This meeting began the tradition of *Katholikentage*, Catholic conventions which are still held today. This first meeting in Mainz was intensely political. On 6 October, following detailed debates, the Assembly formulated

a 'Protest to the German National Assembly', which voiced its criti-
cisms of the institutional guarantee of the state school and the ban on
the Jesuit order.[36]

Pressure from the 'Pius associations' saw to it that the ban on the
Jesuit order disappeared from the Basic Rights, and that the right of
the Church to oversee religious instruction was included. Here were
seen some manifestations of a modern parliamentary system: the
influence of extra-parliamentary organizations; public pressure aug-
mented by means of petitions; and, not least, the responses of some of
the targeted parliamentarians: in Frankfurt this was the inter-fac-
tional agreement between members of the 'Catholic Club', which
held until the controversial issues had been resolved.

The Pius associations' *Katholikentag* established a central organization called the 'German Catholic Association'. It was not a party,
although its political activities were more similar to those of a party
than the 'Vinzenzius associations', for example, formed at the same
time in Mainz. These exponents of Christian social theory restricted
themselves to church and charitable activities.

The Conservative Associations

Conservatism seemed out of date in the year of the revolution; probably rightly so, since change was the aim of the vast majority of
political efforts in 1848. Yet as soon as questions were raised as to the
direction that individual measures should take, traditional value
judgements were revived amongst peasants, craftsmen, small traders,
constitutionally minded civil servants and aristocrats, factory and
agricultural workers. After the onslaught of the revolution, a wide
range of conservative undercurrents emerged. These have been
exposed by recent research into protests, which has taught us to distinguish carefully between the exponents, causes, extent and aims of
individual campaigns. In the context of the dynamics of the revolution, these non-organized phenomena will be described in more detail.

These elements have long been underestimated, and attempts to
categorize them have only recently produced initial findings. The
first significant collection of source material on the beginnings of the
German party system in the 1848 revolution does not yet mention
conservative associations.[37] Yet exist they did, and only future archi-
val research will permit an assessment of their significance. Nor
should research into the Austrian situation be ignored, though it is

already certain today that associations of this kind were concentrated overwhelmingly in Prussia and Bavaria.

Ernst Ludwig von Gerlach, member of the 'camarilla' at the Prussian court and Magdeburg *Oberlandesgerichtsrat*, recognized more clearly and keenly than most liberals that parliaments and parties necessarily go hand in hand. In the *Neue Preußische Zeitung*, which he edited, he wrote:

> The larger the proportion of the people at the helm of government affairs decreed by the constitution, the more necessary is the grouping of citizens of the state according to their political leanings, in other words the *organization of political parties*. The purpose of the formation of a party is to unite in common action all supporters of a general and fundamental political direction, and thus to achieve victory for this direction over those which deviate from it.[38]

Inter-party struggles and the constitutional system were inseparable in his view, although this did not imply that he accepted the system on principle. Like some democrats, he did so only out of tactical embarrassment. While the democrats sought to advance beyond the constitutional system, *these* Prussian conservatives wanted to retreat from it. They wanted to disown the revolution, to dissolve the Prussian National Assembly and to return to the provincial diets and the United Diet, which they saw not as the representative of the people, but of the separate estates. In a literal sense, they should really be described as 'reactionary', and indeed this was the polemical term used at the time, since they sought to reverse the legislation which had been enacted since March.

The conservatives' first party newspaper was Gerlach's *Neue Preußische Zeitung*, nicknamed the *Kreuzzeitung* after the emblem of a cross at the top of its front page. The iron cross, established by King Frederick William III on 10 March 1813, bore the motto *With God for King and Fatherland*. These words appeared on the front of the *Kreuzzeitung*, and were adopted as a slogan by the Prussian royalists of 1848.

At the beginning of July, Gerlach set about founding an 'Association for King and Fatherland', which was committed to the principles outlined above. His appeal was well-received. Fifty individual local organizations have been traced in Prussia bearing the names 'patriotic', 'Prussian' or 'Fatherland' association or 'Association for the Protection of Property'.[39] The 'Association for King and Fatherland' may be regarded as the Prussian conservatives' first central party organization.[40]

The coup of November 1848 was followed by conservative movements on a mass scale. All those who regarded themselves as having
been disadvantaged by the revolution and who supported the monarchy and a strong state, joined the '*Treubund für König und Vaterland*'
(Loyal Association for King and Fatherland), which also bore the
sub-title '*Royalisten-Bund*'. Its statutes declared, 'The aim of our association is the revival of truly constitutionalist convictions, the fortifi-
cation of loyalty and devotion to the King and the Fatherland, and
the promotion of the welfare of the people.' It was founded by the
War Ministry *Geheimsekretär* and former artilleryman, Ferdinand
von Habel. He enjoyed the support of General von Wrangel, who
imposed the siege over Berlin. On 26 March 1849 von Habel submitted the association's statutes to the Berlin police headquarters for
authorization. Just three months later a police report estimated its
membership in Berlin alone to be 10,000. The *Treubund* had a district
committee in each of more than 100 municipal districts. A list of these
committees still exists (see Table 9).

The major concerns of these exponents of royalism were peace, law
and order, increases in rents, sales and orders, and the ability accurately to predict trade and commercial activity in general. Only one
doctor, one pharmacist, not a single lawyer or member of the higher
educated middle classes were to be found on the district committees.
During the course of 1849 the *Treubund* set up 52 branch associations
in the monarchy as a whole, with 500 members in Charlottenburg,
300 in Halberstadt, 1400 in Potsdam and 360 in Halle. Its catchment
area reached as far as Breslau, Anhalt and the Grand Duchy of
Weimar. Approximately a quarter of these branch association committees were in the hands of the clergy, and another quarter were led

Table 9 Social composition of the 102 district committees of the Berlin 'Treubund für König und Vaterland'

Army, police	12
Master craftsmen, craftsmen	18
Traders, merchants, manufacturers	22
Civil servants	23
Teachers	6
Artists	7
Miscellaneous	14

Source: *Staatsarchiv Potsdam*, Pr. Br. Rep. 30 Berlin C,
      Polizeipräsidium Tit. 95, Sect. 5, no. 15476/77.

by civil servants. At the beginning of 1850 a further 40 associations were in the process of being formed.[41] This alliance between the throne and the altar, the army and the commercial middle class heralded the dawn of the reactionary period. The *Treubund* received considerable support from the secret fund of the Interior Ministry.

Since May 1848 the *Treubund's* conservative counterpart in Bavaria had been called the 'Association for a Constitutional Monarchy and Religious Freedom'. In Munich it had an impressive 1600 members, belonging to some 60 local associations. They were usually led by clergymen.[42]

The Middle-Class Pressure Groups

Not just in the political sphere, but in all other areas of social life too, the freedom to form associations gave rise to a host of voluntary associations, formed for specific purposes and regulated by statutes. In each case they sought to organize particular needs, thereby increasing their influence. This became a fundamental characteristic of society as the old system of estates dissolved, and associations took the place of the traditional corporations.

The beginnings of these trade, commercial, agricultural and professional associations date back to the *Vormärz* era. But the year of the revolution provided the opportunity for their unrestricted growth. Hoping that the Frankfurt parliament would have unlimited power and authority, few groups declined the opportunity to articulate their particular concerns in addresses, petitions and manifestos. To do this they needed first to clarify and develop opinion within their associations. In keeping with the general democratization of all levels of society, meetings were organized at which debates and votes were held and decisions made. Typically, like their political counterparts, these associations also organized national congresses.[43]

Whitsun 1848 saw a meeting of approximately 1200 delegates from all universities in Eisenach. In keeping with tradition, this national student parliament called itself the 'Wartburg Festival of German Students'.[44] A second congress was held in Eisenach from 25 September to 4 October. *Privatdozente* gathered in Frankfurt on 27 and 28 August to demand a 'free academic university'. Maintaining a distance from this meeting, a congress of over 120 university teachers discussed university reform in Jena from 21 to 24 September. In the same month a German teachers' conference met in Eisenach. Similar initiatives were undertaken by *Volksschule* teachers, doctors and in general by groups who hoped to find emancipation in the legislation of the new era, including Jews and women.

The first attempts to form the influential national pressure groups, which would become typical of Wilhelmine Germany, were seen in 1848. This was only logical, 'For as modern society became industrialized, organized interest groups increasingly became a fundamental expression of its political and economic structural relations.'[45] The growing opportunities offered by a nationally united market gave rise to boldness, the formation of special interest groups and unleashed defensive reactions against perceived threats. In northern Germany merchants from the Hansa towns and the agrarian coastal regions who had a particular interest in exports joined in a 'German Association for the Freedom of Trade' to defend free trade. Threatened by imports, the coal, steel and textile industries in the Rhineland, in Baden, Württemberg and Saxony joined the protectionist umbrella organization, the 'General German Association for the Protection of Work in the Fatherland'. Supporters of free trade battled with supporters of protective duties in a hail of petitions to the Paulskirche.

Economic expansion provoked counterforces which subsequently joined together, as we saw in the example of the Congress of Craftsmen in Frankfurt referred to above. At the Tailors' Congress, which also met in Frankfurt from 20 to 25 July, calls were made for freedom of trade to be revoked and trade in all cloth and fashion items to be banned. Society became riven by mutually antagonistic interest groups. Prominent amongst them were aristocrats in Prussia, who attempted to stall the impending defeudalization and to safeguard their interests in agrarian property by using the techniques of engagement devised by the middle classes. In July 1848 the landowner, Ernst Gottfried Georg von Bülow-Cummerow, founded the 'Association for the Protection of Property and for the Promotion of the Wealth of all Classes of the People'. On 18 and 19 August the lawyer and *Landrat*, Hans von Kleist-Retzow, founder of the *Kreuzzeitung*, assumed the leadership of the association's first General Assembly. It became known as the 'Junker Parliament' and counted a number of deputies from the former United Diet amongst its members, including Bismarck. Through their links with the court, and with the 'camarilla' in particular, these conservatives had an organization which was both a political campaigning organization and an organization of large-scale agrarian interests. They enjoyed close ideological and personal ties with the political 'Association for King and Fatherland'.

Association politics of this kind represented a degree of modernization: the decorporatization of the economy and the formation of modern pressure groups went hand in hand. ' "Organized capitalism" can be found from the very beginnings of the industrial system, commensurate with its growth and intensification.'[46]

7   Communication and the Public

The Lifting of Censorship and the Problems Experienced by the Book Trade

With the lifting of controls on 'the press' on 3 March, the *Bundestag* abolished the restrictions which had operated a strangle-hold on the production and dissemination of the printed word since 1819. The new freedoms applied not only to the daily press, but to all printed matter, from books and brochures to pamphlets, bill posters, poetry and caricatures. The real implications of the censorship of the press in the *Vormärz* period were made clear by the Frankfurt National Assembly deputies in their formulation of the Basic Rights. Press freedom was defined in terms of a kind of reverse mirror image of the restrictions which had formerly been imposed on the press:

> Every German has the right to express his opinion freely in words, writing, print and pictorial representation.
>
> Under no circumstances and in no way may freedom of the press be restricted, suspended or abolished through preventative measures, namely censorship, licences, the ordering of guarantees (securities), conditions imposed by the state, restrictions on the printing or book trades, postal bans or the inhibition of free communication.
>
> Official investigations into press misconduct will be judged by a jury in a court of law.[1]

Of course, censorship had ceased to be particularly effective in the years preceding the revolution. The invention of the high-speed printing press, and the mass print-runs this made possible, had

110

created a mobility with which the traditional and rather cumbersome monitoring mechanisms had scarcely been able to keep up. The resolutions of the Offenburg Meeting on 12 September 1847, for example, had been printed in the form of pamphlets entitled *The Demands of the People*, thousands of which were distributed to the population of Hesse. As the resigned Prussian envoy in Darmstadt remarked: 'Given the ease with which the means of communication can be created and duplicated, we are deluding ourselves if we think that bans of this kind can work.'[2]

Improved technology and distribution methods stimulated sales and commercial activity. When the Federal Decree of 3 March was enacted, governments fell over themselves in an effort to make it legally binding by issuing press decrees. The Prussian government was dilatory in this respect and on 16 March received a petition from the Berlin book trade demanding the lifting of censorship as soon as possible, since readers and authors were being lost to uncensored publishers 'abroad': 'Every day lost is a new and difficult defeat in the war of literary competition, and one which humiliates us and causes us to suffer material loss.'[3]

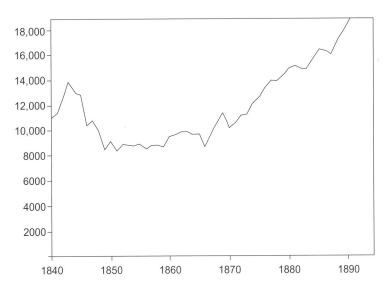

Source: R. Wittmann, *Buchmarkt und Lektüre im 18. und 19. Jahrhundert* (Tübingen, 1982), p. 116.

Figure 5   German book production, 1840–80

Yet business improved only marginally after censorship had been lifted. For the book-sellers then had to face a difficult and persistent recession, made worse by the revolution (see Figure 5).

Contemporaries accurately linked this recession to a change in reading habits which had been exacerbated by the revolution:

> Individuals, who used to spend large sums of money on books, bought nothing, and read only the newspapers. This not only led to a temporary slackening in trade, but to the worst possible situation: for a long time buyers lost the habit of buying altogether. Only later did they start making new purchases again. Rich people who used to buy books held on to their money, for they were expecting a coup at any moment which might force them to leave the state... The newspaper press took advantage of all this: no one had time to read anything else.[4]

It is not surprising that book-sellers in particular soon joined the ranks of the supporters of law and order.

The Press and the Provinces

The newspaper industry, on the other hand, profited from the thirst for up-to-the-minute reading matter. Circulation increased and large numbers of new papers were founded. Many of them, however, proved to be ephemeral phenomena. It might be useful at this juncture to illustrate the explosion in readers with some figures. The number of political newspapers was recorded in the price list of the Berlin Press Office. In the 23 years from 1824 to 1847 this figure had risen by just 22 (from 96 to 118). During the three years between 1847 and 1850 it rose to 184. Before the revolution there were only 79 newspapers in Austria, 19 of which were political. In 1848 this figure rose to 388, of which 306 or 79 per cent were political. A contemporary analysis of the situation in individual states gives the numbers of newspapers, *Intelligenzblätter* and *Volksblätter* (see Table 10). By 1849 their numbers had already peaked.

It is estimated that there were around 1700 newspapers in the whole of Germany in 1849. Now that it had been liberated, society's organizational energies were increased in all areas. This included the press, which no longer simply argued, but now became 'partisan'. 1848 saw the birth of the modern press with its particular political

Table 10 Numbers of newspapers, *Intelligenzblätter* and *Volksblätter*, in individual German states in 1847 and 1849

	1847	1849
Prussia	404	622
Austria	79	215
Saxony	153	183
Bavaria	110	127
Württemberg	60	67
Baden	63	55
Hesse-Darmstadt	22	34
Hanover	23	32
Hamburg	18	24
Frankfurt/M	10	17

Source: F.W. von Reden, 'Statistische Ergebnisse der deutschen periodischen Presse', in *Zeitschrift des Vereins für deutsche Statistik*, 2 (1848), p. 244, and O. Groth, *Die Zeitung*, vol. 1 (Mannheim, 1928), pp. 200f.

leanings. The former distinction between political newspaper and *Intelligenzblatt* disappeared. Most local newspapers no longer simply concerned themselves with satisfying the demand for advertisements, lectures and entertainment. Their readers now wanted to be provided with political news. As early as 25 March 1848, the *Dortmunder Anzeiger* declared that, 'The citizens of Dortmund must now demand that their *Anzeiger* no longer provide them merely with advice on the subject of buying butter or herrings, but also advice on how they might act in the best interests of the town and the Fatherland.' Dortmund might have been anywhere.[5]

The provincial press brought politics large and small into the local communities. When town council meetings became public, their proceedings were reported in local newspapers. Readers of the *Soester Kreisblatt* or the *Heilbronner Zeitung*, for example, received regular reports from their deputies in Frankfurt or Berlin. Printed speeches, appeals, petitions and readers' opinions all found a place in their columns and led in turn to further action. A petition from the Ulm garrison, published in a newspaper, persuaded the Heilbronn garrison to refuse to obey orders and take part in rallies, marches with railway workers and liberations of prisoners.[6]

The democrats above all made use of the press in their attempts to organize. At the first Congress of Westphalian Democratic Associations on 10 and 11 September 1848 in Bielefeld, the president declared that the party should set about founding a democratic newspaper in every town where a publication of that kind did not already exist, even if the cost should be great. What occurred in regions with a rich press tradition, such as Baden or Württemberg, of necessity appeared truly sensational in Westphalia;[7] a brief survey highlights the extent to which the region was mobilized.

The *Volksfreund*, with its motto 'freedom, wealth and education for all' was published in Bielefeld, the *Neue Rheinische Zeitung* in Cologne, which contained countless local items from around Westphalia, the *Waage* in Detmold, the *Westfälische Dampfboot* in Bielefeld, the *Westfälische Volkshalle* in Münster, with the motto 'Everything through the People', the *Volksbote* in Paderborn, the *Märkische Bote* in Lüdenscheid, the *Beobachter an der Lenne* in Hohenlimburg, the *Deutsche Bürgerblatt* in Siegen, the *Volksfreund für den Kreis Altena* in Hagen, the *Märkische Volksbote* in Dortmund, the *Wittekind* in Witten, the *Deutsche Redner für Recht und Freiheit* in Bochum, the *Hahn* in Lemgo, the *Westfälische Zeitung* in Paderborn, the *Freimütige an der Haar* in Werl and the *Recklinghäuser Wochenblatt*, the *Iserlohner Bürgerblatt*, the *Essener Volkshalle*, the *Hagener Kreisblatt*, and the *Rheinisch-westfälische Kurier*, the organ of the Democratic Association of Rhineland-Westphalia. By far the majority were newly established publications. Their titles often reflect the programmes of the time. Other German areas saw a similar revival of the press. There was also a huge increase in the numbers of national newspapers, which stood for one of the newly established party directions and which helped local newspapers in the wording of their own articles.[8]

Leading Political Newspapers

The *Deutsche Zeitung*, the first national 'party newspaper', appeared for the first time on 1 July 1847. It was the newspaper of the German constitutionalists and was edited by Gervinus. Its most prominent readers and contributors belonged to the Frankfurt 'Casino' faction. The newspaper was published until the end of September 1850, its circulation rising at times to 4000. From the beginning, its aim was to influence the provincial and local press.

The various different workers' societies were initially represented by the Berlin *Das Volk*, founded by Stephan Born. After August 1848 this was replaced by the more important *Verbrüderung*, which became the central organ of the 'General Workers' Fraternity'.[9] Born corresponded and worked closely with the *Neue Rheinische Zeitung*, edited by Marx. The *Neue Rheinische Zeitung* soon began to pursue aggressive party politics, and within a few months its circulation had risen to more than 6000, a considerable success when measured against the *Kölnische Zeitung*, the leading paper of the time, which had a circulation of 17,000, but had been published in Cologne since 1798.[10]

The *Mannheimer Abendzeitung*, the Darmstadt *Neue Deutsche Zeitung* and the Berlin *Urwähler-Zeitung* were widely read amongst democrats. The Berlin democrats' Central Committee took Arnold Ruge's *Reform*.

From 30 June 1848 onwards, the conservatives had a successful journalistic champion in the form of the Berlin *Neue Preußische Zeitung* or *Kreuzzeitung*, which was not only read in royalist circles, but also at the Frankfurt *Ober-Post-Amts-Zeitung*, which acted as the mouthpiece of the Central Power.

The political Catholics' newspaper, the *Historisch-politische Blätter* of the Görres circle, was first published in 1838; it was now supported by the Cologne *Rheinische Volkshalle*, later renamed the *Deutsche Volkshalle*, which since 13 May 1848 had become the central organ of political Catholicism. It was issued by the Cologne Catholic publishing house, J.P. Bachem, and August Reichensperger, the Paulskirche representative and future deputy of the 'Zentrum' party.

The Parliamentary Press Agencies

Some of the factions represented in the Paulskirche pursued their own press politics. Robert Blum edited the *Deutsche Reichstags-Zeitung* in Frankfurt, the conservative clergyman Karl Jürgens published the *Flugblätter aus der deutschen Nationalversammlung*, which appeared twice a week. The extraordinary proliferation of the press led the parliamentary factions to take a highly modern step: some of them developed their own press agencies, which were to influence the newspapers with relevant, though obviously partisan, news. In Vienna a *Stenographische Correspondenz* appeared daily, from which the Frankfurt *Ober-Post-Amts-Zeitung* and the famous Augsburg *Allgemeine Zeitung*, for example, took news on *Reichstag* affairs. Berlin National Assembly factions also had their own press service. In the autumn of 1848, when the issue of who would assume the leadership of Germany burned ever hotter, the Frankfurt factions also followed suit. The '*Centrums-Parlaments-Correspondenz*' (C.P.C), led by Rudolf Haym was founded on 7 December. March 1849 saw the establishment of the democrats' '*Lithographische Parlaments-Correspondenz*' (L.P.C.) under the overall control of Karl Vogt, which served 250 newspapers and weekly publications recommended by the 'Central March Association'. At least 50 of them can be shown to have taken articles from it.[11] Finally, another competing Paulskirche news service, the *Großdeutsche Parlaments-Correspondenz*, came into existence on 20 March 1849.

The Press, the Public and Popular Culture

Only some of the close links between newspapers and associations have been researched. But even these testify to the high degree of politicization and the development of political direction in society at this time. But who actually read the newspapers? The existence of at least 1700 such publications would suggest that a great deal of information reached even small village communities. And not every reader was necessarily a subscriber. The classified section of local newspapers often included advertisements for 'co-readers' to share subscriptions. In Württemberg, individuals offered Hecker's *Volksfreund*, Blum's *Reichstags-Zeitung* and the popular satirical newspaper the *Eulenspiegel*. Reading societies ('*Museen*', '*Lesekabinette*', '*Journalistiken*') satisfied the thirst for the printed word. Lists of the publications they subscribed to reveal the astonishingly wide selection on offer.[12]

In 1848–9 the Tübingen '*Museumsgesellschaft*', for example, took 34 periodicals from Germany and Austria and even from abroad. (*Neue Zürcher Zeitung*, *La Presse* and the Basle *National Zeitung*). The entire party-political spectrum was represented: from the *Historisch-politische Blätter*, the *Deutsche Zeitung*, the *Mannheimer Abendzeitung* and the *Neue Rheinische Zeitung*, to the shorthand reports from the parliaments in Stuttgart and Frankfurt. One might, of course, expect a large number of periodicals to be available in a university town; but even in the diocesan town of Rottenburg there were 16 newspapers, including Blum's *Deutsche Reichstags-Zeitung*, the *Deutsche Zeitung* and the shorthand reports of the Paulskirche. Even the reading association in Öhringen took the Augsburg *Allgemeine Zeitung*, the *Ober-Post-Amts-Zeitung*, the *Deutsche Reichstags-Zeitung*, the satirical *Fliegende*

Blätter and the *Eulenspiegel*: the population of Öhringen in the Württemberg district of Jagst, seat of Prince von Hohenlohe-Öhringen, numbered only 3150. The political associations also had their own reading rooms. The Workers' Society in Hanover, for example, owned a library containing some 500 volumes, including Friedrich Engels' *Condition of the Working Classes in England*.

There is no doubt that reading and politics had ceased to be the preserve of dignitaries, and were now matters for ordinary people. But who was able to read? In the generation born since 1800, considerable advances had been made in elementary education following the expansion of the education sector. It is estimated that around 20 per cent of the German population was illiterate in 1848, as against 40 to 50 per cent in Austro-Hungary.[13] Those who were unable to read themselves could attend public readings. Once again, the revolution offered suitable media for this too. Huge numbers of pamphlets and posters were published. They reacted more subtly than the newspapers to the smallest changes in the mood of the day. Colourful, stimulating and partisan political opinion and news was peddled 'at the lowest level'.

It is estimated that 20 to 30 of these printed products appeared daily in Austria, with the majority published in Vienna.[14] Although at the beginning they were primarily democratic in leaning, the counter-revolutionary resistance also made increasing use of the medium. The Prussian lieutenant colonel, Gustav von Griesheim, the 'true spiritual leader of the Prussian counter-revolution of November and December 1848', published a pamphlet anonymously. Its title was widely taken up and used as a slogan: '*Gegen Demokraten helfen nur Soldaten!*' (Only soldiers can help fight the democrats).[15]

The same applies to the large numbers of individual caricatures. In Frankfurt alone it has been shown that at least 93 different caricatures were published in 1848–9, a third on the subject of 'revolution', '*Deutscher Michel*' (the plain, honest German) and 'princes', two-thirds on the Frankfurt parliament and its deputies.[16] They, too, changed from mirrors of surging national hopes to reflections of social disillusionment or anti-parliamentary ridicule. The famous widely disseminated satire on the *Deeds and Opinions of Mr Piepmeyer, Deputy to the Constituent National Assembly at Frankfurt on the Main* was only the mildest of these satires.

Illiterates were also drawn into political events by means of revolutionary songs. Many lyrics were published in pamphlets, and so never appeared in the traditional collections.[17] Pictures and songs encapsulated the experiences and horizons of 'every-day life'; peasants and craftsmen were portrayed in their agricultural lower middle-class settings, and were directly addressed as the supporters, participants and witnesses of the grass-roots revolution. In singing associations and song circles political songs were diligently rehearsed. The '*Marseillaise*' was particularly popular.[18] In order to overcome cultural and educational language barriers, the people's associations sometimes framed their appeals in the local dialect. '*Buer paß upp!*' a pamphlet written in the Low German '*plattdeutsch*' dialect by the Paderborn publisher, Wilhelm Crüwell, called on the peasants to join the campaign for the Imperial Constitution. In Vienna, songs on the social question circulated in dialect; Berlin developed its own 'street corner literature', in which, as on the stage, the Berlin dialect was employed.[19] This revolutionary culture only rarely found its way into print.

There was another medium, long submerged and hardly known today, which provided 'illiterates in practice' (E. Naujoks) with graphic experience of the revolution: the illustrated broadsheet. These were single printed sheets illustrating contemporary history, giving detailed depictions of the events of the day. Their circulation was unusually wide, with print-runs sometimes exceeding 10,000 copies per broadsheet. Centres of production were found in Neuruppin – the mecca of the illustrated broadsheet – Magdeburg, Mainz, Munich, Nuremberg, Stuttgart, Weißenburg in the Alsace and Strasbourg.[20]

It was two publishers in particular, from opposing political camps, which provided Germany with these colourful illustrations. In Neuruppin, Gustav Kühn's publishing house, whose annual production had crossed the million mark in 1832, was initially in favour of the revolution. But in a series entitled *The Remarkable Year of 1848: A New Illustrated Newspaper*, Kühn switched allegiance to the Hohenzollern course, and finally treated the revolution only as an object of ridicule. In contrast, the publishers Oehmigke & Riemschneider, also based in Neuruppin, printed mainly folksy, 'touching' pictures on subjects such as *Workers' Riots in Berlin* (16 October 1848); *Funeral for the Workers*; *Kossuth's Prayer after the Battle*; *Robert Blum on the Vienna Barricade*; *Robert Blum, Deputy of the German Nation, shot in Vienna on 9 November 1848*; and *The Battle of the Volunteer Corps against the Danes at Hardersleben*.

Ballad-singers distributed the illustrated broadsheets, and borrowed material from them for their street ballads. At markets, fairs, pilgrimages and church outings they found a mobile public, primarily the small-town rural population. They changed hands on streets, in inns, were sold by itinerant traders in the countryside and at fixed sales outlets in the towns.

This revolutionary culture of communication operated at a distance from political organization. Yet at the same time it reacted politically. Illustrated broadsheets, pamphlets, posters, songs and caricatures created a 'street public' far from parliamentary dealings, but which reflected the formation of isolated group identities and the disintegration of the revolutionary movement into disparate circles of interests; a phenomenon which will be pursued in more detail below in the context of the dynamics of the revolution.

8   The Paulskirche and the Parliaments

The Composition of the Frankfurt National Assembly

In Frankfurt on the Main
They can't get their washing clean:
Though they scrub and scrub away,
Still the princes remain princes,
And Moors are still Moors,
Despite all the professors –
In the parley parley parliament
Where the talking never ends!

Georg Herwegh composed this poem in the autumn of 1848.[1] As his bitterly sarcastic lines testify, the image of a professorial parliament, a parliament of impractical theoreticians, is as old as the revolution itself. This does not necessarily mean that the image is correct, however. In the 'heyday of the Assembly' in the summer an equally critical eyewitness gained the impression that: 'Ever since the name Germany was first uttered in the world, such a wealth of famous and well-known names, of talented people and characters, such a mix of different professions and spheres of activity has never been seen.'[2]

Seated there, as Wilhelm Zimmermann describes so vividly, was 'a deputy from the far reaches of Prussia, where the Cossack stands on guard, and next to him the Italian Tyrolean, who speaks only broken German, his mother tongue being the language of the land of oranges.' The richest landowner from Upper Swabia, still wearing his princely robes, whose father was said to be as sovereign as the ruler of Prussia or Hanover, sat side by side with a farmer from the Austrian Traun district. Representatives of all religious faiths were there, from the Catholic loyal to Rome, to the renegade German Catholic, the

Protestant rationalist 'Lichtfreund', the bishop, the pietist, the Jesuit and the Jew. Large numbers of former victims of political persecution and political prisoners sat with the lord of the manor from Eastern Pomerania, the member of the Prussian 'Gustav Adolph Association', a well-known economist from Prague, the papist Bavarian assistant secretary, the specialist in oriental studies, and famous writers and scholars. All Germany's peoples were there, together with German Frenchmen and German Slavs; a huge variety of contrasting mentalities and temperaments. Indeed, it was only when the Assembly was gathered in person that many of its members were confronted with the true nature of the Germany which was to be united there.

Colourful though the picture was, there are features which united the deputies across the barriers which appeared to separate them. One of the most important of these features was profession. The more '*bürgerlich*' a deputy was, and the more limited his sphere of life, the more his views, interests and endeavours were influenced by the factors on which his livelihood depended. This is why, again and again, first the historiographer reporters from the Paulskirche itself, and subsequently historians, have sought to classify the Assembly. It is no easy task, since it never achieved the membership of 649 laid down by law, and calculated according to the register of the German Confederation. Constituencies from Bohemia and Moravia, which were members of the Confederation, boycotted the elections because, according to the way they defined their nationality, they were happy to live under a Habsburg Kaiser, but not in a German Empire. The remaining 585 deputies were never all present at the same time: one also held a seat in an individual German chamber; another was on governmental leave; another still was travelling on party business or was absent owing to illness. As a rule, the Assembly only ever had between 400 and 450 members. At one ballot, where every vote was crucial, because the success of the entire constitutional mechanism seemed to depend upon it, the figure reached 540. In April 1849, before the Austrians were recalled, it amounted to 436.[3] According to the latest research, and taking into account the fact that some deputies retired and made room for their replacements, over the entire period of its existence from 18 May 1848 to 18 June 1849, the National Assembly had a total of 812 members.[4] Their distribution among the professions is shown in Table 11.

The figures speak for themselves: despite wide suffrage in some states, few members of the lower middle classes or small farmers, not to mention members of the 'manual working classes', found their way

Table 11   Breakdown of the Frankfurt National Assembly by profession

Senior civil servants, *Landräte*	115	
Middle-ranking civil servants	37	
Mayors, local govt officers	21	
Judges, public prosecutors	110	
Officers	18	
Diplomats	11	
University teachers (49); *Gymnasium* teachers	94	
Other teachers	30	
Total civil servants		**436**
Clergymen		**39**
Lawyers, advocates	106	
Doctors	23	
Writers and journalists	20	
Total freelance intelligentsia		**149**
Large merchants, merchants	35	
Manufacturers	14	
Publishers and booksellers	7	
Total commercial middle class		**56**
Farmers (large landowners and 3 farmers)		**46**
Total craftsmen		**4**
Members with a doctorate, no profession given		**35**
Other professions		**3**
No details known		**44**
Total		**812**

Source: M. Schwarz, *MdR. Biographisches Handbuch* (Hanover, 1965), pp. 43–112; M. Botzenhart, *Deutscher Parlamentarismus in der Revolutionszeit, 1848–1850* (Düsseldorf, 1977), p. 161.

to Frankfurt. Arguments have already been put forward as to why this should have been the case. In terms of profession, the National Assembly was a parliament of civil servants, in terms of education, a parliament of academics (more than 600 had a university education). In terms of the *predominant* education it was a parliament of jurists: 491 or 60 per cent had studied law. It may sound somewhat exaggerated, but it is generally true to say that they owed their understanding and evaluation of the state to the state itself.

If we are looking for factors which influenced the political profile of this parliament, then affiliations between fellow-countrymen and regional and religious factors doubtless played a key role. A university professor thought himself more important than a *Gymnasium* teacher, who in turn thought he was better than a *Volksschule* teacher; a judge believed himself to be more independent than a local government officer – endless differentiations of this kind could be made. But did this have a decisive impact on the Assembly's attitude to the revolution and to the existing state? Certainly it did from time to time, and yet as a rule two factors weighed more heavily than this. The first was the legal education which the deputies had undertaken in the days of the restoration, and which was historical and constitutionalist in colouring, rather than parliamentary and democratic.[5] The second factor was the extent to which the deputies had to safeguard their livelihood, and the degree to which they were dependent. In this respect we cannot accept, as scholars usually do, the separation of the higher teaching professions from members of the state civil service. After all, whether one was a professor, a judge or a diplomat, employment by the state implied dependence, implied a sacrifice of one's post if one's opposition grew too loud. The presence on the parliamentary benches of deputies Arndt, Welcker, Jahn, F. Schüler, S. Jordan, Eisenmann, Behr, Mohl and three of the 'Göttingen Seven' of 1837, Dahlmann, Grimm and Gervinus, was living proof of such experiences. This is not to endorse any crude determinism, but simply to draw attention to the issue of dependencies and main features of political action. This dependence on a civil service post had its advantages too; it meant that the deputy was available to take his seat in the chamber. For how many self-employed businessmen could literally remain far from their businesses for months at a time? However, the implications of the civil servant's dependence were also revealed when the governments illegally withdrew their deputies in April and May 1849, threatening them with disciplinary procedures and removal from office if they did not comply. Civil servant members of the Stuttgart Rump Parliament paid a heavy price for this.

The Paulskirche Factions

Not only its composition, but also the parliamentary actions of the Paulskirche Assembly, refute suggestions that it was merely a parliament of professors or dignitaries. The modernity of this political body, the manner in which it operated in factions, seemed to the deputies to be a necessary evil, for it meant that the Assembly was split into groups. With the exception of Bergsträßer and Valentin, historians have long misunderstood the Paulskirche factions. Indeed, only the most recent research has been able to evaluate them satisfactorily.[6] These factions had already emerged in early June, as the various fundamental political philosophies began to become clear. From then on factions determined the course of business, turned important subjects of debate into 'party affairs', imposed discipline in votes, formed coalitions, limited the numbers of random decisions, steered the plenary debates and influenced the public with their own publications. Factions operated as mediators for pressure groups and for extra-parliamentary political associations; they received impetus from the outside and in turn provided impetus to the public. They even attempted to organize the public, as was seen, for example, in the actions of the 'Central March Association'. It was entirely logical that a society riven by antagonisms should be reflected in parliamentary factions. The development of an organized democratic and pluralistic party system, effective at parliamentary level, was also predictable. The factions named themselves after their Frankfurt inns in which they met. By October the situation had evolved as shown in Table 12. (The percentages given can only represent average approximate figures.)

The 'Café Milani' faction was home to the conservative federalist and legitimist deputies, most of whom came from Prussia, Austria and Bavaria. The most prominent supporters of the constitutional

Table 12   The factions of the Frankfurt National Assembly

Café Milani	Casino	Landsberg	Augsburger Hof	Württemberger Hof	Westendhall	Deutscher Hof	Donnersberg	In no faction
6%	21%	6%	7%	6%	7%	8%	7%	32%
'Right'		'Centre Right'		'Centre Left'		'Left'		
Conservative	constitutionalist-liberal			parliamentary-liberal		democratic		

Source: W. Siemann, *Die Frankfurter Nationalversammlung 1848/49 zwischen demokratischem Liberalismus und konservativer Reform* (Frankfurt, 1976), p. 27.

monarchy from south-west Germany belonged to the 'Casino' faction. At 50 per cent, it was disproportionately represented on the important Constitutional Committee, and therefore had a major influence on the course of the debates. The 'Landsberg' faction laid greater emphasis on the power of parliament and the Central Power than the 'Casino' from which it had split. In diluted form the 'Augs-burger Hof' represented the political leanings of its mother faction the 'Württemberger Hof'. Its members were primarily parliamen-tary democratic liberals from the 'Third Germany'. The 'Westend-hall' united democrats who favoured the tactical tolerance of a constitutional monarchy, but who were united with the 'Deutscher Hof' on the issue of universal suffrage. The 'Deutscher Hof' and the 'Donnersberg' factions embodied the difference between the parlia-mentary democrats and the democrats who favoured plebiscites and were inclined to take direct action, a division that had already become apparent in the Pre-Parliament. Both factions had republi-can leanings. Their supporters came mainly from Baden, the Palati-nate and Saxony. Approximately 150 deputies belonged to no faction at all, operating as 'wild cards' in an impromptu fashion.[7]

As a rule, this apparently confused mass of individual factions formed four broad blocks, which already in 1848 described them-selves according to their seating arrangements as 'right', 'centre-right', 'centre-left' and 'left'. Since these terms are still in use in modern politics, it might be interesting to look at their origins. The terms were taken from the French chamber of deputies in the restora-tion period after 1815, and described the relationship to the existing government. 'Extreme left' referred to an anti-government stance and 'extreme right' to a pro-government stance. After the July revo-lution of 1830 the political fronts were reversed and the original meaning was lost. For the Legitimists, now extreme opponents of the July monarchy of Louis Philippe, remained seated on the extreme right. Since that time the terms 'right' and 'left' had referred to '(the party's) relationship to political freedom';[8] absolutists sat on the right, republicans on the left. When the distinction was no longer adequate, 'centre-right' referred to 'parliamentary rule of the mon-eyed aristocracy' and 'centre-left' to 'a democratic constitution in the monarchy'.[9] With minor modifications, Gottfried Eisenmann, analyst of the factions of the Paulskirche, held this usage to be accep-table, indeed indispensable for the National Assembly.

The social composition of the factions reveals certain patterns,[10] which, viewed from right to left, reflected a growing distance from the existing constitutions in Germany and from the civil service. The right and centre-right, the majority factions, were full of senior civil servants, judges and university teachers. They also included aristocratic landowners and large-scale merchants. The independent professions were less frequently represented. They made up only about 10 per cent of the 'Casino'. The centre left, from the 'Württemberger Hof' to the 'Westendhall' was balanced between the independent professions and members of the middle classes on the one hand, and landowners and large merchants and senior civil servants on the other. On the left, the freelance intelligentsia dominated the 'Deutscher Hof', where they amounted to 40 per cent and the 'Donnersberg', of which they comprised 50 per cent. A considerable proportion – 30 per cent – of lower middle class deputies were to be found in the factions of the left.

The various political leanings of the socially differentiated middle classes have already been explored in our analysis of the constitutionalist and democratic associations. The split in the middle classes was revealed once more in the Frankfurt Parliament, and was also manifested in the formation of majorities. Analyses of important central ballots have shown that, when it came to voting, a generally stable line divided the centre factions. However, there was no single Frankfurt centre: constitutionalist liberals and democratic liberals voted against each other on issues such as:

- the abolition of the aristocracy (constant in three rounds of voting);
- the right to divide land;
- protective tariffs or free trade;[11]
- limited abolition of peasant feudal burdens without compensation;
- the refusal to deal with the mediatization of individual states;
- the absolute veto of the head of state in constitutional issues;
- a president as head of the Provisional Central Power;
- and the establishment of a council of princes ('Reichsrat') as a third state organ alongside the *Reichstag* and the head of state.[12]

Like the middle classes, the liberals were split, with the majority makers lying in the middle. It is not surprising that they were criticized following the break-up of the Assembly, above all by the democratic factions, who had lacked the votes to form a majority but who imagined that, had they actually been in a position to form one, they would have been able to determine the outcome of the revolution.

The Provisional Central Power

The National Assembly's first great act reached far beyond its actual purpose, which was to draft an imperial constitution. In its desire to convene its own national government, which would push aside the *Bundestag* for ever, it revealed its support for the sovereignty of the people, despite the fact that the majority were suspicious of this term.

Given the fact that the overwhelming majority of the Paulskirche wanted to 'conclude the revolution', though not to place themselves at its helm, the demand to form a national government is surprising. Although one should not underestimate the desire for a visible expression of state unity, nevertheless the various calls for the general arming of the populace were part of the revolutionary dynamics of March, as were the calls for the dissolution of the standing armies. When the elected National Assembly established a national state power, the bottom was knocked out of demands of this kind.

Various conceivable models were rehearsed in the wide-ranging debate which lasted from 17 to 24 June. The two major competing ideas emerged as the Directory of Three, favoured by the 'Casino', and a republican Executive Committee. The 'Casino' proposed an agreement with the state governments, the democrats called on the sovereign right of the elected National Assembly. However, the path already mapped out by the Pre-Parliament had shown that a revolutionary Executive Committee could scarcely be achieved. The motion from the left, proposing the transfer of power to a president was defeated (by 355 votes to 171) as was the right's attempt to establish the governments' right to reservation (512 : 31).

In his famous speech of 24 June 1848, the Parliament's President, Heinrich von Gagern, succeeded in achieving this parliament's first major compromise, when he called for the Provisional Central Power to take 'the bold step' of forming itself. At the same time he proposed the Austrian Archduke Johann as *Reichsverweser* or Imperial Regent, 'not because, but despite the fact that he is a prince'. This solution incorporated both the demands for Parliament's sovereignty in decision-making processes and the recognition of the dynastic principle. An extremely broad parliamentary base for the new Imperial Power was thereby created, as the concluding vote testifies (450 : 100)

In a special imperial law (28 June 1848) the National Assembly established the Provisional Central Power, comprised of a *Reichsverweser*, a Minister President and ministers of foreign affairs, home affairs, finance, justice, trade and war: under-secretaries of state were also assigned to the individual departments. The centre-right dominated the cabinet which was subsequently formed.

In doing this, Parliament was determining the future form of state of the *Reich*: a monarchy on a democratic basis. Hopes remained unbroken that Austria could be included. For the moment the proposal to transfer the Provisional Central Power to the Prussian King Frederick William IV was met with 'uproarious amusement'.

In the euphoria surrounding the creation of the Provisional Central Power, the National Assembly took upon itself tasks which robbed it of far more time and energy than the much-criticized and intense debates on the constitution. The politics of the day increasingly proved to constitute a grave impediment to its operations, and this applied both to external and internal executive power.

Firstly, beyond the constitutional debates, the National Assembly was forced urgently to confront the issue of state power before it had even been won. The Central Power wanted foreign countries to regard it as the representative of Germany abroad, and made heavy weather of the issue of winning international recognition. In this respect it enjoyed little more success than the German Confederation. With France, nothing more than the exchange of semi-official representatives was achieved: the French Republic refused to recognize the Central Power. Mistrust towards a strengthened 'Empire Germanique' ran deep. This came as a bitter blow to German liberals and democrats.

Initially the British Queen Victoria, her German husband Prince Albert and her government, led by the Liberal Foreign Minister Palmerston, were sympathetic to the attempts to unify; but in the British Cabinet sympathy turned to opposition when the Frankfurt National Assembly and the German public were brought into the emotional Schleswig-Holstein war. A vigorous, increasingly anti-German press campaign was launched in Britain.[13] The Central Power was unable to effect formal recognition of its diplomatic representatives. The United States of America was the only major power immediately to recognize the Imperial Power. Minor states which followed suit included Sweden, The Netherlands, Belgium, Sardinia, Naples, Greece and Switzerland.

Evaluations of the Provisional Central Power's relationship to other countries usually raises questions as to the chances of success of German attempts to unify in the international power play of 1848–9. Today they are considered to have been rather more favourable than they were in earlier analyses. The revolution did not 'fail because of the a priori resistance of the powers to German unity'.[14]

Secondly, the execution of internal state power represented a further obstacle to the operations of the Central Power. It is often said that the Central Power did not have the means by which its authority could be exercised. It is true that it lacked both an administrative foundation and direct control of the standing armies of the individual states, both of which were the concrete expression of modern state authority. Its weaknesses were laid bare on 16 July 1848, when the Imperial War Minister issued a 'homage edict' to the war ministers of all individual states, in which he claimed supreme command of the armies, and ordered all garrisons to don the German colours and hold a parade to pay homage to the *Reichsverweser*. The medium states either refused to carry out the order at all, or diluted it. But it was Austria and Prussia in particular, which revealed his order to be ineffective and which exposed the fact that imperial policies were unfounded.

Yet to emphasize this point alone is to misjudge the influence of the Imperial Central Power domestically. According to the Imperial Law by which it was appointed, it was responsible for 'the general security and welfare of the German federal state'. To this end it had at its command 'Imperial Troops', which were none other than the army corps of the former Federal Troops, most of which were still stationed in the federal fortresses. On 18 July 1848 the Central Power ordered imperial intervention in Wiesbaden, after March Minister Hergenhahn had requested military aid. Austrian and Prussian troops from the Federal Fortress in Mainz were used. The Imperial War Minister also sent Imperial Troops to put down an uprising in Frankfurt-Sachsenhausen on 6–7 July 1848. He ordered a state of siege following the Frankfurt uprising of 16–18 September 1848. Using Saxon, Hanoverian and Prussian contingents, the Imperial Central Power also intervened in Saxony-Altenburg in October, to put an end to the welfare-state constitutional system established there. Again in October, the *Reich* ordered contingents from Bavaria, Saxony and Weimar to march on Saxony-Meiningen to deal with an uprising amongst salt workers in Bad Salzungen and toy makers in Sonneberg.

The Imperial Central Power acted formally and responsibly in these matters and its orders were obeyed in the cause of law and order. The more they saw Central Power policies countering revolutionary outbreaks, the more submissively the governments of the individual states behaved. But in acting in this way, the Central Power forfeited the good reputation it had enjoyed amongst large sections of the population, as is shown in the increasingly angry and sarcastic polemics found in the newspapers from September 1848 onwards. Finally it even attracted the whiff of the old 'police state', when, in a circular decree of 3 October 1848, the Imperial Justice Minister and the Minister for Internal Affairs asked all individual states 'to give an official account of all associations in their region, together with their political leanings and statutes, any particularly striking resolutions they have made, their influence on popular life, membership and the extent to which they enjoy links with associations in other German states'.[15]

This was nothing short of general police monitoring of political associations. Most states complied wholeheartedly. In their investigations of the winter of 1848–9, they gathered most of the records which enabled them to suppress the associations in the reactionary period which followed. The Central Power had given them a helping hand. Indeed, and this has not previously been recognized, it laid the foundations for a central political state police authority, which had begun its work even before the revolution had ended.[16] Clearly, it would be wrong to doubt the efficacy of the domestic policies of the Central Power.

Excluding the final death-throes ministry of May 1849 for a moment, there were three Central Power cabinets, each directly dependent on the National Assembly. Every change in the leadership of the government attested to the parliamentary method of government which had been put into practice, and this too represents a degree of modernity in the parliamentary history of Germany. To some extent it may be seen as a short-lived anticipation of later hard-won achievements. Only recently has the concrete interplay between Parliament and government in 1848–9 been taken seriously. The first cabinet of 15 July 1848 was led by the mediatized prince, Karl von Leiningen. It was brought down in September 1848 when it accepted the Truce of Malmö in the Schleswig-Holstein conflict, and lost the support of the National Assembly. In December 1848 Parliament forced the resignation of von Leiningen's successor, von Schmerling, when his *Großdeutsch*-Austrian programme was shown to be unworkable. Heinrich von Gagern led the third cabinet which collapsed when Frederick William IV's rejection of the imperial crown exposed its policies as unattainable.

The Frankfurt Basic Rights

The constitution drafted by the Committee of Seventeen gave the Frankfurt National Assembly the chance to reach a rapid conclusion. Although the Assembly later fell back on the essential features of the draft, it seemed out of the question in the elation of recently won sovereignty. On 24 May 1848 the Assembly elected a Constitutional Committee of 30 which assumed a position of key importance in the constitutional debates after 3 July, when it submitted its draft of the *Grundrechte* or Basic Rights. The committee united the eminent authorities of the historical and constitutionalist liberalism of the Vormärz period and the middle-class March movement: Bassermann (chair), von Beckerath, Dahlmann, Waitz, Droysen (secretary), Hergenhahn, Welcker, G. Beseler – all of whom belonged to the 'Casino' faction – R. Mohl, H. Simon and Römer, members of the centre-left. Blum and Wigard spoke for the left, which was generally under-represented.

Again and again the Paulskirche is reproached for wasting 'valuable months' and for placing itself in a position of 'grave disadvantage' by beginning its debates with the Basic Rights rather than constitutional matters such as the leadership issue, imperial territory and suffrage (E.R. Huber). Certainly, it is true that it was wrong to regard the material it began with as lightweight and therefore as an issue that could be dealt with rapidly. However, the Constitutional Committee felt it 'appropriate to find an area which more than any other may be regarded as neutral', in which little 'divergence of opinion' was anticipated.[17] Four factors justify its decision to begin in this way.

1. The March demands (freedom of the press, the right of assembly, trial by jury, people's army) had already placed the focus of attention on the safeguarding of civil rights.
2. The experiences of the police state era of the German Confederation, which, together with national issues represented a major motivation for the middle classes in the revolution, made the guarantee of basic rights vital.
3. The imminent appointment of a Provisional Central Power signified an element in the anticipated constitutional creation of state unity. This created the scope for a discussion of basic rights.

4. In May no one could have predicted such a rapid reassertion of bureaucratic and military power on the part of the states. Only the Paris June Uprising gave an indication of how rapidly the scope for political action could be forfeited.

With the completed list of Basic Rights (in 14 Articles and 60 paragraphs) the National Assembly endorsed constitutional development in Western Europe and devised a concept which remained pioneering through the Weimar Constitution to the Bonn Constitution. The main emphasis of the Basic Rights lay in the safeguarding of personal and political freedoms and of property. The guarantee of freedom of the press, the freedom to assemble and form associations and public, independent jurisdiction constituted strong defences against the power of the state. Freedom of movement and of enterprise, and the right of residence led to disputes on these principles, for the lifting of controls touched on the crisis of pauperism in the *Vormärz* period. The Paulskirche recognized the dangers of increasing competition, the overmanning of the trades and the excessive demands placed on municipal poor relief. It distanced itself from the unrestricted liberalism of the competitive economy, reserving these issues for future imperial legislation.

The freedom of property posed the greatest problem, for here the Assembly found itself confronted with all the problems inherent in the traditional feudal agrarian system. How many of these issues still remained a cause for complaint was demonstrated in a comprehensive report compiled by the 'National Economics Committee' on the petitions submitted by the peasants. For many deputies it was the first time that they gained an insight into the complex legal relationship between aristocratic lords of the manor and the peasant population. Parliament finally abolished all feudal bonds relating to subjects and serfs, patrimonial jurisdiction, the lord of the manor's police, personal services (socage) and levies. Feudal obligations could be exchanged for cash. The democrats' attempt to abolish these without compensation was rejected on the grounds that it smacked of social revolution. In the agrarian world, it was only now, in 1848, that the 'Middle Ages' were finally brought to an end.

The relationship between the state and the church, like that between the state and trade and commerce, gave rise to a well-organized petition movement, which chanelled the pressure of the Catholic public, and led to the formation of new short-term factions in the

Paulskirche. It was not religious freedom and freedom of conscience that were controversial, so much as the integration of the previously privileged denominations into a society in which all religions were equal. The loss of the clergy's control over schools was bitterly lamented. The mixed marriage conflict, which in the *Vormärz* period had led to the emergence of political Catholicism, was defused since, under the Basic Rights, state and canon law were completely separate. Attempts to enforce the democratization of internal church organization and administration from the outside (the election of priests) remained unsuccessful. All in all, this section of the Basic Rights represented a milestone in the secularization of the modern state.

Seen as a whole, the Basic Rights went some way to standardizing Germany's economic, social and legal spheres. It was expressly stated that, 'No regulation in the constitution or in the laws of an individual state may contradict the Imperial Constitution' (§ 194). Beyond the rights of individuals, local authorities were also awarded their own administrations. Individual states were granted constitutions, with representative bodies, ministerial accountability, the right to indict ministers and the opportunity for parliaments to take the initiative on matters of law. The Basic Rights represented 'a powerful counterblow to particularism' (Stadelmann). The proclamation of the Basic Rights Law on 27 December 1848 led to protests, primarily in Austria, Prussia, Bavaria and Hanover, which unlike most other states refused to publish them.

If one examines the social content of the Basic Rights, one is struck by the fact that they contained no trace whatsoever of the social reforming or social revolutionary demands of the time; there was no reference to the particular position of the lower classes, who had formed part of the mass base of the revolution; no mention of the antithesis within society between capital and work, which the Workers' Fraternity had attempted to abolish. This was no accidental omission. It was quite deliberate. For in an important debate on the 'right to work', which did not take place until February 1849, and is therefore often overlooked, the constitutionalist majority was confronted with a number of issues raised by the democrats. They included protection of the unemployed and invalids, the guarantee of a minimum level of subsistence, restrictions on female and child labour and the workers' right to form unions.[18] The speaker of the Constitutional Committee in this debate, the law professor Georg Beseler, recommended that the 'German spirit of association, that is to say, the old institution which inspired and freed the German

Middle Ages' be employed to resolve the social question. The majority accepted his recommendation.

Like the majority of academically educated people, Beseler still thought in pre-industrial and pre-revolutionary terms. The social model of expectations in the Frankfurt Basic Rights largely represented the 'future image of a classless society of "moderate livelihoods" ', as Lothar Gall has put it in the context of early liberalism.[19]

This concept rested on the assumption that a 'harmonious pre-stabilized social order' (Gall) had been distorted by external intervention, be it on the part of the state or the aristocracy. The Basic Rights would protect against such intervention and the harmonious equilibrium would be re-established, once more creating a situation in which everyone would be able to avoid social injustice and material need by autonomous, independent action. The Basic Rights took as an ideal the intellectually and materially free individual, who was responsible for his own life. Independence was the prime feature of middle-class life. There was no room or understanding here for the dependence which comes from waged labour; a characteristic of industrialization.

The proposal that the Basic Rights would resolve the social issue was, therefore, quite typical and only logical: 'Those without means will be guaranteed free instruction at all public educational establishments.' (§ 157) What was meant by a 'classless' society of *Bürger* was actually that everyone could rise by means of education in freedom until there was only one general class in society – the middle class. The growth of the middle classes observed in the *Vormärz* period seemed to confirm this prognosis. The social model underlying the Basic Rights conformed to the historical phase between the dissolution of the *ständisch* social and economic order, and the emergence of industrialization on a major scale. Wherever individual regulations threatened to suppress a competitive economy, the Basic Rights ordered reservations which provided for the evolutionary transition to future legislation on the part of the *Reich* or state, and protected the commercial and lower middle classes: this applied above all to freedom of enterprise, of movement and the liberation and mobility of property.

The majority in the Paulskirche had successfully fended off all attempts to include human rights issues in the list of Basic Rights, on the grounds that such concerns were out-dated. Their basis was purely legal and positivistic: all citizens of the *Reich* would be granted the Basic Rights; they did not correspond to pre-state legal principles, but were statutes derived from the state. This viewpoint, which was challenged by the democrats, relieved those in the Paulskirche charged with drafting the constitution of the need to resolve a particular dilemma: they wanted safeguards *against* state power, but at the same time they wished the state to be strong and unified. For this reason provision was made for the imposition of emergency laws: 'In the event of war or uprising' the Imperial government could suspend the Basic Rights on arrests, house searches and assemblies (§ 197). The revolution itself had given the majority of deputies reason to expect such eventualities. In a decree of 19 September 1848 the *Reichsverweser* had already imposed a siege on Frankfurt, banned all associations and enacted military law.[20]

The Composition of the Berlin National Assembly and its Factions

The social composition of the Berlin National Assembly, which met for the first time on 22 May 1848, differed greatly from that of the German Parliament.

In percentage terms, peasants, even landless *Häusler* and day-labourers, and craftsmen, clergymen and judges were very much better represented. There were few professors and surprisingly, given their high political profile, there were hardly any lawyers, and no writers and journalists at all. But as in Frankfurt, civil servants, such as law and administrative officials and senior teachers, formed the core of the parliamentarians (see Table 13).

In comparison to the Frankfurt Assembly, the spectrum was clearly biased towards the lower middle classes and the lower orders. The underlying reasons for this have frequently puzzled scholars. Certainly, those who had a national reputation and those who were better educated were sent to Frankfurt, whereas the representatives of long-established local interests were sent to Berlin. Recent analyses of voting patterns have led to the surprising conclusion that it was primarily the rural and not the urban populace which had voted 'democratic'.[21] We have already addressed the issues which moved peasants to elect even *Häusler* and day-labourers to Parliament.

The Berlin Parliament also organized itself into factions at an early stage, although numerous splits make it hard to gain an overall picture of the fluctuating situation. As in Frankfurt, there was a split at

Table 13   Breakdown of the Berlin National Assembly according to profession

Administrative civil servants	73	
Judicial Officers	87	
Teaching professions (5 university teachers)	26	
Total civil servants		**186**
Clergy		**51**
Lawyers, advocates	5	
Doctors	12	
Total freelance intelligentsia		**17**
Commercial middle class		**39**
Farmers (27 large landowners; 46 farmers)		**73**
Craftsmen		**18**
With doctorate, no profession given		**2**
Others, and those for whom no details available		**9**
Total		**395**

Source: M. Botzenhart, *Deutscher Parlamentarismus in der Revolutionszeit, 1848–1850* (Düsseldorf, 1977), p. 517.

the centre. By autumn the groups shown in Table 14 had formed, some of which were named after their parliamentary spokesmen.

The right combined the opposition of the First United Diet, the *Großbürgertum* (Camphausen, Hansemann), East Prussian aristocrats and Westphalian Catholics. In terms of political leaning it may be

Table 14   The factions of the Berlin National Assembly

Right	Harkort Faction	Centre-right Duncker-Kosch- Unruh faction	Centre-left Rodbertus faction	Left
c. 120	*c.* 30	*c.* 40	*c.* 90	*c.* 120

Source: M. Botzenhart, *Deutscher Parlamentarismus in der Revolutionszeit 1848–1850* (Düsseldorf, 1977), compiled from pp. 441–53.

compared with the Frankfurt 'Casino' faction. The Harkort faction, which split from the right, remained essentially on the right, developing an independent profile only to a limited degree. Like the Frankfurt 'Württemberger Hof', the centre-right was home to democratic liberals and defenders of the parliamentary principle. Under certain circumstances the centre-left formed the majority. It therefore assumed a key position on many issues. It can be compared to the 'Westendhall'. The left also split into a parliamentary and a republican and actionist wing, but in the main was less distanced from the democratic parliamentary monarchy than the Frankfurt 'Deutscher Hof' and 'Donnersberg' factions.

The Constitutional Policies of the Berlin National Assembly

The Berlin National Assembly was appointed to agree a constitution with the monarch. Yet from the very beginning some of its deputies, conscious of having emerged from the revolution, pursued constitutional policies which went beyond the negotiations on the constitution. The controversies focused on the attitude to the revolution, and to the events of March in particular, and on the binding nature of the principle of agreement with the monarch. Both these issues led to the formation of factions within the Assembly.

This was seen for the first time on 8 June 1848, when the printing works owner, Julius Berends, proposed his famous motion asking that, 'in recognition of the revolution, the Assembly put on record that the fighters of 18 and 19 March had rendered outstanding services to the Fatherland'.[22] The majority rejected the motion in accordance with the wishes of Camphausen's government. This provoked extraparliamentary agitation, which culminated in the storming of the Berlin Armoury on 14 June. Nevertheless, the Assembly decided on 15 June that it did not require armed protection. Camphausen's ministry regarded this as a defeat and resigned on 20 June.

Recognizing the right to a revolution implied a commitment to the principle of the sovereignty of the people. Behind the apparently empty dispute about principles stood the issue of power. This brought the controversy surrounding the 'agreement principle' out into the open, for agreeing the constitution meant recognizing the right of the crown as a political power, a notion which was unacceptable to the democratic factions. Typically enough, a motion that the constitution be accepted by the National Assembly alone, without the agreement of the crown, was rejected on 16 October 1848 by 226 votes to the left's 110. This fact is frequently overlooked when the Berlin National Assembly is called to account for being 'considerably more radical' than its Frankfurt counterpart.[23] The Paulskirche was also asked to make a similar decision on whether the Provisional Central Power should be established 'subject to agreement with the German governments'. The motion was defeated by 512 votes to 31, and the agreement principle thereby rejected.[24]

However, the Berlin National Assembly also refused to work with the constitution drafted by the King alone, which the government placed before it on 22 May. Instead, it appointed its own Constitutional Committee, which on 26 July produced a draft which became known as the 'Charte Waldeck' after the Committee's chairman Benedikt Waldeck. Its considerable deviations from the government draft all touched on the issue of power. In addition to the standing army and a reserve *Landwehr* or militia, the Charte Waldeck proposed a general right to arms and a people's army which would be assigned to parliament. It also demanded a say in the signing of foreign treaties, proposed only a suspensory right of veto for the monarch, far-reaching anti-feudal regulations and an extension of parliament's right to monitor the government by means of investigating committees.

The draft attacked the very heart of monarchic power: the army and diplomacy. It led to agitation amongst royalist and conservative associations, who now began to prepare themselves for a coup. The King became ever more bitter and ready for counter-revolution when the National Assembly passed a series of resolutions in the spirit of the 'Charte Waldeck', including the elimination of the expression 'by the grace of God' from the royal title and an end to aristocratic and other titles, honours, orders and decorations: in short the 'abolition' of the aristocracy. All these issues concerned the Frankfurt National Assembly in a similar manner (Article II of the Basic Rights), though the phrase 'by the grace of God' was not a subject for them at all. As Huber rightly points out, these resolutions did not merely affect matters of prestige and etiquette, but 'were consciously targeted at the symbols of the traditional monarchical, aristocratic and bureaucratic and military order.'[25] To royalists it all seemed like a coup pure and simple: the force with which the old ruling structures were able to assert themselves against the advance of the middle classes is revealed in the events leading up to the counter-revolution.

The Vienna Reichstag

The Vienna *Reichstag* was formally opened on 22 July 1848 by Arch-duke John, representing the Kaiser who had fled. It was comprised of a total of 383 deputies from all Habsburg states with the exception of Hungary and Lombardo-Venetia. With the Romanians, Ruthe-nians, Italians from Southern Tyrol, Czechs and Poles, the Germans formed one minority amongst many. The problems which arose as a result were described by the Württemberg envoy, Freiherr von Linden, in his vivid, though uncomprehending, report on the first official session:

> The president by seniority appointed as chairman appeared in the person of a man from Bukovina, who doesn't really speak any language at all; he spoke in the Romanian dialect, an idiom which has its origins in the ancient Roman colonizers from Dacia and is therefore said to have retained some similarities with Latin; he was followed by Slavs, and finally an Italian. The mythical times of the Tower of Babel seemed to be returning.[26]

The deputies reacted to one another with a mixture of amazement and incomprehension. Their reactions were often recorded in pictur-esque descriptions, frequently mixed with arrogance. This was one aspect of the multi-ethnic state of Austria. The other was the function of the *Reichstag* within the Austrian revolution, and we will examine that here. As was already clear in the elections, the *Reichstag* and the structure of the agrarian world were closely linked. It was the possibi-lity that the old feudal relics might be abolished that had awakened the peasants' interest in the revolution in the first place. This was reflected in the social composition of the *Reichstag*: 92 deputies were farmers or small landowners, representing almost a quarter of the Assembly. Of these, 31 came from Galicia alone, which had seen vio-lent peasant revolts in 1846 during the great agrarian crisis.

Despite the differences in nationalities, a decisive advance was made on 26 July, when the young Viennese doctoral student, Hans Kudlich, submitted a sensational motion on this issue. He proposed: 'From now on the subservient relationship, together with all the rights and obligations which spring from it, will be abolished, subject to decisions as to whether and how compensation should be awarded.'[27] The issue of whether the abolition should be carried out without compensation led to bitter inter-party wrangles. The matter was finally resolved by the *Reichstag* on 31 August 1848, in a resolution which stated that all subservient relationships were to be abolished without compensation. However, services and levies (socage, referred to as 'Robot', and feudal obligations) were to be abolished in exchange for compensation. Provincial funds were to support the peasants. The outcome represented a victory for liberalism over the social revolution.

The Kaiser ratified the resolution in a law of 7 September, and a new social order was proclaimed in Austria, in which the old feudal Austrian aristocracy was robbed of part of its power over the rural population. Already on 15 September the Council of Ministers issued an announcement to the rural population explaining how the law was to be implemented. On 24 September the peasants fêted Kudlich in a massive torch-lit procession through the streets of Vienna. For them the revolution was over and their interest in the *Reichstag* began to wane. In October the Vienna revolutionaries would feel the lack of peasant backing.

After the October revolution and the coup the *Reichstag*, which had been transferred to the small Moravian town of Kremsier, met again from 22 November 1848 to 7 March 1949, when it was dissolved by the army. As the reaction took hold, their second great achievement vanished: a draft constitution, which seriously addressed the problems of federalism and centralism, and which envisaged a political organization of Austria which would do justice to all nationalities.

The Chambers of the 'Third Germany'

The attention accorded to the parliaments in Frankfurt, Berlin and Vienna make it easy to forget that parliamentary life in Germany was in fact far more complex than that. In the medium and small states too, as well as in the city republics, there were representative bodies which inspired, and at the same time absorbed, the political forces of the middle classes. Under the onslaught of the March movement the princes and senates had been prepared to appoint diets or '*Bürgerschaften*', so that they could transform the promised March achievements into laws on the press, on the formation of associations and on trade and agrarian issues.

It soon became clear that the March revolution 'halted before the benches of the chambers' and not just 'before the thrones'.[28] As in Frankfurt, Berlin and Vienna, one might have expected the medium and small states to have formed constituent 'national' assemblies according to new suffrage regulations on the broadest democratic basis. In fact, almost everywhere it was the princes who appointed the chambers, and once again they did so according to the old *Vormärz* type, with unequal suffrage based on the payment of taxes and special representation, awarded in particular to large numbers of privileged or hereditary members of the first chambers. The March ministers behaved passively, and only in the late autumn and winter of 1848–9, following public pressure, did chambers elected according to new election laws materialize. Sooner or later they were dissolved again in conflicts with the government, and the majority of the modernizing laws were reversed to their pre-March basis. The reactionary decrees of the Confederation in 1851 saw to it that this situation was re-established as uniformly as possible in all German states.

9 Nation-Building and the Crisis of Nationalities

O. Dann has described the development of the national movement as a progression 'from the nationalism of élites to a national mass movement'. This movement emerged on an organized level for the first time after 1806, supported by a small group of intellectuals. Already in the anti-Napoleonic Wars of Liberation the craftsman middle classes had joined the volunteer contingents in large numbers, but as a rule their horizons were limited to devotion to the ruling house and the immediate homeland, and to loyalty to the motto 'with God for King and Fatherland'. In this sense the German national movement of '1813' was a 'nationalism of élites'. ('Nationalism' in this context refers to a common European phenomenon and has no pejorative connotation.) Its spokesmen Arndt and Jahn, and many a former *Burschenschafter* later took their seats on the benches of the Paulskirche.

Since the Rhine crisis of 1840, exacerbated by the conflict surrounding Schleswig-Holstein, the issue of nationalism had grown into an increasingly broad popular movement, which was now also supported by the middle and lower middle classes, who were active in their own associations and festival culture. Fundamental social changes fostered this alliance; the massive expansion in elementary education, decreasing illiteracy rates, growing book and newspaper production, improvements in transport networks and the integration of the economic sphere: all these factors created scope for supra-regional German communication networks.

To a large degree the German national movement also formed in opposition to the existing territorial states and the German Confederation. Whilst in the 1840s the governments became ever more embroiled in a legitimation crisis, national feeling became ever stronger. It grew particularly animated during the March revolution. Although on the surface it seemed united, the movement already contained its own contradictions. 1848 saw the emergence of 'competing groups agitating side by side on different national issues' whose integration was no longer possible.[1]

In all the Paulskirche debates, controversies arose on the issue of what constituted the German nation. This was expressed in two competing ideological perspectives.[2] The *national democratic* variant was based on the principle of the national right to self-determination, usually conceived in ethnic terms. Its supporters thought in parliamentary, republican and international terms; that is to say, they employed their nationalism as a doctrine of liberation and independence against the forces of 'reaction'. They expressed their solidarity with the Greeks of the 1820s (as 'Philhellenes'), and with the Poles after their uprising of 1830. In the Paulskirche, their spokesmen belonged to the democratic factions.

The second perspective was the *antagonistic nationalist* variant: it was formed in 1813, and was also a liberation movement. However, it was characterized by its reference to German history and to rights genuinely or putatively founded in it. It stood for the aggressive assertion of German self-interest, for national prestige and the claim to German superiority. Antagonistic nationalism was manifested not on an international level, but as an 'integrative ideology'. It was already expressed in extreme terms in Arndt's writings. For example, his famous song includes the lines: 'This is the German Fatherland,/ Where anger destroys the French dross,/ Where every Frenchman is our foe/ And every German is called friend.' Antagonistic nationalism grew after the Rhine crisis of 1840. In the Paulskirche its mild and more intense forms were represented by the centre and centre-right, respectively.

In 1848 there were two fundamental problems associated with the issue of nation-building.

1. Nationality and state territory could rarely be reconciled without conflict with neighbouring nations. The German nation's right to self-determination clashed with that of non-German ethnic groups.
2. Every resolution passed by the National Assembly which sought to standardize the future territory of the *Reich* was influenced by the politics of the day; the growing counter-revolution weakened nation-building attempts, and made it ever more difficult for the Central Power successfully to assert its primacy over the individual states.

In the early summer of 1848, the overwhelming majority in the National Assembly believed that the traditional territory of the German Confederation should serve as the basis for the outlying borders of the future nation state. But this was based on a pre-national construct which, as a loose federation of princes and city republics, had incorporated constitutional hybrid relationships which ran counter to the nationality principle. As Duke of Holstein, for example, the King of Denmark was a member of the German Confederation, as was the King of the Netherlands in his capacity as Duke of Luxembourg and Limburg. To the north, east and south, the borders of the Confederation followed the frontiers of the old *Reich* of 1806. Yet the *Reich* had not been nationally homogeneous: in the border areas the inhabitants of German nationality mixed freely with Danes, Poles, Czechs, Slovacks, Hungarians, Slovenes, Croats, Italians and Dutch.

All non-Confederation areas which were perceived as being clearly or predominantly German were also included in the great national unification efforts. They were therefore asked to elect deputies to Frankfurt; this occurred in East and West Prussia, in Posen and in Schleswig. This expansionist tendency, recognizable at an early stage, which obscured traditional state and international laws, together with the jumbled nature of German and non-German areas, made conflicts with foreign countries and with national minorities inevitable. It was reflected in the five nationality issues dealt with by the Paulskirche: those of Posen, South Tyrol, Bohemia-Moravia, Limburg and Schleswig-Holstein.

Posen

Large tracts of the eastern provinces of Prussia and Austria had been settled by Poles. For many liberals and democrats, and for large sections of the public in the *Vormärz* period, the re-establishment of an independent Poland had been part of the programme of liberal politics in opposition to the Prussian, Austrian and Russian powers which had divided it. Friendship towards Poland stood for progressive politics. A majority in the Pre-Parliament had voted in favour of a resolution stating that 'the Assembly declares the division of Poland to be an ignominious injustice. It recognizes the sacred duty of the German people to help effect the re-establishment of Poland.'[3] This enthusiasm for the 'Peoples' Spring' collapsed in the negotiations of the

Frankfurt National Assembly, when antagonistic nationalism scored a success over the nationalist democrats. The Polish problem became a party issue when 16 deputies from the left submitted a motion on 24 July 1848 calling for the Province of Posen's membership of the German Confederation to be denied and for its 12 deputies to be excluded from the National Assembly.[4]

The great confrontation between the Hegelians Arnold Ruge and Wilhelm Jordan saw an almost stereotypical clash between the antagonistic and democratic conception of nationalism. Since then Jordan's speech has always been cited as the prime example of the inherently aggressive nationalism of the German revolution.[5] Dismissing Germany's support for the national rights of Poland as an expression of 'cosmopolitan liberalism', Jordan contrasted it with the modern 'healthy national egotism' which had replaced 'Poland euphoria', 'cosmopolitan idealism' and 'feeble-minded sentimentality'. He referred to the principle that 'might is right' and to the national superiority of the Germans.

In contrast to Jordan's chauvinistic speech, the majority focused on the principle of nationality which would make a division of Germans and Poles in the province possible. They agreed to the demarcation line laid down by the Prussian government on 4 June 1848. But in doing so they made a pact with the counter-revolution and weakened their own position, or so the minority in Frankfurt must have understood matters. For them strengthening Poland would imply international support for the independence movements against 'the reaction'. At the beginning of May Prussian troops had put down the Polish uprising in Posen. On 4 June 1848 the Prussian government commissioner General von Pfuel then divided off two-thirds of the province, calling it 'German Posen', consigning to the realm of the impossible the Prussian March promises on the 'national reorganization' of Poland. The Frankfurt National Assembly sanctioned this policy with a division decree, demonstrating how little of the original enthusiasm for Poland remained. This was seen in stark terms when the democrats reiterated the Pre-Parliament's declaration of support for Poland: the Paulskirche now rejected the motion by 331 votes to 101.[6]

South Tyrol

Here, too, the international nature of the revolution engendered a confrontation; for it was impossible to separate a decision on a nationality issue from its repercussions on the driving forces of the revolution. The South Tyrol issue exposed the Frankfurt democrats' sympathy for the Italian War of Independence.

From Lake Brenner to Lake Garda, the whole of South Tyrol was part of the German Confederation, including the region south of the Salurner Klause, with the Districts of Trient and Rovereto, which was settled mainly by Italians; this area was referred to as 'Welsch-Tirol'. Five of the deputies from this region submitted a separation motion on 3 June 1848, declaring their wish to leave the German Confederation. The democrats supported this proposal, for they viewed the issue in the context of a reinforcement of revolutionary Northern Italy. A few days before the debate was held, the Austrian Field Marshal von Radetzky had reconquered Lombardy. During the debate, the majority factions came under attack for being inconsistent; for making demands on ethnic grounds in the north and east, yet refusing to make corresponding territorial concessions in the south. Indeed, it was maintained, the National Assembly was behaving in an utterly opportunistic manner in the fixing of borders. An Austrian deputy objected, voicing his own 'machiavellian programme' (G. Wollstein): 'I have just one thing to say: *beati possidentes*; we own South Tyrol and we will keep it; that is my right under international law.'[7] The historian Friedrich von Raumer's motto 'Germany would rather die than surrender and give away the soil of the Fatherland'[8] was warmly received.

Justified by self-interest in a strong German position south of the Alps, the majority ignored the ethnic principle and came down in favour of the victory of the Austrian troops in northern Italy. The Prussian politician von Radowitz's reference during the debate to von Radetzky's successful armed campaign brought forth 'continuous' applause from the factions of the centre and the right. This took place on 12 August, when the majority rejected the 'Welsch-Tirol' motion.

Bohemia and Moravia

In contrast to Posen and South Tyrol, the conflicts surrounding Bohemia and Moravia did not lead to the polarization of parties. The ratio of Germans to Czechs in Bohemia was two to three. Although the revolution had begun with the emotional alliance of Germans and Czechs under the banner of the 'Peoples' Spring', the Czech middle classes soon began to distance themselves from a German nation state in favour of an independent Bohemian evolution under Austrian sovereignty. The Prague historian and champion of Bohemian autonomy, Franz Palacký, rejected an invitation to join the Committee of Fifty on the grounds that joining a German nation-state would jeopardize the independence that Bohemia had always enjoyed. In his famous written response of 17 April 1848 he declared that the 'people's association of nations' of the Danube monarchy was the natural protector of small nations. 'Truly', he wrote, 'if the Austrian imperial state had not existed for a long time already, one would have to make haste to create it in the interests of Europe, and indeed in the interests of humanity itself.' In keeping with these sentiments, 48 of the 68 Bohemian and Moravian constituencies refused to send deputies to Frankfurt.

For all Paulskirche factions on the other hand, it was taken as read that these former Confederation areas belonged to the *Reich*. They did recognize the concerns of the non-German minorities, however. On 31 May 1848, with the Habsburg monarchy in mind, they voted almost unanimously for wide-ranging measures to protect minorities. During the Prague uprising of 12–16 June 1848, however, no faction was willing to regard as legitimate the Czech nation's claim for independence from the former German Confederation. Indeed, the overwhelming majority of deputies regarded this demand as an attack on the Germans in Bohemia. Even some democrats welcomed Windischgrätz's defeat of the Prague Uprising, although doubts were voiced as to whether the success of the German nationals in Prague was not paid for by the victory of reactionary forces. The *Bundestag* was still in session and passed a resolution to hold troops ready for intervention (20 June 1848). For many deputies this resolution did not go far enough. They demanded the immediate invasion of Bohemia by German troops. These events testify to the militant explosive force inherent in the attempts to unify the nation, already in its early stages, a force which would shortly be unleashed in Schleswig-Holstein.

Limburg

Although it could be argued that Bohemian affairs were an internal Confederation issue, the National Assembly's claim to Limburg signified an intervention in matters of international law. For the integration of this Duchy (resolution of 19 July 1848) was inconsistent with the fact that constitutionally it was a Dutch province. It may have seemed a mere trifle in terms of size, but the Limburg conflict had grave international repercussions. To a greater extent than has previously been recognized by scholars, England, France and Russia now began to follow the policies of the Central Power and the National Assembly with growing mistrust and displeasure, and made reassuring undertakings to The Netherlands.[9] The Central Power's careful manoeuvrings came under attack from Parliament, and once again it found itself subject to accusations of lack of energy in national politics.

Schleswig-Holstein

The Central Power was criticized most sharply for its lack of national drive in the Schleswig-Holstein issue, which threatened the very existence of the parliament and its unification attempts. Complex chains of motives were intertwined, which must be teased apart if we are going to examine the issue in detail. First of all it is necessary to look at the events themselves.

Schleswig-Holstein was ruled by the only revolutionary provisional state government which had openly rebelled against the state's sovereign, but which nevertheless was recognized by the other German governments and the *Bundesversammlung*. Denmark's annexation decree on 21 March 1848 and the subsequent advance of Danish troops into Schleswig, marked the beginning of a military confrontation which threatened to turn into a European war. Prussia initially responded on its own initiative with military intervention in Holstein. In a decree of 12 April 1848 the *Bundesversammlung* declared the conflict to be a *Bundeskrieg* against Denmark. Although the supreme command was awarded to a Prussian – General von Wrangel – it had become a German rather than simply a Prussian war. The Provisional Central Power took it on as an 'Imperial war'. Prussian troops were joined by forces from the Tenth Federal Army Corps (Hanover, Mecklenburg, Oldenburg, Brunswick and the Hansa towns). While these Federal Troops, supported by volunteers from all over Germany, successfully advanced as far as Jutland, the Danish fleet proved its superiority by blockading German coasts and shipping. Demands for a mighty German fleet grew ever louder. Almost on a daily basis the Paulskirche clerk announced the receipt of contributions to the fleet fund. Large numbers of public collections were held.[10] Here we see the beginnings of the mobilization of national and imperialist feelings, which came to the fore in the 'place in the sun' hysteria of the Second Kaiserreich. The Bergzabern Song Circle sent in a contribution accompanied by the motto, 'Was bringt zu Ehren? Sich wehren!' (What will bring honour? Arming ourselves!) Debates in the Paulskirche were filled with descriptions of Germany's claim to be 'a world power', the 'honour' of Germany and its prestige on the oceans of the world.

There were five aspects to the 'German War'. In terms of their potential for conflict they overlapped to some extent and were mutually reinforcing. They are: firstly, the relationship between the Central Power and the European powers; secondly, between the Central Power and Prussia; thirdly, between the National Assembly and the revolution; fourthly, between the Central Power and the National Assembly; and finally, between the National Assembly and the public.

1.   The conflict was a test of the Provisional Central Power's foreign policy, for Germany's international standing and external recognition of German unity depended on it. Russia and England, guarantors of the Schleswig-Holstein position under international law, regarded the absorption of Schleswig into a German nation-state as the forcible annexation of a territory which was under Danish rule. It risked becoming a *casus belli* which might turn into a European war.

2.   The primacy of the Central Power over the individual states was challenged on 26 August, when Prussia agreed the Truce of Malmö with Denmark. Following its own analysis of the international situation, Prussia came down in favour of the compromise suggested by the English; to divide Schleswig according to nationality. Von Wrangel gave the order to withdraw from Jutland and to retreat far enough to enable Northern Schleswig to fall into Danish hands. The retreat was seen as a national betrayal and led to an extraordinary storm of public protest. It had, moreover, been carried out in a high-handed manner and by circumventing the Central Power. The Central Power had been unmasked; without its own instruments of power it was helpless against Prussia.

3.   The British plan to divide the territory, a plan which, incidentally, was rejected by the Danes, would have annexed the overwhelmingly Danish North Schleswig to Denmark, with the remaining two-thirds of the Duchy falling to the Confederation. Deputies from all factions of the National Assembly dismissed this suggestion. The centre-right and the right, which was dominated by antagonistic nationalist claims, referred to Germany's historical and legal right to the whole of Schleswig, to their shared history and Germany's honour. Given the democratic understanding of national issues, one might have expected the left and the centre-left to recognize the right to self-determination, as it had for the Poles in Posen and the Italians in 'Welsch-Tirol'. But unlike the Schleswig situation, in these latter cases there was no conflict between the reinforcement of the revolution and the principle of nationality. When the revolution was at stake, loyalty to the principle of nationality was less important: the Truce provided for the dissolution of the provisional state government and the lifting of its laws. For the democrats this constituted a betrayal of the revolution. The Schleswig-Holstein issue provided an opportunity to secure the revolution internally by means of an external war. They wanted 'to centralize and dynamize the revolution, to prevent it from becoming too moderate and seeping away'.[11] The democrats were shrewd in their calculation of the heights of national excitement on this matter. Social divisions had opened up on all sides; general agreement on this issue might bring about a new unity and cohesion.

4.   The conflict led to a test of strength between the Central Power and the National Assembly. The law of 28 June 1848 (when the Central Power was appointed) provided for Parliament's right to a say in foreign affairs. As early as 9 June 1848, the historian Waitz had garnered wide support for his motion stating that the Schleswig-Holstein question was a national issue and therefore the responsibility of the national parliament.

In the passionate debate on the Truce, which had been taking place since 4 September 1848, a gulf had been widening between deputies and the imperial cabinet, which was prepared to ratify the treaty on the grounds of political expediency. The rift was exposed when Parliament decided by 238 votes to 221 to halt ('adjourn') all measures undertaken to implement the Malmö Treaty. This was designed primarily to prevent the withdrawal of troops from the Duchies. The left, centre-left and sections of the centre-right and right voted in favour of the adjournment.

Von Leiningen's defeated cabinet resigned. The government had been brought down by the Paulskirche according to the principles of parliamentary rule. But the *Reichsverweser*'s instructions to Dahlmann, the leading anti-truce campaigner, to form a new government, resulted in a fiasco. For the coalition on the national issue which extended from right to left, was untenable in matters of constitutional politics: the issues on which the factions would not yield – freedom, equality and sovereignty of the people – remained as entrenched as ever. Dahlmann was forced to admit defeat. Renewed negotiations from 14 to 16 September forced the majority to adopt the course of *realpolitik*. On 16 September 1848, Parliament rejected a motion calling for a continuation of the Imperial war by 258 votes to 237. They then voted in favour of the Truce (257:236). The Austrian von Schmerling assumed the leadership of the Imperial Cabinet.

5. Public hostility towards the Central Power and the National Assembly had been building up for some time. It was now unleashed by the resolution of 16 September. The acceptance of the Truce sparked renewed outbreaks of revolution in Germany, beginning with the Frankfurt uprising of 17 September. Asserting all the influence it could muster, the Central Power tried to suppress these movements. In doing so, it joined the ranks of the European Powers which brought about the turning point of the revolution in the autumn of 1848. Now, instead of an external national war, civil war reigned in Germany. A majority in the Parliament voted to surrender the initiative, handing it over to Prussia, which set about implementing the armistice. The majority, and with it the Paulskirche as a whole, lost the support of the population, forfeiting the opportunity to use the spectre of a continuation of the revolution to put pressure on the governments, and relinquished Frankfurt's primacy over the princes. The alternative presented by the defeated minority would have posed too high a risk, and might have resulted in a European war and the uncontrollable continuation of the revolution.[12] But the history which did not come about must remain open and unwritten. Disputes as to what might have happened are not appropriate here. But we should not forget that the fate of the revolution was not decided exclusively, indeed perhaps not even decisively, by votes taken in Frankfurt. The dimensions were far more complex and larger than that – particularly in the context of Europe. In this context, September 1848, with the ambivalent option of a truce, should be regarded as a turning point in the revolution, which was inextricably linked with the general European turning point of the revolution that autumn.

The debate on the formation of the nation highlights the risks that the middle classes elected to Frankfurt were prepared to take when Germany's power and honour were at stake. The National Assembly provoked crises with non-German nationalities, broke treaties with foreign powers and laid claim to regions beyond the German-speaking borders. Its need to demonstrate its power and unity, honour and might to foreign powers was great. During the debates, central European projects were voiced which were based on a kind of 'magnetic theory' (Wollstein), according to which an attractive economically powerful *Reich*, constitutional and liberal in nature, would draw neighbouring regions and states to it like a magnet, and keep them in a position of dependence. Demands for comprehensive military action, against Bohemia for example, had grown loud; emotional proclamations that the 'honourable' defeat of the German people would be preferable to its continued existence in bondage, 'ignominy' and 'humiliation' were enthusiastically received; the emotional pathos linked with a claim to world prestige was focused on the 'fleet euphoria'. There was a clear readiness to sacrifice internationally agreed ties to the principle of national power. It is true that at the end of the day the resolution on the Schleswig-Holstein issue was a moderate one, but it was passed by a narrow majority. Beneath the surface were hidden phenomena which show that the desire for power on the part of the dominant middle classes of 1848–9 and for their projected *Reich* actually brought them far closer to the Second *Kaiserreich* than is usually assumed.[13]

10   The Turning Point in the European Revolutions, Summer/Autumn 1848

Just as the outbreak of the revolutions in the spring of 1848 had been a European event, so too did the turning point in the summer and autumn assume European dimensions. Revolution and counter-revolution were scattered over many different centres, and just as success in one region in the spring had provided the impetus for others, from the summer of 1848 onwards, a chain of government reactions could be observed. The consolidation of state power in one European metropolis stimulated reactionary activity in others, restricting the room for manoeuvre in the remaining centres of action.

The image of a chain reaction has a very real background. Since the outbreak of the revolutions, senior diplomats in the capitals had been meticulously documenting the development, features and internal weaknesses of the events of the revolution. Valentin owed much of his detailed information to the reports compiled by the embassies. In Dresden they had a clear picture of the Paris June Battle, just as in Paris details were known of the May Uprising in Dresden in 1849.[1] Thanks to their ambassadors, the princes were able to experience and record the chances and successes of the counter-revolution as a European event. Nineteenth-century monarchs rarely wrote their memoirs. Those of the Saxon King Johann document his experience of the European reaction in the summer and autumn of 1848 as a gradually intensifying sequence of events.[2]

Crakow, Posen, Prague, Paris and Northern Italy

Crakow, 26 April 1848

The first example of ruthless and successful military suppression was seen in Crakow. Already in the *Vormärz* period the town had been the focus of the Polish national movement. After the outbreak of the February Revolution in Paris it became the meeting point for returning émigrés from western European countries. Attempts to prevent their return led to an uprising on 26 April. The revolt was put down that same day, when the town was bombarded on the orders of the Austrian fortress commandant.

The Polish Uprising in Posen, 2–9 May 1848

In its announcement of a royal cabinet order of 24 March, the Prussian transitional ministry of von Arnim-Boitzenburg had promised the Poles a 'national reorganization'. Before that, on 20 March, under the impact of the Berlin March revolution, the Polish officer Ludwig von Mieroslawski had been freed from Prussian imprisonment, together with those found guilty with him in 1847. Von Mieroslawski now assumed the leadership of the Polish struggle for independence in Posen and formed a revolutionary government (a National Committee). He recruited soldiers for a national Polish army with the slogan: 'Let us go into action against Tsarist Russia in an alliance with liberated Germany!'[3] Countless small farmers enlisted. But a conflict of interests between the aristocracy (*szlachta*) and the democrats caused a rift in the committee, with one section favouring the limited autonomy promised by Prussia, and the other calling for active fighting. Von Mieroslawski wavered and finally reduced his troops to around 4000 men, despite protests from the peasants.

At the beginning of May Prussia abandoned its policy of careful restraint and ordered military intervention. Under the leadership of General von Pfuel the Prussians forced first von Mieroslawski (2 May) and then the remaining forces (9 May) to capitulate. Prussian troops had passed their first test of reliability in the fight against the revolutionaries. From 4 June onwards, a demarcation line divided the province. The Frankfurt National Assembly immediately accepted this outcome.

The Prague Uprising, 12–16 June 1848

Prague became the focus of Slav efforts to achieve political independence. These efforts culminated outwardly in the Slav Congress which met in the city from 3 June onwards, over which Palacký presided. A manifesto to the European people proclaimed freedom, equality and fraternity and demanded a general European People's Congress which would be better able to settle international issues than the old diplomatic channels.

As in Vienna and Berlin, the urban population became politicized in the rallies which were held daily, and which the workers and lower middle classes attended in large numbers, supported by a student legion formed on the Vienna model. Organized book-printers and textile workers (cotton printers) voiced their complaints about low wages, unemployment and social demotion.[4] The successes of the Vienna May Revolution inspired events in Prague too. They culminated, as so frequently in situations of this kind, in a demand for the arming of the populace. The commanding general, Prince Windisch-grätz, refused to distribute arms and ammunition. Demonstrations and protests were held on 12 June; following the massive Whitsun Rally of 13 June, barricades sprang up and open fighting broke out. The unorganized uprising rapidly collapsed when the town was bombarded. Windischgrätz ordered a state of siege, imposed martial law, dissolved the student legion, ordered mass arrests, suspended the current elections to the Bohemian Diet and extended the military dictatorship to encompass the entire country. Prague represented the first example of a military victory over a popular movement in a capital city, which was subsequently followed by a general reaction. The Paulskirche overwhelmingly perceived the uprising as an attack on the integrity of the *Reich*, and welcomed its suppression.

The Paris June Battle, 22–6 June 1848

The June uprising in Paris represented the first turning-point for the European revolutions. In contrast to the military campaigns in Crakow, Posen or Prague, in Paris a republican government which had emerged from the revolution turned the army on its own people, exposing the social gulf which existed in the once united pre-revolutionary oppositional front. Paris saw a rehearsal of events which the Provisional Central Power in Frankfurt completed soon afterwards.

The uprising in the French capital was sparked by measures proposing to abolish the national workshops, which employed proletarians in sewage and excavation work. Both the bourgeois middle class and the peasants had grown tired of bearing the immense costs of these job creation schemes. In a decree of 21 June, unmarried workers between the ages of 17 and 25 were sacked or enlisted in the army. Workers took to the streets on 22 June. The demonstrations soon grew into an armed uprising. According to the lists of those later arrested, the 'workers' included activists from many groups which ought really to be described as lower middle class: metal workers, construction workers and cabinet-makers joined with members of the trade and commercial lower middle classes, including master craftsmen.[5] On 26 June the uprising was violently suppressed in an enormous military operation by the Mobile Guard, the National Guard and the regular army under the leadership of War Minister Cavaignac. More than 10,000 people fell victim to the ensuing persecution.

Northern Italy, 25 July–6 August 1848

The decisive turn of events for Austria in favour of the unity of the multi-ethnic state under the Habsburg Kaiser took place in northern Italy. The impetus came not from the March ministry in Vienna, which was prepared to accept the separation of an independent Lombardy, but from the army. More particularly, it came from Field Marshal von Radetzky, who pushed through the decision to re-establish Austrian rule in northern Italy by means of a violent armed intervention. He ordered his Field Marshal Lieutenant, Felix Fürst zu Schwarzenberg, to procure the appropriate authorization from the court in Innsbruck. The court and the army were thus able to circumvent the policies of the Vienna ministry.

Indeed, the army guaranteed the cohesion of the monarchy. The decisive victory at Custozza (25 July 1848) was owed to the loyalty of the Croat regiments, that is to say, the competing nationalities had a stabilizing effect on the cohesion of the troops. On 6 August Austrian troops once again entered Milan, where Schwarzenberg took over the administration until he had successfully implemented the political reaction in the state as a whole, as representative of the *Großösterreich* concept and Minister President. On 12 August the court returned to Vienna from Innsbruck. This, too, was a reflection of the the significance of the victory in northern Italy.

The September Revolution in Frankfurt and Baden

Just as the social question had provided the fundamental stuff of conflict for the insurgents in Prague and Paris, in Germany too it kept the lower middle classes, peasants and the democratic freelance intelligentsia in a state of growing unrest which culminated in revolutionary tension in September. The social policies of the March ministries and the parliaments had increasingly been shown to be the self-interested policies of the educated and propertied middle classes, and as such they were not enthusiastically received amongst those broad sections of the population which had been the driving forces of the March revolution. Efforts on the part of people's and workers' societies to organize had also helped to shape social consciousness on a regional level, and to co-ordinate political actions, thereby ensuring their greater efficacy. In September in Schleswig, Saxony, Bavaria, the Badenese Oberland, the Odenwald (Wertheim, 13 September) and even in Mecklenburg, renewed socially motivated protests erupted amongst peasants and agricultural workers because it had become clear that the abolition of peasant levies and services was proceeding too sluggishly for their liking. Calls for a 'social republic' were heard in mass demonstrations in the Rhineland cities of Düsseldorf and Cologne (7 and 13 September), in Mannheim and at a rally in Worringen (17 September).

In this September movement social disillusionment, locally bound protest, national enthusiasm, anti-Prussian resentment (over Schleswig-Holstein) and the democrats' fears of the victory of 'the reaction' culminated, as they had in March, in a series of separate actions. The signal for the revolution then came from Frankfurt. When the National Assembly submitted to the Truce of Malmö on 16 September, the city's Democratic Association and Workers' Society organized a rally on the Pfingstweide at Frankfurt, which was attended by at least 15,000 people from near and far. Deputies from the Paulskirche Left also took part, although they refused to comply with requests that they should resign from parliament. The rally adopted the following 'resolution'.

1. That the majority of 258, which accepted the shameful truce on the 16th of the month be hereby declared traitors to the German people, to German freedom and honour;
2. That this resolution be made known to the German nation as quickly as possible; and
3. That a deputation inform the National Assembly of the above resolution tomorrow.[6]

This manifesto, which was read out in the Paulskirche on 18 September, evoked historical memories of the Jacobin tribunals of the

French Revolution. Von Schmerling, who was also Imperial Minister for Internal Affairs, had during the night of 17 – 18 September requested 'Imperial troops' from the Mainz Confederation fortress. As always during the revolution, the military presence whipped up emotions in some of the urban population. Their displeasure was first expressed when a crowd of people attempted to force its way into the Paulskirche and gain a hearing. Troops used violence to clear the square in front of the parliament. Spontaneous protest meetings turned into an uprising, with barricade battles in which more than 1000 people took part. It was later possible to identify as many as 600 of them by name, and to try them in a court of law. A clear social conflict emerged here. The *Großbürgertum*, the businessmen and educated classes disapproved of the events. The gymnasts, the workers' association, members of the civil guard, manual workers, journeymen and craftsmen – the lower middle classes in general – stood on the barricades. The failed uprising claimed 80 lives.

During the fighting, though some distance from the battles, deputies Prince Felix von Lichnowsky and General Hans von Auerswald were killed. The murders aroused the fear of revolutionary terror amongst the middle classes, and made them more ready to acquiesce in the demands of the old powers. Both deputies had been involved in the battles in a military capacity; both had been on a reconnaissance expedition on which von Lichnowsky, experienced in Spanish guerilla wars, had advised the commander-in-chief General Nobili on how it might be possible to circumvent the barricaders and attack them from the rear. He too had been armed and had fired into the crowd.[7]

It has rightly been suggested that the political repercussions of the murders of these deputies were no less important than the consequences of Sand's murder of Kotzebue. Windischgrätz's march on Vienna and von Wrangel's entry into Berlin could 'not be more strongly legitimized than by extreme actions'.[8] The same occurred in Frankfurt. The *Reichsverweser* ordered a state of siege over the city, dissolved all associations and issued 'wanted posters'. On 10 October 1848 the National Assembly enacted an 'imperial law for the protection of the constituent Imperial Assembly and the civil servants of the Provisional Central Power'; it was a 'law for the protection of the constitution' (E.R. Huber).[9]

The Central Power also issued the circular decree referred to above, which ordered the systematic monitoring of political associations. In order to be in a position to oppose the revolutionary consequences of the Frankfurt uprising firmly and immediately, on 19 September the Central Power had also decided to assemble the 'Imperial troops' at its disposal in five surveillance camps. More than 12,000 men gathered at Ulm, in the Central and Upper Rhine areas, in Frankfurt and Thuringia, 'for the rapid and forceful suppression of anarchic movements and uprisings'.[10]

They were supported by troops from the individual constitutional state governments who could be sure of the moral support of the Central Power. Peace was re-established in the Prussian Rhine Province when the government responded to the riots and the building of barricades in Cologne (25 September) by ordering a state of siege.

The situation in south-west Germany was more difficult. Even after the failure of the April revolution, the democratic republicans there had not entirely lost the support of the small commercial middle classes and the rural population. As early as June, their spokesman, Gustav von Struve, had issued a pamphlet containing his 'plan for the revolutionization and republicanization of Germany', and had announced the break-up of the National Assembly.[11] Von Struve's programme promised a 'social republic': 'wealth, education and freedom for all', the arrest of monarchists, the elimination of peasant manorial obligations. His supporters included journeymen, students, Swiss irregular volunteers, craftsmen and peasants. After the Truce of Malmö was accepted, in an echo of the Frankfurt Pfingstweide proclamation, von Struve wrote in his *Deutscher Zuschauer*, 'Triumph! The Frankfurt Parliament is unmasked! There is no longer a German parliament – only an angry population, and opposite it a handful of rogues.'[12]

On 21 September, in the mistaken belief that the Frankfurt uprising had been successful, he proclaimed the German republic from the Town Hall in Lörrach. However, the insurgents were only able to hold out only until 25 September, when they were dispersed by regular Badenese troops under March minister and War Minister General Friedrich Hoffmann. The following day military law reigned in Baden. Amongst von Struve's papers, lists were found predicting uprisings on 25 September in Kassel, Cologne (as did in fact occur), Berlin and Vienna, and on 28 September in Cannstatt in Württemberg. Unlike the March–April movement, the undertaking had clearly been better planned, even if the planning did not finally pay off.

The events of September were apparently crystallized around the Schleswig-Holstein crisis and were riven by internal social revolutionary leanings. Their outcome decided the test of strength between revolution and army in favour of the military forces. The gulf between the constitutionalist and democratic middle classes had widened. (In the Paulskirche Bassermann had demanded the arrest of left-wingers. Von Struve intended the same fate for the liberals.) Internal divisions between the parliamentary and the revolutionary democrats had made matters even more uncertain.

The Vienna Counter-Revolution in October

As in no other capital in the German Confederation, the revolutionaries in Vienna had been able to seize genuine power during the summer. Seven different forces competed for political influence: the court, with the Imperial Army in the background; the ministry; the National Guard; the 'Academic Legion'; the Vienna district council; the democratic associations and workers' societies; and finally (after 22 July), the *Reichstag*. This created an extremely complex dynamic, which was biased in favour of the revolutionaries from the end of May onwards.

If, as Stadelmann once suggested, there was ever any doubt as to whether the events of 1848 constituted a revolution, they will be refuted by the situation in Vienna, where the revolutionary democrats were able to organize the power they had won and to consolidate it on a military basis with the support of 10,000 armed men. After the most recent successes of counter-revolutionary forces in Frankfurt in September, democrats from the other states of the German Confederation looked to Vienna as the last bastion of the March achievements. This is why Blum, Fröbel and two further Frankfurt deputies became involved in the Vienna revolution.

Although the Vienna revolutionaries were better equipped than most, two fundamental weaknesses brought about their downfall: firstly, the conflict within the middle classes on the social question, and secondly the different nationalities in the monarchy, which had a mutually paralysing effect. The Vienna 'June battle' took place on the Prater on 23 August. It was not as violent as that of Paris, but its psychological consequences were just as damaging for the unity of the revolutionaries. As in Paris, the unemployed earned a living wage through public excavation and construction work. In total they numbered more than 20, 000 people.[13] Statistics from the Security Committee (Table 15) show who these 'proletarians' actually were.

Table 15 Breakdown according to profession of the workers employed in public works in and around Vienna, supported by state and local funds. From the Committee of Bürger, National Guard and Students for the maintenance of peace, security and the safeguarding of the rights of the people, Department for public works

Type of worker	Total workers	
	Men	Women
1. House painters	48	
2. Bakers	61	
3. Book printers	16	
4. Book binders	32	
5. Flower makers	9	19
6. Brush binders	13	
7. Coopers	43	
8. Sculptors	32	
9. Surgeons	8	
10. Chocolate makers	8	3
11. Wood turners	282	
12. Servants	359	392
13. Printers	405	
14. Butchers	102	
15. Dyers	89	
16. Engravers	44	
17. Gardeners	64	9
18. Gold, silvers, etc., workers	224	
19. Tanners	14	
20. Glaziers	16	
21. Traders	103	28
22. Manual workers	116	2861
23. Potters	28	
24. Hat makers	17	
25. Glove makers	50	56
26. Instrument makers	47	2
27. Leather workers	62	
28. Artists	101	
29. Bricklayers	603	
30. Millers	22	
31. Trimmers	89	41
32. Plasterers	285	
33. Rope makers	30	
34. Soap makers	7	

Table 15   *(continued)*

	Total workers	
Type of worker	Men	Women
35. Locksmiths	8	
36. Bobbin makers	8	462
37. Tailors	178	18
38. Shoemakers	240	39
39. Joiners	390	
40. Day labourers	2501	2930
41. Watchmakers	67	
42. Weavers	2703	346
43. Washers	14	237
44. Armoury workers	382	385
45. Carpenters	61	5
46. No profession	227	385
Total*	**10,343**	**8218**

* Total workers 18,561. Added to these are the workers currently employed on the railway link: 1450. Therefore, the total is 20,011.

Source: W. Häusler, Von der, *Massenarmut zur Arbeiterbewegung, Demokratie und soziale Frage in der Wiener Revolution von 1848* (Munich, 1979), pp. 250f.

Unskilled workers (servants, manual workers, day labourers, no profession) represented 52.6 per cent of the 18,561 workers (which included 8218 females), and 0.7 per cent were shopkeepers. This means that the remaining 46.7 per cent were qualified male and female workers. The statistics list 41 different trades, from bakers to wood turners. At 16.4 per cent, weavers represented the largest group, followed by bricklayers and printers. These were the crisis trades of the year of the revolution.

These qualified workers were acutely conscious of having been demoted in terms of their social status; they were more politically responsive than the pauper who had never known anything other than being poor, and who accepted his position as his lot in life. In Vienna the crisis in the craft trades had created an army of workers which could easily be revolutionized. As in Paris, the workers' demands for an improvement in their social situation clashed with the economic and political demands of the middle classes. Open conflict erupted on 23 August when the excavation workers held a mass demonstration to protest against wage cuts. The armed National Guard advanced on them, though the 'Academic Legion' remained passive. Also on 23 August the Security Committee dissolved itself on the grounds of the conflicts which had emerged on the workers' question. The 'Academic Legion' and the 'Democratic Club' went over to the workers' side. Most of the middle-class National Guard and the upper middle classes declared their support for the government. The Ministry gained political weight.

The Hungarian-Croat conflict – the second weak point – strengthened the counter-revolution still further, since the anti-Magyar Independence Movement in Croatia provided the most energetic support for imperial power in the form of its representative, the 'Banus' or governor, Joseph Freiherr von Jellačić. In a manifesto of 3 October 1848 the Kaiser dissolved the Hungarian Imperial Diet, ordered a state of siege over the whole of Hungary and appointed von Jellačić as his representative and supreme commander of all Hungarian troops. The counter-revolutionary recipe for success was to 'bring the nationalism of one nation to bear against that of another'.[14]

This constellation also proved to be decisive for the German revolution in Vienna. For von Jellačić, beaten by the Hungarians, was in urgent need of aid from Austrian troops. This was provided by War Minister, Graf Latour. The revolution broke out in the capital on 6 October, when the units stationed in Vienna refused to fight the Hungarians. The troops which defended the revolution were made up of the Vienna units, the democratic associations, the Workers' Club, the Student Legion and a newly formed Mobile Guard, formed from members of the unpropertied population, armed with weapons from a storming of the armoury. They are estimated to have totalled 100,000 in Vienna alone. Government troops and the National Guard were powerless against them.

The military counter-offensive came from Prince Windischgrätz's troops, who advanced on Vienna from Prague. Windischgrätz had been appointed supreme commander of all Austrian troops (with the exception of von Radetzky's army) in an Imperial Manifesto of 16 October. The attack on Vienna began on 26 October. By 31 October Windischgrätz had taken the centre of the city.

The Hungarians had wanted to rush to the aid of the Viennese, but they hesitated too long over the dilemma of fighting troops under the same commander-in-chief. By the time Kossuth arrived to urge them to intervene, it was already too late; on 30 October they lost the battle of Schwechat. Windischgrätz used Czech and Croat troop units. For unlike the Vienna units, there was no danger of them expressing solidarity with the insurgents.

According to official calculations, 843 civilians were killed in the battles and 928 wounded; 189 soldiers lost their lives and 817 were wounded. But there were large numbers of unreported cases too: fear of persecution had taught people to keep quiet about such matters. If anything, contemporary estimates of 2000 civilian victims are probably on the conservative side. Hospital statistics are available which allow a detailed analysis of the dead and wounded defenders of Vienna (see Table 16).

Small craftsmen, journeymen and day labourers formed the majority of the victims, followed by servants and students. The conquest of Vienna laid the foundations for the restoration of the Habsburg monarchy. With the appointment of Prince Schwarzenberg as Minister President and Foreign Minister (21 November 1848), the defender of a centralist *Großösterreich* took the helm. The unification of Germany as a nation-state favoured by the Frankfurt Paulskirche – with or without Austria – was now shown to be unworkable. Schwarzenberg demonstrated his attitude to the Frankfurt National Assembly on 9 November 1848; the date of Blum's execution, which he had been in a position to prevent.[15] The impotence of parliament could not have been revealed more starkly than in the open and conscious disregard of one of its laws: the imperial immunity law, which was designed to protect the elected representatives of the people.

The Berlin Counter-Revolution in November

While the struggle for power in Vienna took place in open military confrontation, in Berlin it was primarily a constitutional battle in the Berlin National Assembly, under the influence of extraparliamentary forces. More emphatically than in Frankfurt, attempts were made in Berlin to assert the Assembly's supreme authority over the army, following a violent clash between garrison troops and the civil guard in the small Silesian town of Schweidnitz on 31 July 1848. Having broken up a demonstration, and without being ordered to do so, soldiers fired into the crowd, which included members of the civil guard. Fourteen were killed.

Table 16 Survey of the October revolutionaries identified and/or treated at the General Hospital in Vienna

	Dead	Wounded
Bürger, craftsmen, commercial traders, manufacturers	105	45
Independent occupations		25
Journeymen	139	339
Apprentices	17	22
Shop assistants	3	10
Actors, singers, musicians, draughtsmen, artists, lithographers	11	24
Factory managers and foremen	5	
Servants	38	39
Day labourers	31	106
Peasants and farm labourers	1	3
Public civil servants	5	5
Private officials	3	7
Doctors of law and medicine	4	2
Students	13	23
Elite Corps		1
Polish Legion		3
Swiss Corps		1
Mobil Frank Corps	2	18
Graz Legionaries		2
Steier Volunteers		3
Linz Guards		2
Marksmen	1	4
Municipal guards and revenue investigators	1	7
Privates	2	8
Surgeon's assistants	6	
Hungarian National Guard	1	
Soldiers	3	27
Women	20	22
Total	**411**	**748**

Source: W. Häusler, Von der, *Massenarmut zur Arbeiterbewegung, Demokratie und soziale Frage in der Wiener Revolution von 1848* (Munich, 1979), pp. 395f.

The Prussian public regarded such actions as symptomatic of the attitude of the army and as a harbinger of the counter-revolution. The National Assembly took up the conflict as a matter of principle, and on 9 August attempted to decide the issue in a bitterly controversial resolution on a motion proposed by the senior school teacher Dr Julius Stein. A large majority voted in favour of demanding a decree from the War Minister, 'that the officers distance themselves from all reactionary efforts, and not only avoid conflict of any kind with civilians, but also demonstrate, by *rapprochement* with the *Bürger* and uniting with them, that they wish to co-operate respectably and devotedly in the achievement of a constitutional legal situation'.[16]

The resolution touched the very heart of the power problem in 1848: the military's support for and loyalty to the new state order, and the right of parliament to issue the army with orders. (Even in the constitutional system the army was outside parliament's sphere of authority.) The motion was given a sharper edge by a further demand that the War Minister should 'make it a matter of honour' that those officers whose political convictions did not allow them to do so 'should resign from the army'. This passage, narrowly accepted by 180 votes to 179, led deputies from the right and centre-right to protest against the 'beginning of a political inquisition'.

In Berlin a parliamentary majority attempted to use legislation to integrate the modern state's instruments of militarily enforced power into the process of democratization. These events were of exemplary significance, for they demonstrated the limits of the evolutionary path of legalism. In the Prussia of 1848 this could not be achieved without an armed struggle. The *großbürgerlich* von Auerswald–Hansemann ministry failed on this very point. It refused to carry out the anti-reaction decree which the National Assembly had once again adopted on 7 September by a clear majority (219 votes to 143). The ministry resigned the following day. Even though, according to the 'agreement principle', the National Assembly was not entitled to do this kind of thing, in doing so it proved the power of the parliamentary system when put into practice. On the other hand, these measures also exposed the fundamental weakness of the March ministries in their delicate position between the princes' waning readiness to make compromises and the parliaments' increasing demands.

Every new change in ministry brought Prussia a step closer to counter-revolution, whose forces used the time to reassert themselves. Stein's motion and the course adopted by the National Assembly had brought forth pure indignation in the court – on the part of members of the 'camarilla' – in aristocratic and officers' circles, and above all on the part of the King. The collapse of the von Auerswald–Hansemann ministry on 8 September also decided the fate of the National Assembly. Under pressure from the military faction, but also as a result of his own convictions, three days later, on 11 September, Frederick William IV formulated the steps he intended to take in the imminent coup:[17]

- the revocation of the anti-reaction decree on the part of the National Assembly;
- the transfer of the National Assembly to the small town of Brandenburg;
- the dissolution of the National Assembly in the event of public protest and the suppression of indignation in Berlin with 'unrelenting severity';
- consideration of the imposition of a constitution.

The King also put into place the necessary military measure in the programme: on 13 September he appointed General von Wrangel commander-in-chief 'in the Brandenburg Marches'; this was nothing short of the preparation of a military coup focused on Berlin and its environs. The ensuing ministry of civil servants under General von Pfuel (21 September to 28 October 1848) was little more than a shadow cabinet, which enjoyed even less support in court circles since it attempted to enforce the anti-reaction decree.

As in Vienna, the Prussian metropolis provided the arena in which the revolution was decided. Here, too, the counter-revolution was facilitated by the deep rifts in the middle-class opposition, which had emerged as a result of its confrontation with the 'proletariat' of the capital. The class conflict was expressed in the battle for the civil guard. The storming of the Berlin armoury on 14 June already had this social dimension; when the civil guard was formed it was proposed that workers be excluded from the 'general arming of the populace' because they lacked the means of the 'independent' *Bürger* to arm themselves. Supported by the students, the workers then decided to help themselves. The rebellion collapsed following the combined intervention of the army and the civil guard.

The issue split the liberal and democratic middle classes in the Prussian National Assembly when, against the will of the left, the factions of the right and centre pushed through the civil guard law on 13 October 1848 (by 233 votes to 116). The civil guard was dominated by the craftsman middle classes. It competed with countless 'mobile associations' of students, artists, workers and journeymen. The new law eliminated these independently organized defence associations.

On 16 October Berlin canal workers stormed machinery in typical pre-industrial fashion. Tensions were heightened to the point of armed barricade battles in which the civil guard emerged as the protector of law and order. The conflict was fuelled during these weeks by further extra-parliamentary action, including the meetings of the revolutionary counter-parliament, the second Democratic Congress and the incoming news of the Vienna October revolution. Agitation spread to the Berlin National Assembly, culminating on 31 October in an unsuccessful motion calling on the State Ministry to undertake direct action in support of the Vienna revolutionaries.

Further heralds of the coup came on 1 November, when the reaction cabinet under Minister President Graf Brandenburg was appointed. Shortly afterwards, the King adjourned the National Assembly until 27 November and transferred it to Brandenburg (Royal Communication of 8 November).[18] The Assembly declared his actions to be unlawful and continued with its debates. Yet it lacked all instruments of power. The mobile associations had given up, and amongst the members of the civil guard and the middle classes in general, the desire for peace, security and order had increased. The civil guard simply refused to comply with the government order to take action against the National Assembly. This passive resistance provided the formal legal grounds for the advance of von Wrangel's troops (10 November). The automatic mechanisms of reaction followed, though in a bloodless fashion, in contrast to Vienna: a state of siege and martial law were declared (12 and 14 November), the civil guard was dissolved, all political associations were banned and restrictions were placed on the freedom of assembly and the press.

The March movement was by now so paralysed that initially no one responded at all to the 227 National Assembly deputies who called for taxes to be withheld 'while the National Assembly is not able to continue its debates in Berlin unhindered'. The resolution smacked of revolution and placed the burden of risk on individual tax payers, the majority of whom belonged to the propertied classes, who at this stage wanted nothing more than peace and the re-establishment of law and order. Nothing pacified the Berliners more than the fact that von

Wrangel allowed the Christmas market to go ahead, despite the state of siege; displays in cake shops and public halls, all part of the everyday life of the city, were also permitted.

The response to the resolution on the withholding of taxes was similarly split. The 'Constitutionalist Association' in Stettin, the 'Patriotic Association' in Herzberg and the district of Strohsdorf in Pomerania welcomed the policies of the Brandenburg ministry; parts of Silesia on the other hand, Erfurt, the Rhine province and Westphalia saw resistance on the part of the *Landwehr*, proclamations and civil guard campaigns in support of the tax boycott. The dependability of the Prussian officers, the garrison and rank troops, however, remained unchanged.

The National Assembly's *bürgerlich* attempt to assert control over the standing army failed because of the army's deeper loyalty to the monarch, which had been nurtured over generations. The constitutional movement, moreover, undermined the rights of the army in the state. The criticism of the standing armies, the demand for a 'general arming of the populace', the preferential treatment of the civil guard and *Landwehr*, the abolition of aristocratic titles, orders and distinctions, the army's oath of loyalty to the constitution and the conflicts arising from the 'double oath of loyalty' to both monarch and constitution,[19] all had a profound effect on a class with rights and interests, acquired long before, and with its own code of honour which the March movement was unable to break.

The King was now determined to make unrestrained use of his power. '*Now I am sincere again*', he declared to the Bavarian Ambassador, Graf Lerchenfeld, in mid-November.[20] The National Assembly, which had met again on 27 November in Brandenburg on the Havel, was allowed only to stage a farce lasting a few days before the King dissolved it on 5 December and imposed a constitution.

Public indignation at this infringement of the law was tempered by surprise at the progressive and liberal nature of the constitution. In the spirit of the hard-fought 'Charte Waldeck', it promised universal and equal suffrage. On closer inspection, however, around 40 changes had been made and the opportunities for a royal right to enact emergency decrees had been extended. For this reason the spirit of the document has rightly been described as 'crypto-absolutist' and the entire process as a 'skilful move on the part of the ministry',[21] aimed at appeasing those sections of the middle classes which were inclined towards 'political expediency'. It was the evolutionary path to reaction. But it was not so much the constitution itself, as the state of siege, martial law and the imposition of the constitution which were the signals for the true turn in events.

Power rested in the troops, and Frederick William IV's statements from these weeks point to the fact that he was no longer prepared to yield a single inch. This is why all the Provisional Central Power's attempts at diplomatic intervention were unsuccessful. In November it sent imperial commissioners (Simson and Hergenhahn) to Berlin to act as mediators; Parliamentary President von Gagern followed soon afterwards. More than anything else it was the Prussian policy of issuing *faits accomplis* which snubbed the Frankfurt efforts. Frankfurt's impotence was revealed whenever it tried to work not *with* the individual state powers but *against* them. In a call to the people on 21 November on the subject of the tax boycott, the *Reichsverweser* declared:

> I will not tolerate that resolution which endangers the welfare of all Germany by a cessation in the levying of tax in Prussia. But I will enforce the guarantee of the rights and freedoms of the Prussian people. As in all German states, the Prussian people must retain them in unatrophied form.[22]

Displays of this kind provoked the scorn of the oppositional press and fired the imagination of the caricaturists. The victory of the army in Berlin virtually ended the European turn in the revolution. A few pockets of resistance remained in Venetia, Rome and Hungary. At any rate, the Frankfurt constitutional efforts still contained a dynamic which it had not been possible to evaluate in December 1848, which possibly eluded the Provisional Central Power and the March ministers.

11   The Dynamics of the Revolution

The year of the revolution was characterized above all by 'move-ments'. 'Forces' were unleashed, 'tensions' released, 'unrest' broke out, 'mobility' and 'progress' encountered 'inertia', dams burst their banks, reservoirs 'emptied' – we are all familiar with these graphic descriptions from accounts of the revolution. To some extent they are probably unavoidable, since language can never be entirely stripped of its metaphors. We cannot complain about that. But it is worth examining the dynamics of the revolution themselves in more detail. In doing so, many traditional viewpoints are put to the test, as is the image of the revolution as a 'part of a longer-term historical development'.[1] Seen in this light, 1848 appears as a kind of intermedi-ate stage on a long-term developmental trend which might be called 'national unity', 'the creation of the parliamentary system' or 'the formation of classes'. That these trends existed can be proved beyond doubt, but if we focus on them and them alone, we overlook phenomena which do not conform to them, which were 'not in keep-ing with the times' and which then run the risk of slipping through the net of interpretation.

Examined more closely, the dynamics of the revolution actually reveal the '*dissimilarity* of its movements', the differences 'in terms of region, time, motive and intention, in terms of form and symbol'.[2] Events may often have occurred simultaneously, but they took place in isolation from each other. Actions which took place concurrently were sparked by conflicting motives. Urban popular unrest, driven by craftsmen, took place alongside traditional agrarian revolts, where entire village communities supported the peasant campaigns, and these in turn occurred alongside 'modern', highly organized mass movements, with carefully targeted petitions, and association

171

and assembly activity. The simultaneous events of March 1848, for example, were not bound together by any cohesive force.

Similarly, there was a wide gulf between the objectives of different individual campaigns, despite the universal March demands. The actions of peasants and craftsmen, which seemed revolutionary, were aimed at re-establishing the 'old law'. Workers demanded the formal organization of the relationship between 'capital and work'. The middle classes wanted political power on a parliamentary basis. Recent protest research in particular has highlighted the contradictions inherent in the dynamics of the revolution, and the internal distinctions between individual social groups. The traditional distinctions between the 'people', the liberal 'middle classes' and the forces of 'reaction' have proved to be not subtle enough. Internal social tensions and paralyses and resistance on the part of the 'silent majority' have come into our field of vision. No 'class' was homogeneous in terms of the expression of its interests. Each developed internal counterforces which were detrimental to the 'movement'. The fact that it awoke defensive fears may be attributed to 'modernization'.

The dynamics were not only revealed in the splits in the revolution, but also in its escalation. Wherever people met in 1848–9 we can expect to find mobility and action, not just on a parliamentary level or in associations, but also, and often more fundamentally, at rallies, popular festivals, on streets and in inns. The railway revolutionized the experience of measured time and distance. Everything acquired a political dimension. If one could not take part in elections, read or speak, it was necessary to harness and channel the political desire for action: this gave rise to the petition *movements* typical of the time. This particular dynamic was new. It was difficult to assess. It was easily incited. It was a fundamental element of the 'revolution' which spread to 'everyday life' in its many different features, and is as much an integral part of the image of the revolution as the events in associations, factions and cabinets.

Rallies, Festivals and 'Rough Music'

An astonishing phenomenon, witnessed again and again in the early days of the revolution, was the transformation of news into a political gathering. On 22 February the revolution broke out in Paris. On the evening of Saturday 26 February the first messengers arrived bearing the still vague tidings which acted, in von Struve's words, like 'an electric spark'. Hecker was sitting in the 'Pariser Hof' in Karlsruhe with his political friends when he heard the news. The courier had first approached an actor from the theatre, and it was this actor who brought the news to the people in the inn. Afterwards Hecker recalled that 'people leapt from their seats, embraced each other, raised their glasses in jubilation, shouting, "Let us quickly work for Germany's liberation, let us act now!" '[3]

By the following day, 27 February, Hecker and von Struve were already leading the speeches at the rally in Mannheim where the March demands were formulated and which acted as a signal for the whole of Germany. Zimmermann gave a contemporary evaluation of Baden's 'significant position' as the political seismograph of the time: 'Alongside Paris, attention turned above all to Karlsruhe, Mannheim and Heidelberg.'[4] The subsequent course of events has already been described. We are specifically interested here in the dynamics of these events. We should not forget that the political resolutions which emerged from the now frequent rallies were first prepared by a small circle of people – perhaps even at an inn – then read to a massive crowd, which could barely understand them. Without further debate, which would hardly have been possible anyway, they were adopted.[5]

The railways and the inn played a key role in the exchange of ideas and mobility.

Of all the phenomena of the modern era, it is the railway which enables us to perceive how fast our lives are. I use the word in the positive sense, that in the shortest possible time a host of important new phenomena emerges, through which we experience the most rapid expansion of our intellectual[!] knowledge.[6]

The expansion of intellectual knowledge by means of the railway – an incredible notion today – was a reality of life at those moments in which the political calendar was marked in hours rather than years. In Wiesbaden, Karlsruhe, Frankfurt, Cologne and Berlin, the railway was a popular method of transport, and the only one which could enable large crowds to gather in the shortest possible time. During the September uprising, the Central Power imposed bans on and strictly monitored the management of the railway lines into Frankfurt, specifically in order to prevent demonstrations of that kind.

On 26 February an extra issue of the *Hanauer Zeitung* announced the abdication of Louis Philippe.[7] Tension was not released until the evening of Sunday 27, however, when travellers arrived at 6 pm bearing news of the 'revolution in Paris'. The landlord of the 'Große Krone' heard the news. He had been banned by the police from holding meetings in his rooms, and had resorted to issuing invitations to 'evening entertainments' instead. All the freedom songs which had previously been banned, the Marseillaise, the Poland and the Hambach songs, were now sung without restraint. Young people and gymnasts took to the streets with flags made from handkerchiefs. The following day a mass meeting was held quite openly at the 'Weißer Schwan' inn, organized by members of the Gymnasts' Association, but with participants from all classes. The police presence went unheeded. On Tuesday 29 the tobacco manufacturer, August Rühl, the future Hanau deputy in the Paulskirche, gave an impressive speech in the 'Große Krone' and submitted a petition to the Elector which he had drafted himself. The Hanau March demands began to take shape.

It is not the anecdotal, but the typical nature of these events that is significant, for the news spread quickly and there were inns everywhere, just as everywhere there were speakers who emerged in these hours, who came to the attention of the public and who helped it to formulate its political demands. Everywhere March demands made their way to the ruler.

Rumours developed a particularly unpredictable dynamic, and the air was thick with them. In the general excitement of the Hanau meeting referred to above, a rumour began to circulate that a shoemaker who had been imprisoned for insulting the ruler some weeks before, was to be broken out of jail that evening. The police got wind of the rumour and released him as quickly as possible. The appearance of the freed man on the streets was greeted with jubilation. The day-to-day events of the revolution are full of rumours of this kind, which have hardly been researched at all. One of the more notorious is the great '*Franzosenlärm*' in Baden. A terrifying rumour spread that thousands of Frenchmen, German workers and vagabonds were moving through the countryside, murdering and setting fire to property as they went. They had already reached . . . (the next but one town to the west was then named). Initial panic gave way to the population arming itself, setting off to halt the rabble, followed by disappointment and then carousing in inns when they realized their fears were unfounded.[8] It is hardly possible to overestimate the significance of rumours such as this in these delicate situations, where the army and civilians stood opposed to each other.

The physical proximity and the feeling of being part of a group at these popular rallies engendered a particular form of campaign on the part of the so-called 'proletarian public'. Rough music, as it was called in England, '*charivari*' in France and '*scampanate*' in Italy, was a traditional form of punishment campaign; 'a kind of non-*bürgerlich* "counter public" ' of the underdogs.[9] In the absence of other means of articulating dissatisfaction, it represented an old-fashioned vent for pent-up aggression. Gathering in front of the houses of unpopular people, a crowd would begin shouting, whistling, making noises, smashing windows and hurling insults and obscenities. These 'rough musicians' sought out their victims very carefully. They were usually deputies, such as Johannes Fallati in Tübingen, who had been the only Württemberg deputy to vote for the acceptance of the Truce of Malmö in the Frankfurt Parliament. Whether parliamentary debates, the election of the *Reichsverweser*, the September crisis or the Berlin coup, the expression of displeasure, or more rarely sympathy, from the streets remained a lively form of action which was found in almost every district.[10] An analysis of protest actions reveals the numbers of 'rough music' campaigns so far discovered (see Table 17).

Table 17 Structure of political actions, 1848–9

Type	March–April 1848 Cases		May 1848–June 1849 Cases	
	(Number)	*(%)*	*(Number)*	*(%)*
'Rough music'/punishment campaigns	75	50.0	70	20.8
Mass rallies, demonstrations, uprisings	38	25.3	95	28.4
Clashes with the forces of law and order	27	18.0	146	43.6
Counter-revolutionary activity on the part of the lower orders	10	6.7	24	7.2
Total	**150**	**100.0**	**335**	**100.0**

Source: M. Gailus, 'Soziale Protestbewegungen in Deutschland, 1847–1849', in H. Volkmann and J. Bergmann (eds), *Sozialer Protest: Studien zu traditioneller Resistenz und kollektiver Gewalt in Deutschland vom Vormärz bis zur Reichsgründung* (Opladen, 1984), p. 99.

Amongst the various reactions to the outbreak of the revolution, agitation and the desire to celebrate frequently went hand in hand, unless violent barricade battles were followed by accusatory funeral processions. In all cases they turned into mass events. The population experienced the events of the March revolution as a decisive political turning point. The festival atmosphere, particularly in the 'Third Germany', was frequently justified, in that the March demands could be wrung out of the rulers without bloodshed. Rallies were followed by popular festivals such as the one celebrated on 8 March in Mainz after the ruler had solemnly agreed to fulfil the March demands two days before. Bells were rung, singing and music was heard from the tower of Mainz Cathedral, the town was lit up, 30, 000 people took part in an enormous torchlit procession, and the song '*Heil dir Moguntia*' was sung before Gutenberg's statue. Finally, a public oath was sworn 'to live and die for freedom'. Such scenes were typical of the course of the revolution following its apparent victory over the old system.[11]

This picture was repeated at all major events. The editor Ludwig Bamberger reported in the *Mainzer Zeitung* on 30 March, the day before the meeting of the Pre-Parliament in Frankfurt:

> Good heavens! – Shouting! Firing! Frankfurt is awash with black, red and gold. For the moment the city has an air of euphoria about it! They are overloading themselves with such feelings of hope and triumph that the victory might become a side issue. It looks as if an innocent Whitsun festival is being held here. The houses are covered in foliage, carpets and flags, the streets are filled with people dressed up to the nines. Elegance in plenty, but terribly few members of 'the people'. Germans of all kinds and from all areas come together in great numbers; those who were once hounded out and who will soon be hounded out again.[12]

The readiness to believe the spoken word of the ruler and to celebrate a victory which only more perceptive sceptics like Bamberger could see rested on extremely questionable foundations, was a fundamental feature of people of all political persuasions. The guilelessness, the well-meaningness and hope documented at festivals was a psychological factor which influenced even the deputies in their political decisions, and which for a long time caused them to trust in the constancy of things. And this expectation was reinforced by the rulers, including on many occasions the Prussian King Frederick William IV: on 14 August 1848 at the Cologne Cathedral festival marking the 600th anniversary of the laying of the cathedral's foundation stone, he had himself magnificently celebrated together with the *Reichsverweser* as guarantors of a united Germany. This too was an integral part of the revolutionary dynamics of the time; a period so rich in intentional and unintentional 'misunderstandings'.

Mobilization by Means of Petitions

The revolution politicized the population at a fundamental level. As early as 23 March 1848, the editor of the *Breslauer Zeitung* had expressed his surprise:

> Just eight days ago the majority of our population behaved as if it was quite indifferent to political and social questions; now everyone is interested in the issues of the day, and it is quite normal to hear men from the lowest classes, and even women, developing clear and healthy opinions on political and social issues, as if they had been studying these subjects for years.[13]

This eagerness needed a channel. To some extent it was provided by the elections, associations and the political press, but to an extraordinarily high degree it found an outlet in petition movements which translated mass action into political activity and provided a channel for interests, hope and anger. The storm of petitions[14] began already in the spring. It was directed first at the individual chambers and the governments, then at the Pre-Parliament, the Committee of Fifty and finally at the Frankfurt National Assembly.

These petitions were taken seriously as expressions of the will of the people. The Paulskirche Economics Committee, for example, compiled a comprehensive report for the plenary debate on the petitions which had been submitted by peasants demanding the elimination of feudal obligations. Nowhere else were the misfortunes and wishes of the peasants catalogued in such a detailed manner and broken down into individual areas.[15]

Approximately 17,000 petitions were submitted to the Paulskirche; 13,451 were received by the Berlin National Assembly. Of those received in Frankfurt, approximately 30 per cent related to economic and social problems, with an emphasis on trade policy (protective tariffs or free trade), 28 per cent referred to the relationship between state and church, 20 per cent to the restructuring of Germany, and around 18 per cent to the Basic Rights.

Conflicting information exists on the exact number of petitions received.[16] This is due to the fact that all petitions were not the same. There were 'group petitions', such as those submitted by the butchers' and tailors' central committees, each containing 200 lists of signatures. Others combined lists of signatures from various different towns. One of these was signed by approximately 10,000[!] master craftsmen from the Bavarian district of Swabia and Neuburg.[17] The total 1200 craftsmen's petitions underline the highly organized development of informed opinion, which had been refined above all at congresses and in national organizations. In addition to individual petitions, there were those from entire corporations, towns or areas. If the group lists are divided into individual groups, the total number increases.

The petitioners liked to ensure the support of the local council. In Tölz in Bavaria, all 103 master craftsmen appeared before the town concil in order to impress upon it the detrimental effects of freedom of trade. To increase their impact, several petitions were sometimes submitted simultaneously and on a mass basis to the constituency's deputy.

Petitions were compiled following calls in newspapers or General Assembly resolutions. Sometimes individual congress deputies gathered personal signatures. Trade associations tried to persuade the guilds in smaller towns to adopt their way of thinking. Thus, the Heidelberg Trade Association worked on its counterpart in Tauberbischofsheim in Baden by claiming that 'a hostile enemy party... craves unrestricted freedom of trade'.[18] The petition movement exercised a 'knock-on effect on the undecided, the less politically committed' (Simon), and mobilized craftsmen in the smallest villages. Working through the petitions submitted to Frankfurt,[19] the crisis areas of the craft trades figure prominently: the Prussian province of Saxony, the Rhine-Main region, Baden, Württemberg and Bavaria, all of which were regions in which the trades were overmanned. These regions would lie in the catchment area of the later campaign for the Imperial Constitution.

The commercial petition movement was organized to a similar degree; approximately 90 per cent were submitted as group petitions, that is to say, they were carefully planned and prepared and rarely spontaneous.[20] The industrial middle class, independent traders, commercial workers, farmers and merchants had formed coordinating authorities, as might be expected in a society developing pluralistic economic associations. Although these groups differed in terms of their interests and their social composition, they acted against the backdrop of a common national basis.

The political aims of the various petition movements varied too. The excellent organizational forces of the 'Pius associations' were put to good use by the Church hierarchy. They collected a total of 1142 petitions with 273,000 signatures.[21] The methods they used underline the way in which the storm of petitions was able to create as well as channel mobility. The impetus for a petition usually emanated from the 'Pius Association' in Mainz. It was taken up by the bishop's palace and spread to the lower priesthood. The priests then set about persuading their parishes and sometimes even the peasants in the fields, of the necessity of the Church's continuing influence on schools, on children and teachers. Or, like one priest in Riegel in Baden, they allowed the entire parish to vote during the church service. After a unanimous vote in its favour, this priest set out the petition for people to sign. Then, in the interest of neatness, he copied it out again himself. When one of the 77 parishioners voted against religious schools, the priest described him to the dean as a 'drunkard and a braggart'.[22]

Here too we encounter 'well thought-out, highly organized efforts' (Bergsträßer), whose methods reveal the considerable extent to which psychological group pressure was exercised. Although the Protestant Church did not organize a comparable petition movement, most of the priests preached political sermons from the pulpit which were close to the government line, and which sometimes verged on the royalist.[23]

In both denominations groups split from the main church and soon found widespread support: they included the Protestant-rationalist 'Lichtfreunde' and to a greater degree the German Catholic movement, which had been organized in 'councils' since 1845, and which had already gathered some 60,000 supporters in 250 parishes by 1847. Petitions and pluralism went hand in hand in matters of faith, too.

Movements and Resistance within Social Groups

The Peasants

The peasants' horizons were limited by the village life they experienced. It was a religious life, without political perspective, but rich in experience of the lord of the manor's power. Peasant actions were aimed at the objects of their displeasure: offices, documents and the castles of the mediatized princes, but not at the state ruler himself. Cases were reported of them storming aristocratic bursaries whilst simultaneously singing, 'Long live our Grand Duke!' The latter was regarded as an honoured patron, the lord of the manor as a villain.

They translated the middle-class concepts of 'press freedom', 'equality' and 'republic' into their own concrete sphere of experience. This led to a curious 'confusion of terminology' (R. Wirtz), which ceases to be so strange after all when it is understood as a result of the clash of middle class life with 'plebeian culture' (E.P. Thompson).

For them 'press freedom' became freedom from pressure or oppression, or even more directly: 'It is the freedom to put pressure on all those who have always done the same to us.'[24] This in turn justified the withholding of all services and levies to the lord of the manor and the landowner in the name of 'press freedom'. In some areas 'freedom' came to mean the expulsion of officials; 'equality' and 'republic' could be interpreted as taking from those who seemed to have more than them, and frequently resulted in the storming of Jewish homes.

A 'confusion of terminology' of this kind was seen in the Odenwald, in Prussia and in Silesia. It explains the extent to which these terms, which had suddenly begun to circulate in the villages at the beginning of the revolution, encouraged the peasants to take action. It even led, as the example of Sinsheim shows, to unity of action between peasants and middle-class democrats. The Sinsheim pharmacist had been holding daily meetings, reading aloud from the democratic *Mannheimer Abendzeitung*, and speaking of liberty, equality, the republic and America. Thus educated, on 24 April 1848, the peasants set off for Heidelberg, armed with rifles, scythes and flails 'to come to Hecker's aid' and join the Badenese April revolution. Women carried sacks with them to relieve the town inhabitants of their surplus property in the name of the 'equality' of all citizens in the state. The Heidelberg Civil Guard explained the 'misunderstanding' to the peasants, who had raised three cheers for the republic on the market square, and sent them packing. Disappointed, they returned to the village, with the suspicion that they had been betrayed. The Grand Duke's authorities showed no understanding whatsoever for the peasants' interpretation. They insisted on regarding the campaign as a 'republican' revolt, and were correspondingly draconian in their punishment of it.

'Rude awakenings' of this kind, coupled with the later lifting and dissolution of peasant services, are at the root of the fact that the

German peasants, like their counterparts in Austria after Kudlich's success, could no longer be persuaded to take part in great revolts. A protest analysis may corroborate this important aspect of the dynamics of the revolution: whereas, in the spring of 1848, peasants participated with great enthusiasm, later they were lost as a significant group. With isolated exceptions, such as the 'rustic associations' of Silesia, alliances between the middle classes and the peasantry were often fleeting phenomena. The latest research has uncovered lively cooperation between democrats and peasant associations in the Rhine-Main region. But as a rule the political aims of the middle-class legal world were irrelevant to the peasants (see Table 18).

In addition to these revolutionary, mainly traditional actions, peasants also took part in actions which proclaimed their loyalty to the King and which were openly counter-revolutionary. In a letter of 4 May 1848 we read, 'We peasants from West Prussia hereby declare to you Berliners that if you do not soon re-establish discipline and order in your cursed dump, and restore the rights of our beloved King, we peasants will come to his aid and you blackguards will lose the power of hearing and sight.'[25] We do not know who incited the peasants to write this. We do know that such sentiments most certainly existed.

Table 18   Categorization of protest in Germany, 1848–9

Type	March–April 1848 Cases		May 1848–June 1849 Cases	
	(Number)	(%)	(Number)	(%)
Peasant actions	85	17.4	11	2.3
Agrarian underclasses	88	18.0	24	5.1
Urban underclasses	94	19.2	34	7.2
Craftsmen	6	1.2	8	1.7
Labour conflicts	49	10.0	47	9.9
Political action	150	30.7	335	70.6
Miscellaneous	17	3.5	15	3.2
Total	**489**	**100.0**	**474**	**100.0**

Source: M. Gailus, 'Soziale Protestbewegungen in Deutschland, 1847–1849', in H. Volkmann and J. Bergmann (eds), *Sozialer Protest: Studien zu traditioneller Resistenz und kollektiver Gewalt in Deutschland vom Vormärz bis zur Reichsgründung* (Opladen, 1984), p. 98.

Conflict sometimes emerged between small farmers and landless peasants on the one hand, and medium and large farmers on the other. The wealthy behaved actively or passively, depending on whether their interests were affected. In the Paderborn region they tolerated 'extremes of behaviour' directed against forest officials which took place in woods which belonged to the aristocracy or the state. However, they clashed with day labourers and small property owners when similar events took place in communal woods or if the formerly collective wood and grazing rights were involved.[26]

Wherever fallen foliage and stray wood collecting had been a matter for the whole community since time immemorial, the modern understanding of the concept of property gave rise to a typical 'confusion of the term' 'communism'. As a knowledgeable observer in the Duchy of Nassau ascertained:

> On the subject of ancient rights, the peasants have inherited a very communist conception of forest property. They don't need sermons on modern theories of property to come up with the idea that property should be generally distributed. When the popular movement broke out in 1848, and this idea immediately went through the whole of the Nassau peasantry, it was based *far less on revolutionary than conservative inclinations*: they wanted to re-establish a convention which has existed since ancient times with respect to the wood, and, if need be, to extend it to cover a number of other things too.[27]

The existence of conservative revolutionaries was a difficult concept to grasp in 1848, unless, like the observer cited here, one understood the particular peasant experiences in which it was rooted.

The 'communism' of the rural workers and small farmers conflicted with the interests of the wealthy farmers who had profited from the distribution of common lands. In Oldenburg it was expressed at a gathering of rural workers who submitted a petition to the ruler of the state in which they accused the *Landstände* of blackmailing the prince. They offered to protect him and to 'shed our last drop of blood for the ruler and father of our state and to remain loyal to him until death'. In their petitions these rural workers openly expressed their desire 'for the beloved days of old to be re-established wherever possible'.[28]

Workers

A 'return to an old, familiar situation and not its replacement with something new' (Langewiesche) was also the root cause of the numerous machine-stormings carried out by workers in the year of the revolution. As with the peasants, protest was not expressed in terms of an attack on the business itself, but was personalized or objectified and aimed at individual building officials or industrial plant.[29] This led to the most absurd outbreaks of violence, as witnessed in Berlin on 12 October 1848, where canal workers attacked the steam machine on the Köpenicker Feld, which was needed to pump water from the trenches before their work could begin. Believing that it would ultimately put them out of a job, the workers destroyed it, whereupon a hundred of them were sacked. The conflict, which again had arisen from 'a confusion of terminology', assumed class-war dimensions in turbulent Berlin, and culminated in the bloody workers' uprising of 16 October 1848.[30]

Workers also took action against the politically active associations, perceiving 'the revolution' or the 'agitation of the democrats' to be responsible for their miserable material situation. Armed with cudgels, they attacked a meeting of the 'Democratic Club' in Berlin. Similar incidents occurred in Danzig and Butow in Eastern Pomerania. Workers and seamen in Memel demanded that the local authority order the arrest of the chairmen of the 'Constitutionalist Association', 'because they have caused rebellions in the state and preach disloyalty to the King'.[31]

These by no means isolated incidents force us to reassess the notion that a progressive learning process gradually shaped solidarity and class consciousness amongst the workers in the revolution. It may have been expressed as such in the efforts of the workers' societies and the General German Workers' Fraternity, but the revolution also provoked defensive attitudes amongst the workers. 'A young worker' gave a commentary in the *Zeitung des Arbeiter-Vereines zu Köln* on the widespread storming of machines, describing the almost stereotypical perspectives of retrograde, spontaneous violence and enlightened, politically organized action:

> They smash up machines, set factories alight and destroy production materials and instruments. But this doesn't help them much; after all, machines and factories can be rebuilt, but they themselves will simply be oppressed even more severely. Experience then makes them wiser; everywhere they found permanent societies and, following the example of their despots, they attempt to unite. This gives them greater strength and they have even enforced the recognition of individual workers' interests in the legal reforms.[32]

The Middle Classes

It was above all members of the commercial middle class who soon became worried about the economic losses they were suffering as a result of the revolution; and when business falters, enthusiasm quickly begins to evaporate. Book sellers, provoked by the competition of the daily newspapers, raised their voices at an early stage. As early as the beginning of April, they complained, as we saw above, that the political events of the day had 'had a very disturbing and inhibiting effect on all branches of trade and industry, above all on the German book trade'. They were particularly concerned about the flood of 'writings and verses which indulge in immoderately impudent and often vulgar phrases'. Before it had even been in existence for a full month, they were already attacking 'abuses of the freedom of the press'.[33] By July, openly counter-revolutionary sentiments could already be read in the press:

> *We don't want*
> *This revolution,*
> *Where shameless crows*
> *Peck at the eagle's throne.*
> *Our dear father of the state*
> *Is the refuge of the Fatherland.*
> *May law and order see off*
> *The swarm of people's advisers.*[34]

Accompanying currents of the revolution like this were by no means restricted to the efforts of the Berlin '*Kreuzzeitung*' Party, but had their roots in the pre-revolutionary royalism of the provinces. They heralded a change in mood which was growing ever stronger, and which was registered in detail by the Prussian King, who was acutely sensitive to the public mood. For him counter-action was simply a matter of waiting for the right time. The effect of a constitution imposed at too early a stage had been shown in the Austrian May revolution, following the enactment of the Pillersdorf Constitution. This and other indices of the counter-revolution were carefully assessed by Frederick William IV. They had a direct influence on him when he penned his detailed programme for the coup of 11 September. A petition of 8 September had found its way into the King's cabinet files, which made reference to the old Prussian royalist slogan 'with God for King and Fatherland' and urged him to 'coax the spark from the steel', to build on old Prussian loyalty and 'to observe the good of the state in this way'.[35]

The same file contained a newspaper article from 10 September with an address from the 'Constitutionalist [!] Association' in Elberfeld; with reference to the Berlin National Assembly, the signatories demanded that 'the threatening power of absolute parliamentary rule be removed and the people's freedoms be protected from all kinds of despotism'. They demanded the immediate dissolution of the Assembly and new elections.[36]

Just as Dahlmann was prepared to justify the imposition of the Prussian constitution of 5 December 1848 as the *'Recht der rettenden Tat'* (right to perform an act of rescue), in an address of thanks to Prince Windischgrätz, the committee of the Vienna book-sellers' association voiced its support for the coup in the Austrian capital.[37]

These internal divisions within the middle classes, some of whom were in favour of armed action against the population, was revealed at grass-roots level in the internal conflicts in the civil guards. Frequent clashes were seen between the magistrates of the towns and the Free Corps, who were in favour of a 'democratic' arming of the populace. This situation often led to divisions within civil guards into a pro-'order' and a pro-'movement' wing, as was seen now and again in Vienna or Dresden. Sometimes a self-help corps of conservative *Bürger* was formed, notoriously in Hamburg in the form of the *'Knüppelgarde'* (cudgel guard) – that is if the civil guard did not come down on the side of the police and the army from the start, as it did in Hanover, Berlin, Augsburg, Munich and Elberfeld.

The campaign for the Imperial Constitution constituted a test in which some civil guards openly supported the revolutionaries, as in Breslau, Heilbronn, Düsseldorf, Karlsruhe, Hanau, Mainz and Solingen. But the situation varied considerably, and little research has been carried out on the subject as yet. A key factor in the structure and political stance of the civil guards was the conditions of acceptance into their ranks. The exclusion of workers or journeymen who were defined as 'dependent', as occurred in Berlin, for example, gave rise to a dramatic conflict which transcended class barriers. For although exclusions of this kind conflicted with the March demand audible up and down the land for a 'general arming of the populace', there was no clear view as to how this might be realized in reality. Issues of this kind raised questions on the 'constitution of the *Bürgertum* as a class'. It was this very image of the civil guards – varied and inherently contradictory – which mirrored the split in 'the middle class' itself, which had become evident in parliaments and political associations. At all levels there were people who were in favour of damping down the revolution and who were prepared to employ armed counter-revolutionary force to do so.

Jews

Women and Jews were among the groups most heavily discriminated against in the pre-revolutionary legal system. They took part in the general movement in ways typical of the time: they tried to fight for legal and social equality in rallies, in their own associations and publications. Both groups encountered vehement opposition.

Already during the early days of the March revolution, anti-Semitism had been evident amongst the peasant population. It was based on economic concerns and exacerbated by Christian and nationalist discrimination. Jewish businesses were attacked in approximately eighty towns in Baden, Württemberg, Bavaria, Hesse, Upper Silesia and Posen. These attacks did not lead to organized self-defence or a united Jewish position, however. In Germany the Jews put their trust 'in the *Bürgertum* and the "good people", who, unlike the "riff-raff", who were inclined towards pogroms, offered the hand of friendship to the Jews'.[38]

Events appeared to justify this hope. Jews emerged as active political campaigners and elected deputies for the first time in the parliaments. They were among the March victims in Berlin and Vienna. Moritz Heckscher, Johann Hermann Detmold, Johann Jacoby, Adolf Fischhof, Gabriel Riesser or Eduard (von) Simson assumed positions of leadership in the Vienna, Berlin and Frankfurt parliaments.[39] Marx and Stahl were the most prominent in a long list of political journalists. The Basic Rights resolutions of the Frankfurt Parliament (Article V) granted full legal emancipation and total freedom of religion and conscience. When the revolution failed, some of this emancipation was curtailed, although it was not lost altogether.

Already during the revolution, however, the legal emancipation, the integration into the middle classes of the Jewish people and their identification with the national movement assumed an ambivalent character, for in the process Jewish bonds and the sense of community were weakened, creating a crisis in communities where individual Mosaic orthodoxy tried to resist assimilation.[40] Here, as in other social groups, 'modernization' brought with it profound anxieties of being under threat.

Women

The beginnings of the German women's movement, with its own press, politics and independent associations can be traced back to the year of the revolution. This long overlooked fact has only recently received the recognition it deserves, as the modern women's movement has carefully researched its own history.[41] The organization of women forms part of the general organization of associations during the revolution.

Women often accompanied public consecrations of flags, they sewed flags, encouraged their men to take risks; they collected donations to provide weapons, ammunition and bandages for the fighting revolutionary troops. In Vienna and Berlin some even became involved in the fighting on the barricades and were killed or wounded. Emma Herwegh, Amalie Struve and Mathilde Franziska Anneke accompanied the Volunteer Corps on their campaigns. Recently discovered sources provide insight into the 'Humania' Mainz Women's Association, which had a membership of 1700 and was led by Kathinka Zitz, into the correspondence with political emigrants and into the problems experienced by women's associations in general (G. Hummel-Haasis). The numbers so far unearthed are considerable. As far as we know, however, the emancipation of women was not yet a central theme in 1848.

Louise Otto's women's periodical with its slogan, 'I am recruiting *Bürgerinnen* to the realm of freedom' was founded in April 1849, during the counter-revolutionary period. Her newspaper met the same fate as every other decisively democratic political paper. 'If an account of these days is ever written with historical accuracy, the "women of Rastatt" will assume an honoured place in it.'[42] A sentence like this, published in 1850, could bring its female author close to high treason. House searches, confiscation of the association's funds and bans on all associations put an end to this organized liberation movement. But even in 1848, where women's emancipation was discussed openly, it encountered expressions of open hostility in pamphlets which held themselves to be particularly close to 'the opinion of the people'.

12   The Imperial Constitution and the Election of the Kaiser

The first reading of the Basic Rights took place in the National Assembly between 3 July and 12 October 1848. On 19 October the plenum began to debate the constitutional organization of the *Reich*, concentrating on three major issues: the territory covered by the *Reich*, the distribution of power within the state organization, and the issue of the head of the *Reich*.

None of these subjects could be addressed in isolation from current political developments, and in this phase of the revolution these changed almost weekly. The renewed rise of the 'Austrian and Prussian autocracy' (Faber) between October and December 1848 coincided directly with the parliamentary debates, which thereby became part of current constitutional and power politics. It is nothing short of astounding to see how such a large body was able to keep up with the fast and furious pace of events, not least because actions were taking place simultaneously on several levels: in Parliament itself between the factions; at the Provisional Central Power and the representatives of the states; in the diplomacy between the princes and individual states; and finally in the extra-parliamentary popular movement.

The Question of Unity – the Territory of the Reich

The deputies experienced the effects of power politics most acutely during the debates on the territory which was to be included in the *Reich*. Many of them had arrived at the Paulskirche in May with only vague and emotional ideas as to where the frontiers of the *Reich* should lie. As Arndt's famous song of 1812, '*Des Deutschen Vaterland*'

(Fatherland of the Germans), implored, 'It should be the whole of Germany', 'wherever the German tongue is heard'. The problems associated with demands of this kind had become abundantly clear during the summer in the territorial disputes in Posen, Bohemia, Italy, Limburg and Schleswig.

Now the issue was Austria. During the Vienna October revolution, when the debates began, there was no question that Austria was part of the *Reich*. On 27 October the overwhelming majority, including the Austrian deputies, voted for the so-called *großdeutsch* or greater German solution, whereby the Habsburg monarchy would be constitutionally divided into German areas which belonged to the *Reich*, and non-German parts which would remain outside it. The latter also included the states of Galicia, Hungary, Croatia and Lombardo-Venetia, which had previously been outside the German Confederation. It was envisaged that they would simply be linked to the German–Austrian heartland by means of a personal union. There was no intention of absorbing the Habsburg monarchy as a whole into the German *Reich*.

Yet the Habsburg monarchical state had emerged from the military campaigns in Prague, Custozza, Milan and Vienna more strengthened than might have been expected. Following the victory of the Austrian counter-revolution, the new leader, Schwarzenberg, was in a position to dictate terms to the Paulskirche, which was now forced to adopt the *kleindeutsch* or smaller German solution. The subsequent regrouping of factions left its mark on the constitution.

Schwarzenberg blazed the trail on 27 November 1848 with a declaration made in the small Moravian town of Kremsier, to which the Austrian *Reichstag* had been transferred. The decisive passage read: 'Austria's continued existence as a united state is a German as well as a European necessity'.[1] This frustrated the efforts of the *großdeutsch* party in Frankfurt, and von Schmerling, champion of the *großdeutsch* solution, saw no option but to resign his post as Imperial Minister President on 15 December 1848.

His successor, von Gagern, placed some hope in the idea of a twofold union, in which a restricted confederation of states without Austria would still be linked to the Habsburg monarchy by means of a wider alliance of the states. This settlement would not contradict the Kremsier declaration, nor, in the light of the later alliance between the German *Reich* of 1871 with Austria in the *Zweibund* of 1879, does it seem so unrealistic. Von Schmerling, however, now put all his energies into thwarting the double union plan. His personal intervention with Schwarzenberg was successful; on 28 December the Minister President decisively rejected von Gagern's plan. Austria, Schwarzenberg said, 'remains a German federal power' and demands a say in the 'future formation of the previous confederation of states'.[2] Schwarzenberg was thus committing himself to the idea of a supranational Central European 'empire of 70 million people' (40 million Austrians and 30 million Germans), an untimely notion for the Paulskirche, given its adherence to the idea of a strong nation state. A *Reich* such as this would only have been able to constitute a loose confederation of states as had been represented by the former German Confederation, whose revival seemed now to be foreshadowed.

Finally, on 7 March 1849, Austrian policies decided matters once and for all when the Kremsier *Reichstag* was dissolved and a constitution imposed (dated 4 March). This document established the constitutional unity of the monarchy as a whole. On 9 March Schwarzenberg combined his coup with a further ultimatum: he demanded the incorporation of the Austrian state as a whole into the association of German states;[3] however, he did not allow for a national parliament of any kind, but simply a consultative *Staatenhaus*.

Austrian policies thus intentionally prevented a parliamentary and nation state unification under Prussian hegemony. This should always be considered when we are tempted to form too harsh a judgement of the outcome of the Frankfurt constitutional efforts following Frederick William IV's decision.

Factional Regrouping

The Austrian policy of obstruction had the paradoxical effect of suddenly increasing the weight of the factions on the left and centre-left in deciding votes, as the balance of power began to shift. As the *großdeutsch-kleindeutsch* conflict grew more intense, the relatively stable ideological factional frontiers which had emerged during the debates on the Basic Rights were redrawn, as the '*großdeutsch*' and '*erbkaiserlich*' factions formed opposing camps (see Figure 6).

The *großdeutsch group* was created when a number of deputies led by von Schmerling split from the 'Casino' to form the '*Pariser Hof*' faction. Before long it had approximately 100 members, most of whom were conservatives, Austrians and Southern Germans, frequently Catholic and primarily particularist in leaning. The *left* was mainly *großdeutsch* and unitarian. It had about 160 members. In February

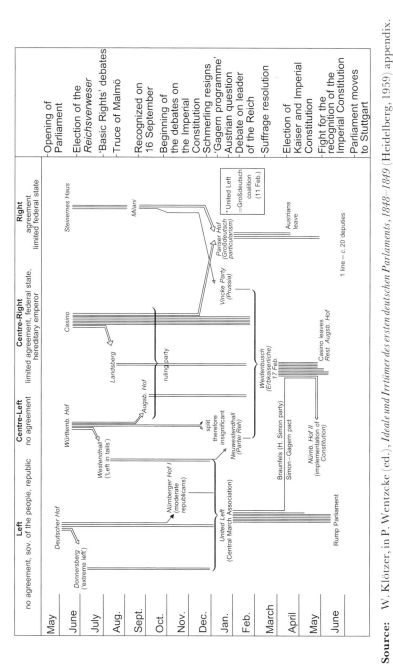

Figure 6 Factional regrouping in the Frankfurt National Assembly

Source: W. Klötzer, in P. Wentzcke (ed.), *Ideale und Irrtümer des ersten deutschen Parlaments, 1848–1849* (Heidelberg, 1959) appendix.

it joined with von Schmerling's *großdeutsch* supporters in a tactical alliance, which went by the name of '*Mainlust*'.

The 'Casino', 'Landsberg' and 'Augsburger Hof' on the other hand gained deputies from the 'Württemberger Hof' and even some members of the 'Westendhall'. In February 1849 these factions formed the '*Weidenbusch*', an alliance of approximately 220 primarily North German, Protestant, *kleindeutsch* supporters of the hereditary emperorship.

The *großdeutsch* alliance between the factions of the left and right could agree only in its negation of certain issues, for democrats and conservatives had no common constitutional programme which would have been able to resolve the dilemma as it had stood since the Kremsier declaration. Nor did they have a positive conception of the way in which the Habsburg state as a whole could be integrated into a German national state. The coalition of convenience proved stronger than the traditional majority factions.

This paved the way for the formation of the 'Westendhall', a small faction of liberals and democrats. Heinrich Simon and his supporters ('*Braunfels*') were prepared to reach a compromise with the '*Erbkaiserlich*' faction, albeit at the price of more extensive democratic components in the Imperial Constitution. The position of the imperial leader, expressed in terms of the definition of his right of veto, and the issue of universal suffrage were particularly close to their hearts.

The need to form an alliance of this kind was clear, for in the first reading the Assembly had manoeuvred itself into an unbreakable deadlock on the question of the Kaiser. The hereditary nature of the title of emperor had been rejected by 263 votes to 211; but Parliament also failed to reach a *positive* decision on the four other different forms of an elected emperor suggested. The draft constitution went to a second reading in which the leadership question was still unresolved.

In order to achieve a clear majority of votes, von Gagern, the leader of the *Erbkaiserlichen*, formed a 'pact' with Simon and his splinter faction, in which 114 *Erbkaiserlich* deputies declared in writing that they would allow the suspensive veto in questions of law and universal suffrage to be passed. For his part, Simon committed 15 party friends to a written counter-declaration to vote in favour of a hereditary emperor. As one of the signatories said, 'Like so many others I am sacrificing almost all my convictions, but this has to be done if anything is going to be achieved.'[4]

The importance of the 'Simon–Gagern pact' is reflected in the result of the vote of 27 March 1848: the hereditary nature of the imperial title was accepted by 267 votes to 263. They included four votes from democratic Austrians who voted with the *kleindeutsch* party in protest at Schwarzenberg's policies.

The Distribution of Power within the State Organization

The deputies filed away all plans to reduce the number of small states ('mediatization'), not least because of all the governments it was the small states who showed most support for the unification efforts. Nevertheless, the individual states were to renounce considerable sovereign rights. Frankfurt was in favour of a strong *imperial power*. Foreign representation, the declaration of war, the making of peace, the right to sign internationally binding treaties and authority over the Imperial Army were thereby transferred to the jurisdiction of the *Reich*. Unity of trade and commerce, of customs, coinage and the postal service created the framework for an integrated economic sphere. The *Reichstag*'s power to enact laws, the basic principle that 'Imperial law overrides state law', the generally binding Basic Rights of all citizens of the *Reich* and the creation of an Imperial Constitutional Court lent the state organization strong unitary features, which were offset by the federal counterweight of the intended *Staatenhaus*. The balanced structure of its constitution united national, constitutionalist and democratic elements. It was rightly regarded as one of the most progressive of the European constitutions of the middle of the century, and provided a model for all subsequent German constitutions. It was not the quality of the constitution finally agreed by Parliament that brought about its failure in 1849.

As a result of the 'Simon–Gagern pact' the hereditary monarchy acquired the character which the poet Ludwig Uhland famously couched in the following terms during the leadership debate: 'No head will shine above Germany that has not been anointed with a full drop of democratic oil.' The issues of veto and suffrage became crystallized as the two democratic 'essentials'. Debates on these subjects exposed many aspects of the constitutionalists' understanding of democracy and their attitude to state power.

The debate on the sovereign's *right of veto* with regard to *Reichstag* resolutions came during the week following the Berlin coup and the imposition of the constitution. The centre-right sought to fight 'parliamentary absolutism', the centre-left and the left to prevent 'the despotism of princes'. Events in Berlin provided the backdrop. Dahlmann, as speaker for the Constitutional Committee, regarded the behaviour of the Prussian King as the actions of a 'rescuing power', the 'right to perform an act of rescue'. His words were warmly received. The debate documented the fundamental readiness of the constitutionalists of 1848 to accept even a *coup d' état*, and to justify it on the grounds that the nightmare of anarchy was imminent.

Any analysis of parliament's vote on this issue should distinguish between the right of veto over all general laws and the right of veto over constitutional changes. The latter was of greater import, for future opportunities to establish a republic would depend upon it. In the first reading, the majority rejected the concept of an absolute veto in matters of law, but granted the sovereign the right of veto in constitutional matters. In the second reading, influenced heavily by party tactics, the suspensive veto was pushed through.

The social objectives of the majority factions were made clear in the *suffrage debates*. The lower orders were to be excluded from the electoral process. Hermann von Beckerath, leading exponent of the commercial middle class, regarded two-thirds of the population as politically uneducated. Von Gagern declared, 'The prevailing trend of our time is to safeguard the predominant influence of the middle classes in the state.'[5] These deputies had themselves been appointed under extremely wide suffrage regulations. They now attempted to safeguard their supremacy.

The 'Casino' suggested denying around half of all mature adults the right to vote. This was to be accomplished by means of hurdles based on the payment of taxes. They also submitted a sensational proposal to compile a 'discriminatory list of entire professional groups'; a suggestion which made the 'middle class ideology' (Botzenhart) of the constitutionalist wing of the liberals abundantly clear. Servants, commercial assistants, wage earners, the supported poor, and all those who were not subject to income tax, or who had an annual income of less than 300 *Gulden* were to be excluded. All the attempts to restrict suffrage, and to hold open rather than secret ballots, failed as a result of the *großdeutsch 'Mainlust'* coalition, in which some of the deputies who usually voted with the right had the casting votes. This was widely interpreted as obstruction. The writer, Heinrich Laube ('Augsburger Hof'), asked 'what could drive conservative monarchists from the right to such a betrayal of their principles?'[6] It was a purely rhetorical question. The answer was plain, even at the time: a group of rebels was intent on making the constitution as democratic and, therefore, unacceptable in their eyes as possible. On 2 March 1849 the law as a whole was accepted by a majority of 256 votes to 194. Although it proved unworkable in 1849, the principle of a general, equal and secret majority vote was adopted in the election law of the North German Confederation and subsequently in 1871 in that of the German *Reich*.

The final constitution was more democratic than would have been tolerated by the original majority. However, this was attributable to the issue of the Prussian hereditary emperor. For it was only by reaching parliamentary compromise that it was possible to reach a solution on the leadership issue. In doing so, the deputies learned how to operate in a modern parliamentary manner. Astoundingly, given all the differences they experienced, they proved themselves up to the task. It would not have been at all surprising if Parliament had broken up without reaching a definite result, given the pressures it was subjected to and the internal disintegration it experienced. However, the deputies revealed that they possessed a political maturity which is only now being recognized. For too long failure to understand the Parliament has led to the stereotypical portrayal of the Frankfurt National Assembly as a professor's parliament, populated by impractical theoreticians. Fingers have been pointed at the conflicts and break-ups into factions it experienced, whilst the political achievements of the young Parliament have been ignored. The deputies put to the test a representative system based on majority decisions; they managed to overcome the necessity of the factionalization vital for the formation of informed opinion and for the structuring of parliament; they experienced the decisive influence of small minorities; they learned how to conduct politics with changing majorities and negative coalitions which blocked progress; in important votes they practised the discipline necessary for parliamentary compromise.[7]

The Prussian Hereditary Emperorship

After Austrian policies had fought vehemently against the unification of the nation state and the possibility of a Habsburg emperor had been excluded, the Paulskirche increasingly concentrated on the Prussian king as a realistic sovereign of the future Reich. But what did the monarch himself want? Although the chances of winning him over appeared doubtful to many, on the other hand there were plenty of favourable indications, too. Sceptics recalled how, in April 1847 at the opening of the United Diet, he had announced that he would never tolerate a constitutional relationship between prince and people, the forcing of a 'written sheet of paper' between the two, which replaced 'the ancient, sacred loyalty'.[8] But, the confident could object, had he not granted a constitution in December 1848, and a liberal one at that, which included universal suffrage? The sceptic might point to the fact that in May the King had rejected the title of Kaiser without Austria, when the Committee of Seventeen produced its draft constitution, and that in November he had expressed similar sentiments to von Gagern; and, moreover, that Prussian primacy would only be acceptable with the agreement of the other princes, if at all. The confident on the other hand, recalled the King's presence at the festivals of the Cologne *Dombauverein* in 1842 and 1848, the nationalist declarations he had made, the March procession when he wore the German colours, and his announcement that Prussia was merging into Germany.

Today we know the King's frank opinion of the Frankfurt constitution, expressed as early as December 1848 in a confidential letter: he did not want *the* crown 'with its whorish smell of revolution', the 'imaginary trinket baked from dirt and clay', not he, 'a legitimate king by the grace of God'. The crown of the Ottos, the Hohenstaufens and the Habsburgs could also be worn by a Hohenzollern. This, he said, showed 'God's stamp', the holy anointing gave its bearer 'the grace of God'. He was concerned with 'the thousand-year crown of the German nation',[9] not with that of a constituent National Assembly.

The King was unable to read the signs of the times; the ideology he subscribed to was that of medieval pseudo-sacred rule by princes, as propagated by the 'camarilla' circle. In January 1849 this idea, in competition with the work of the Paulskirche, even assumed the form of a 'draft constitution' for Germany. It was to be composed of six duchies, each with a king at its helm, superior to the other princes. He claimed the privileged office of 'Reichs-Erzfeldherr' for Prussia, and the Imperial Roman majesty of the Habsburgs was to stand in solitary splendour above all else.

Schwarzenberg's ministry accepted this proposed plan on 17 January 1849, because it promised nothing other than the close agreement with Prussia in the struggle against Frankfurt. On 23 January 1849, under the influence of his ministry, the Prussian monarch completely changed tack and in a circular issued to all governments, declared himself willing to accept von Gagern's plan of a double wider and narrower union.[10] But did that not presuppose his readiness to accept the crown? It might have been seen as such by the public. The dispatch demanded that every German government co-operate in achieving 'a successful outcome' to the work on the constitution in Frankfurt.

After the conclusion of the first reading of the Imperial Constitution, von Gagern's Imperial Ministry invited all German individual states to make clear their position on it clear. Austria and the four kingdoms of Bavaria, Württemberg, Hanover and Saxony rejected it, Prussia, together with 30 other German governments, voted in favour. Eighteen states voiced open support for a hereditary emperorship, some of them expressly with reference to Prussia.

From Frankfurt's point of view it might have looked like a growing wave of support from the individual states, from which Frederick William IV was ultimately unable to distance himself. The signs of inconstancy in his character gave rise to hopes that he would be weak at the decisive moment. His long-term determination to win back the monarchical monopoly on rule, and his deployment of military force were either misunderstood, repressed or condoned. At an early stage deputies from the democratic factions asked parliament to consider the fact that under certain circumstances the Prussian king might not want the crown at all. But his personality seemed to contemporaries to be sometimes unfathomable, sometimes complex, sometimes patriotic, sometimes emotional, sometimes weak, sometimes militant – so that it did appear that there were grounds for hope, especially if desires were allowed to obscure the facts.

The Rejection of the Imperial Crown

On 28 March 1849 the Frankfurt National Assembly elected the Prussian King German Kaiser by 290 votes to 248 abstentions. Sections of the right, the centre-right and centre-left, half of the 'Westendhall' and even individual deputies from the 'Deutscher Hof' and the 'Donnersberg' factions formed the majority. On 3 April in Berlin an elected delegation of 32 deputies, led by the Parliamentary President, Eduard Simson, offered the crown to Frederick William IV.

The King's response was hedged in restrictive clauses. He would accept the crown, but only if the 'free agreement of the crowned heads, the princes and the free cities' was acquired. This implied further negotiations amongst the German governments as to 'whether the constitution avails the individual as it does the whole'.[11] According to the National Assembly's understanding of the law, there was no longer any question of agreement. The delegation therefore rightly interpreted the answer as a refusal.

The King's confidential views on the constitution in December 1848 had already shown that the idea that the Prussian King would become emperor, a notion which had emerged during the revolution, was unlikely to succeed. After the delegation had been received, Frederick William IV sent a letter to the Prussian envoy Bunsen in London, confiding what was really hidden behind his answer of 3 April:

> The meaning of the decision is this: 'I cannot answer yes or no. One can only accept or refuse something which *can* be offered – and you have nothing to offer: I will settle this matter with my own people, but to finish with, the truth: only soldiers can help fight democrats'.[12]

In the same letter he described the constitution as a 'dog-collar'.

Against this background even the recognition of the Imperial Constitution by 28 governments in a collective communication of 14 April 1849 cut no ice. Austria and the kingdoms of Bavaria, Württemberg, Saxony and Hanover were not amongst them. Of course the position of the reluctant medium states was delicate: under the pressure of the campaign for the Imperial Constitution which was just beginning, the Württemberg King announced his recognition of the constitution (25 April); at the beginning of May the provisional revolutionary governments from Saxony and the Bavarian Rhineland-Palatinate followed suit.

The Prussian King's decision is frequently interpreted as fateful or tragic. It is attributed to the excesses of the revolution or to the dubious democratic colouring of the Imperial Constitution, without which, it is argued, it might have stood some chance of success. On the other hand, we should take seriously the real political substance of Frederick William IV's romantic imperial ideology and his determination not to allow the instruments of a royal monopoly on rule to be taken away from him. The King asserted the position of the monarch in the system of rule; his supremacy over the army, diplomacy and the internal administration. He stood for a political system which was now being challenged to surrender part of its power by the movements within society. All the post-revolutionary police-state policies of Prussian crypto-absolutism exacerbated this profound conflict. It was not a single clause in the Imperial Constitution in particular that led Frederick William IV to refuse the crown, but the fact 'that on principle, as the representative of all the more important German ruling houses, he did not recognize the constituent power the National Assembly claimed'.[13]

It may have seemed inappropriate or presumptuous to the delegation, but the King's offer of military power was a logical response to the 'sovereignty of the people'; 'If the Prussian shield and sword are required against enemies from without and within [!], I will not fail; even if I am not called upon to do so.' This was the Prussian counter-revolutionary programme in Germany; he had informed Bunsen about it in no uncertain terms. On 28 April 1849, in a dispatch meant for the Central Power, the King definitively rejected both the crown and the Imperial Constitution.

13 The Campaign for the Imperial Constitution, April–July 1849

Crisis and the Break-up of the Frankfurt National Assembly

In April 1849 it was clear that the Prussian King was not minded to assume the leadership of the new *Reich* voluntarily. But could he perhaps be forced to do so? The Frankfurt deputies felt a mixture of disappointment, bewilderment and determination to take extra-parliamentary action, added to by the frantic diplomatic efforts of the Central Power, which attempted to move those governments which had not yet done so to recognize the constitution, by holding the spectre of renewed outbreaks of revolution over their heads. The question was raised as to how Parliament should proceed, now that the actions at governmental level and that of the delegation to the King had proved unsuccessful. Once again, the Assembly was challenged to make a fundamental decision on its role and position in the revolution. On 23 April Welcker wrote: 'We had hoped that we were at the end of our great work. We had hoped that we would succeed in concluding the revolution... now it seems that an even larger, more terrible and difficult revolution than that of 1848 is presenting itself to us.'[1]

Unlike the Pre-Parliament, however, the Paulskirche had legality on its side. As far as the National Assembly was concerned, the consti-tution decided on 28 March 1849 and published in the imperial law gazette was legally binding. Should the governments which were resisting it be forced to recognize it and to implement it? The deputies now had to clarify their position on power and on the popular move-ment. For, from the last week of April 1849 onwards, following the revolutionary waves of spring and September 1848, Germany experi-enced a third wave of uprisings which were largely dependent on the

Paulskirche decisions and which took as their programme the implementation of the Imperial Constitution. For this reason the wave of protest has gone down in history as the 'campaign for the Imperial Constitution'.[2]

This issue led to a rift in the National Assembly, which, on 4 May voted by the narrowest of majorities (190:188) to take political action. The following resolution was passed: 'The National Assembly calls on the governments, the constituent bodies, the local authorities of the individual states and the entire German people to recognize and implement the Constitution of the German Empire of 28 March this year.'[3] The elections to the *Volkshaus* were set for 15 July. The *Reichstag* would meet for the first time on 22 August. If Prussia refused, the ruler of the largest state represented in the *Staatenhaus* would assume the position of Imperial Governor.

In doing this the Assembly went beyond the governments, directly addressing the parliaments, local authorities and the population as a whole, and heralding the future course of events. Von Gagern changed tack and voiced his moral support for the campaign for the Imperial Constitution. His government programme of 8 May 1849 contained a passage directed at Prussia, stating that the Imperial Ministry would, 'however, oppose any intervention by one or several individual states to suppress any movement which might arise for the purpose of achieving recognition of the Imperial Constitution in other individual states'.[4] *The Reichsverweser* rejected the programme on the grounds that it was illegal, and could lead to civil war. Archduke John now developed a consistently counter-revolutionary strategy. As a result, von Gagern resigned on 10 May 1849, and the National Assembly lost its widely respected figure of integration.

Other National Assembly resolutions reinforced this course. They included a protest against Prussian intervention in Saxony (10 May) and a declaration of protection for the Palatinate uprising movement (15 May). The call penned by Uhland on 26 May demanded the 'active co-operation of the entire population'. He expected measures, he said, 'to ensure that the people would be equipped with arms and schooled in their use'. He called for people's guards to be formed and for the standing armies to commit themselves 'to upholding the Imperial Constitution'.[5]

With each new resolution, a further section of Parliament turned its back on it. The Prussian government had already regarded the call of 4 May as a breach of the agreement principle, and had declared it unlawful. The Austrian government had recalled its deputies on

5 April. Now other deputies were recalled from Prussia (14 May), Saxony (19 May), Hanover (23 May) and Baden (12 June). Huber refers to these recalls as 'a new link in the chain of *coup d' état*-like measures on the part of the governments of the individual states'.[6] The legitimization of the revolution in the spring was followed by its de-legitimization in decline. The civil servants amongst the deputies had least grounds for refusing the recall, since apart from the legal consequences of doing so, they were also threatened by disciplinary consequences and removal from office. Conservatives and constitutionalists were also opposed to taking extra-parliamentary action. The majority rejected a motion to form an Imperial Army from the troops of the states under the Imperial Constitution, so that the National Assembly would not be solely reliant on the civil guards and volunteer corps.

The first signal was given on 20 May, when a collective declaration was signed by 65 deputies – the core of the 'Casino' faction – including Arndt, Beseler, Dahlmann, von Gagern and Simson. A resolution on 26 May was followed by others. This completed the break in the middle classes, as it had been represented in this Parliament. The campaign for the Imperial Constitution lost its centre. The so-called 'Rump Parliament' remained behind. On 30 May 1849 it resolved to move to Stuttgart. The proximity of the Mainz fortress, the soldiers stationed anyway in Frankfurt since September 1848 and the advancing Prussian troops posed an acute threat to the meetings of the parliament.

The *Reichsverweser* remained in Frankfurt, however. Following von Gagern's resignation, he had formed a right-wing cabinet, which lacked any parliamentary support, and on 17 May was even forced to submit to a damaging vote of no confidence (191:12). The cabinet sought to oppose 'all unlawful movements which have as an excuse or cause the implementation of the constitution' by all means possible; and that included military means. Indeed, the major task of the continuing Central Power consisted in deploying 'Imperial Troops' against the campaign for the Imperial Constitution in south-west Germany.

Features of the Campaign for the Imperial Constitution

The uprising movement for the Imperial Constitution was more than an epilogue or episode, despite the fact that it is usually misjudged in these terms: for once again it demonstrated the power and limitations of a popular movement which gripped large parts of Germany. It was focused on the states which had refused to accept the Imperial Constitution: Prussia, with centres in Silesia, and Rhineland-Westphalia; Württemberg; Saxony; Bavaria, with the focal point in Munich; Franconia; Bavarian Swabia and the Palatinate; the regions left of the Rhine; and, finally, Hanover; that is to say, the states in which, together with Austria (which was not affected by this movement), political power, monarchic inertia and particularist weight were most concentrated. Baden was a special case, for it developed into a bastion of the movement despite the fact that its government had recognized the Imperial Constitution.

Although the campaign appeared to repeat the events of the March revolution, there were some marked differences.

- It was driven and co-ordinated by the highly developed political people's associations and workers' societies. The 'Central March Association' operated at a national level, steering and controlling the movement, although the extent of this is not yet clear.
- The attitude of the army had a decisive impact on the success of the movement in an individual state, and the soldiers of the medium states above all had not emerged from the last year of the revolution untouched.
- There were no supporting agrarian revolutions. In some cases the peasants came down on the side of the princes, as in the Bavarian mountain regions, for instance. In addition, approximately 80 per cent of the Prussian troops in the campaign for the Imperial Constitution were peasants loyal to the King.[7]
- The movement was inclined in favour of republican coups. Instead of halting before the thrones, it forced monarchs to flee their residences. The Württemberg monarch fled to Ludwigsburg, the King of Saxony to the Königstein fortress, that of Baden to the Mainz fortress. The Bavarian King was on the point of making a similar decision. Provisional revolutionary governments of the kind that only Schleswig-Holstein had seen since March 1848 (and here the relevant person was no German monarch) now showed that the revolution had taken on a new quality.
- The movement could no longer rely on the undivided support of the middle classes. In contrast, the compliant announcements made by the state parliaments, the address movements and popular rallies had all been part of the superficial image of the March revolution.

Hanover and Württemberg

In Hanover a strong movement arose which opposed the stalling policies of refusal of Stüve's March ministry. In Celle 75 *Volksvereine* or
people's associations agreed on the measures to be taken. The King
answered the insistent demands of the deputies by dissolving both
chambers (25 April). Encouraged by the Frankfurt 'Central March
Association' the movement gripped the state: councils, rallies in
Eystrup and Hanover, and most civil guards agitated in favour of the
Imperial Constitution. A delegation from the people's associations
demanded that the King sack the ministry. However, the *Zeitung für
Norddeutschland's* demand that a revolutionary state committee should
be introduced went unheeded. Further difficulties did not arise, since
on the critical days from 6 to 8 May the railway stations were occupied
and the army was standing by in the barracks.[8]

The popular movement in Württemberg forced the King to accept
the constitution – in an equally non-violent but more vigorous
manner. To a deputation of the chamber of deputies he declared
that he would later retract any promises which had been forced out
of him. Volunteer corps were formed, civil guards took up arms and
the central committee of all the people's associations set about arming
the populace together with the 'Central March Association'. Soldiers
were forced to swear to remain loyal to their oath to the constitution.
Officers told the King in Ludwigsburg that they would protect him,
but would not undertake action against the constitution.[9] Most of the
reliable monarchical troops were under the command of General
Moritz von Miller on the Badenese border. A republican coup was
imminent. Under this pressure William recognized the Imperial
Constitution on 25 April 1849; the first king to do so.

Saxony

King Frederick August II and the Saxon government under the
newly appointed Foreign Minister, Graf Beust, were determined not
to follow suit, preferring to allow matters to come to a head in a
battle. The split in the middle-class front was extremely useful to
them. Parliamentary democrats and social republicans were agitating in the 'fatherland associations', supported by the journeymen,
factory workers, miners and gymnasts; the constitutionalist middle

classes were active in the 'German associations', supported by the town councils, the municipal guards and Leipzig University. On the other hand, the government was weakened by the army's position. Most of its soldiers were fighting in Schleswig-Holstein and only about 2000 men were available in Dresden. It was not possible to predict how some of them would act. Here, too, the political associations carried the movement. More than 200 of them had reached an agreement at a large rally held on 22 April. The chambers also committed themselves to the Imperial Constitution. When the King dissolved them, public agitation increased. News that Prussian troops had been requested was met by public outrage and the construction of barricades. With the co-operation of the court architect, Gottfried Semper, and kapellmeister, Richard Wagner, the Russian, Michael Bakunin, steered the work.

Following the flight of the King, the lawyers, Samuel Tzschirner and Otto Heubner, and the mayor, Karl Gotthelf Todt, formed a provisional government. It was recognized by 24 towns, as the movement took effect in the heart of the state. In the capital it could rely on the support of 3000 genuine fighters. Two-thirds of the incoming 6000 were unarmed and could hardly be deployed. Saxony now followed Württemberg as the thirtieth state to recognize the Imperial Constitution.

The reaction followed swiftly, and the railway made it even faster: Prussian troops arrived on 5 May. By 9 May the battles had already been decided. Even the leader of the Workers' Fraternity, Stephan Born, stood on the barricades. Armed with modern breech-loading needle-guns and plenty of artillery, the superiority of the Prussian troops was clear. Thirty-one soldiers died and 97 were wounded, against approximately 250 dead and 400 wounded revolutionaries. The violent manner in which the Dresden May uprising was suppressed acted as a deterrent in the rest of Germany.

The 869 participants who had been arrested and placed in custody in Dresden by 25 August 1849 included 262 journeymen, 201 'workers', 16 soldiers and a further 106 members of the lower orders.[10] After the victory of the counter-revolution, the authorities' work began. More than 6000 people were indicted for their actions between March 1848 and the campaign for the Imperial Constitution. Many were able to flee; 727 were sentenced to long periods of imprisonment. Of these, 97 per cent came from Saxony. This refutes in no uncertain terms the thesis held at the time that foreign demagogues had staged the Saxon revolution. A breakdown of those sentenced allows more detailed analysis of the classes who were the mainstay of the Saxon revolution (see Table 19).

The vast majority of those sentenced were craftsmen; masters, journeymen, apprentices and other craftsmen together made up

Table 19   Breakdown of revolutionaries sentenced in Saxony, according to profession

Profession		Number	%
Civil Servants[1]	senior	11	(1.5)
	middle-ranking	29	(4.0)
	lower	9	(1.2)
Independent[2]		72	(9.9)
Masters		139	(19.1)
Journeymen		192	(26.4)
Apprentices		1	(0.1)
Craftsmen[3]		90	(12.4)
Assistants		22	(3.0)
Workers		89	(12.2)
Army		52	(7.2)
Trainees[4]		13	(1.8)
No details given		8	(1.1)

[1]   The breakdown into senior, middle-ranking and junior civil servants is extremely difficult and can only give us approximate values. Senior civil servants include university teachers, patrimonial court administrators, councillors of justice ('*Justizräte*') and graduate civil servants who had finished their traineeships ('*Assessoren*'). Middle-ranking civil servants include *Gymnasium* teachers, councillors, vicars. *Volksschule* teachers, town clerks, post-office officials and town hall porters were described as lower-ranking civil servants, even if they did not officially have civil servant status.

[2]   Manufacturers, merchants, pensioners, traders, landowners, freelance professions.

[3]   This group comprises all craftsmen who did not use the prefix 'master' 'journeyman, or 'apprentice'. It is not possible to categorize them exactly. It is probable that most of them were journeymen. Use of the term 'master' does not mean that that person was necessarily employed in a craftsman business. He might also have worked in a factory.

[4]   Pupils, students, academic and other trainees.

Source: H.-J. Rupieper, 'Die Sozialstruktur der Trägerschichten der Revolution von 1848/49 am Beispiel Sachsen', in H. Kaelble *et al.*, *Probleme der Modernisierung in Deutschland* (Opladen, 1978), p. 93.

58 per cent. This highlights the fact that, even in the most heavily industrialized state of the German Confederation, there was a revolutionary link between socio-economic structural crisis and political movement.

Prussia

As the chosen hegemonic power of a unified Germany, Prussia was particularly affected and challenged by the campaign for the Imperial Constitution. Consistent in its policies, on the day that the Imperial Crown and Imperial Constitution were definitively rejected, the von Brandenburg ministry declared Prussia to be the leading counter-revolutionary power (28 April 1849). Prussia, it said, was 'prepared powerfully and energetically to counter the destructive and revolutionary efforts on all sides'. Prussia offered military aid to the other governments and declared it to be its 'calling' 'to intervene in the days of danger wherever and however it is necessary'.[11] Indeed, all that was needed was an invitation to intervene, and in an emergency – as events in the Palatinate proved – even that was not strictly necessary.

First, however, the government had to deal with the popular movement within its own borders. Elections had now taken place following the imposition of the constitution, and the chambers had met for the first time on 26 February 1849. Yet the second chamber's description of the Imperial Constitution as 'legally valid' was sufficient reason for Frederick William IV to dissolve it again one week later.

In Prussia, too, the attitude of the army played a key role in the campaign for the Imperial Constitution. Berlin was still under a state of siege and the city remained calm; troops put down a barricade uprising in Breslau (6–7 May 1849). However, Prussia's 'calling' in Germany was announced by its intervention in Saxony which occurred at the same time, and which required the mobilization of the *Landwehr* or militia. Yet this mobilization had the opposite effect to that intended, for the militia became the driving force of spontaneous resistance. In Prüm and Gräfrath the militia's armouries were stormed. The 'Central March Association' activated the political clubs in Düsseldorf, Iserlohn, Solingen and Hagen. In a proclamation of 8 May at the Rhineland *Städtetag* in Cologne, 303 communities called for the recognition of the Imperial Constitution and protested against the deployment of the militia. Unlike the young generation serving in the ranks of the standing army, the militia generation participated in political life: some of their officers belonged to the leading strata of the liberal and democratic movement. In Elberfeld there was an armed militia uprising, after which the town found itself under the control of a revolutionary security committee. At a General Assembly on 3 May 1849, militiamen declared that they would view 'the ministry around the crown as one which was hostile to the people, and regard themselves as released from the absolute crown'.[12] They threatened to take up arms and hound every soldier from the town.

But such actions remained restricted to isolated regions. 'The law-enforcing troops of the middle-class centre' (Huber), the civil guard, put down the uprising, as 'one defence organization of middle-class society overcame another'.[13] The young Friedrich Engels from Elberfeld had advised in vain for the civil guard to be disarmed. Where military intervention was necessary, rank troops finished matters off. The most bloody intervention was seen in Iserlohn, where 100 people lost their lives.

Bavaria and the Rhineland–Palatinate Uprising

The Congress of March Associations in Frankfurt had resolved to focus its actions on Bavaria, which saw the greatest resistance on the part of a medium state government to the Imperial Constitution. 'I want to prevent a *Kleindeutschland*', King Maximilian had declared. An assembly of March Associations in Munich (27 April 1849), attended by more than a thousand members, demanded the unconditional recognition of the Imperial Constitution; 12,000 people signed a petition set out in the town hall. In Erlangen, Nuremberg, Würzburg, Füssen and Lindau the people's associations organized rallies which were attended by up to 10,000 people. By mid-June 283 political associations had joined the district committee of democratic associations in Würzburg alone, where, within a few days, 10,000 signatures had been collected.[14] The movement spread even to small country towns.

When the chamber of deputies adopted a resolution on the unconditional recognition of the Imperial Constitution, the King responded by dissolving the chamber. This heightened agitation and led to an uprising in the Palatinate area left of the Rhine. Here, too, the initiative lay with the people's associations, whose executive committee proclaimed on 1 May, 'If the government has become a rebel, the free citizens of the Palatinate will become executors of the law.'[15] At a rally on 2 May in Kaiserslautern, attended by more than 12,000 people, a ten-man State Defence Committee was formed, which swore in civil servants on the Imperial Constitution and introduced the general arming of the populace. The uprising as a whole succeeded because, with the exception of the Landau and Germersheim fortresses, the garrison troops joined the revolt, including those called from Frankfurt, and because the soldiers on leave did not respond to the district administrator's appeal, he was forced to flee.

Imperial Commissioner von Gagern sent the Saxon manufacturer Bernhard Eisenstuck ('Deutscher Hof') to the Palatinate to discipline the state committee in the name of the Provisional Central Power. Instead, Eisenstuck legitimized it as a public body and managed to persuade the fortress command of the Landau federal fortress to agree not to allow in any Prussian troops. This sole case of intervention from Frankfurt in support of the revolution showed that the Central Power would have been in a position to offer effective support to the Imperial Constitution movement.

On 17 May a provisional government comprised of five members was formed. They included the editor, Friedrich Georg Kolb, the lawyers, August Ferdinand Culmann and Friedrich Schüler, and the notary, Joseph Martin Reichard: all four of whom were members of the 'Deutscher Hof' or 'Donnersberg' Paulskirche factions. The Palatinate declared itself an independent republican state. Although there was no uprising in Franconia, owing to the pressure of the Dresden fighting, Prussian troops under the command of Prince William of Prussia, the future Kaiser William I, marched into the Palatinate. Only afterwards did the Bavarian government submit a request for aid. On 14 June the provisional government was forced to flee, and the entire state found itself in Prussian hands.

Baden and the End

With the intervention in south-west Germany, the days of the revolution were numbered, although initially in Baden it seemed as if the third attempt might be successful. The republicans' seizure of power mirrored the stages seen in the Palatinate. Although the government had recognized the Imperial Constitution, the movement went beyond what had been achieved elsewhere. An alliance between the freelance intelligentsia and the lower middle classes, already recognizable in the *Vormärz* period, pressed for power.

The agitation started from the people's association spokesmen, from mayors, innkeepers, local councillors, lawyers, doctors, pharmacists; local dignitaries who were backed by gymnasts, journeymen and country people. Central leadership came from the Central Committee of the People's Associations, to which the 'Central March Association' was linked; the Mannheim lawyer and Paulskirche deputy Lorenz Brentano ('Donnersberg') was its chairman.

The soldiers' uprising in the fortress of Rastatt on 12 May 1849 was decisive for the coup. The soldiers demanded the release of political prisoners held there since the two uprisings of 1848. As in Vienna in October 1848, it was when sections of the standing army went over to the revolution that the swing was triggered. At the Offenburg State Assembly of Democratic Associations, attended by some 40,000 people the following day, the Central Committee was supplemented by soldiers and the programme for a social and democratic republic already outlined in April 1848 was proclaimed. This time, too, the arming of the populace was included in the programme. The Archduke fled on 14 May and the Central Committee appointed an 'Executive Committee'; a provisional government led by Brentano. Subsequent measures consolidated the power of this first German state governed on republican lines. The government resolved an increase in soldiers' pay, the election of officers, the swearing-in of civil servants on the constitution and elections to a constituent state assembly. The social composition of the parliament which now met mirrored the leading stratum of the people's associations and included virtually no senior civil servants or professors. Advocates, self-employed businessmen, lower civil servants (mayors, teachers) were most heavily represented. There were also editors, doctors, priests, a single peasant, but no 'dependent people', such as workers or journeymen.[16] Despite numerous internal disputes, the government had genuinely acquired the support of the population and the apparatus of state power. The army, administrative civil servants and judges placed themselves at its disposal.

The counter-revolution came from the outside. From Mainz the Archduke requested the aid of Prussian and 'Imperial troops'. On behalf of the Provisional Central Power in Frankfurt, the former Imperial War Minister sent Imperial troop contingents from Hesse, Nassau and Württemberg to Baden, to back up the Prussian troops under the command of Prince William. Soldiers from Bavaria,

Württemberg and Austria were also put on stand-by to the east and the south. Given these troops' superior numbers, the position of the united Badenese militias, civil guards and rank soldiers was hopeless, despite the skilful leadership of commander-in-chief Ludwig von Mieroslawski. The defeat at Waghäusl on 21 June decided the battle. By 15 June Mannheim was in Prussian hands, three days before the Rump Parliament in Stuttgart was forcibly broken up.

Although the Rump Parliament had appointed an imperial regency as executive body on 6 June 1849, in fact there was nothing left for it to rule. The popular movement, steered by the Württemberg State Committee of People's Associations, organized the great Reutlingen Whitsun Rally of 28 May, attended by 20,000 people, where open imperial war against Prussia and support for the National Assembly and for Baden were declared. The Heilbronn civil guard wanted to protect the National Assembly 'from princes and governments practising high treason'. However, Württemberg troops who had previously been stationed on the Badenese borders had now been ordered to withdraw, and had been strategically distributed in the state. The state of siege over Heilbronn ended the resistance there and on 18 June 1849 the Württemberg March minister Römer ordered the violent break-up of the Stuttgart Rump Parliament.

The German revolution ended on 23 July 1849 with the written capitulation of the approximately 6000 revolutionary fighters incarcerated in the fortress at Rastatt. Unlike in Saxony and the Palatinate, Prussian drumhead courts martial liquidated the revolution. Regular courts martial and law courts also issued approximately 1000 verdicts. Valentin estimated that 80,000, or 1 in 18 of the Badenese population, emigrated. Almost every family was affected. Memories of the events lived on amongst the population, as testified by the lyrics of the Badenese Lullaby, which began with the verse:

> *Sleep, my child, sleep quietly,*
> *There's a Prussian outside the door.*
> *He's killed your father*
> *And made your mother poor.*
> *And if you don't sleep peacefully and quietly*
> *He'll come and close your eyes.*
> *Sleep, my child, sleep quietly,*
> *There's a Prussian outside the door.*[17]

The German campaign for the Imperial Constitution once again demonstrates the European character of the revolutions of 1848–9, for after the suppression of campaigns in non-German states, foreign revolutionaries fled to the German arena. The Russian officer, Bakunin, in Dresden, the Polish General, Franz Snayde, as commander-in-chief in the Palatinate, the Hungarian Colonel, Stefan Türr, also in the Palatinate, the Polish General, von Mieroslawski, in Baden, refugees from Austria, including Kudlich, political refugees from Swiss and French exile, including the Prussian officer from Posen, August Willich, and his élite 'Besançon' company; Poles, Frenchmen, Swiss and Hungarians formed their own legions.

From a European perspective, the revolutions finally ended in Italy and Hungary, with the complete restoration of the Habsburg imperial state. The first stage was the defeat of Sardinian troops on 22 March 1849 at Novara. In April Austrian troops occupied the northern parts of the Papal State and Toscana. On 3 August Garibaldi's and Mazzini's Roman republic fell following bombardment by French corps. On 22 August 1849 Venice, too, was forced to capitulate to the Austrian besiegers. The republics of Rome and Venice became symbols of the national Italian revolution against foreign rule.

In Hungary, however, aid from Russian troops was requested. Windischgrätz and von Jellačić were forced to accept defeats against the Hungarian revolutionary army, paving the way for the Hungarian declaration of independence (14 April 1849). However, the invasion of Tsar Nicholas's troops in June helped the return of Habsburg rule here too. With the Hungarian capitulation at Világos on 13 August 1849, the fate of the European revolutions was finally sealed.

14 From Erfurt Union to Reaction

With the revolution over, the state organization of Germany remained as an unresolved political problem. Initially there was no question of a reconvening of the old *Bundestag*. This was due to Prussia's bizarre initiative to introduce 'from above' a unification of the *Reich* without Austria, though with the agreement of the other German princes. It was bizarre, because von Gagern's plan of a double union was now taken up in Berlin, despite the fact that Austrian and Prussian resistance had previously caused it to fail.

Once again it was diplomats who took matters into their hands. Conferences and the exchange of dispatches, memoranda and draft constitutions were all part of unification politics. This is still part of the final phase of the revolution, because it took place through reference back to the Imperial Constitution of 28 March and entangled the Paulskirche '*Erbkaiserlichen*' in constitutional politics for a last time. Frederick William's close adviser, Joseph Maria von Radowitz, the former leader of the 'Café Milani' faction in the Paulskirche, emerged as the spokesman of a *kleindeutsch*, Prussian hegemonic unification policy. For some of the time he acted without official function, from September to November 1850 as Prussian Foreign Minister.

During the campaign for the Imperial Constitution, at the invitation of Minister President von Brandenburg, representatives from Prussia, Bavaria, Saxony, Hanover and Württemberg gathered for a conference in Berlin on 17 May 1849 under the leadership of von Radowitz. The so-called 'Alliance of Three Kings' (26 May 1849) signalled that support from Bavaria and Württemberg would not be forthcoming. The allied partners Prussia, Hanover and Saxony agreed an Imperial Constitution (28 May), which came literally close in parts to that of Frankfurt, but which differed in three fundamental ways.

213

1. Alongside the imperial leader, the *Staatenhaus* and *Volkshaus*, a fourth body involved in legislation would consist of a Prince's College of Six; this corresponded to the originally planned '*Reichsrat*', which the '*Erbkaiserlichen*' had demanded as an additional federal element in the Paulskirche, but had been unable to push through in the second reading of the constitution.

2. The Imperial sovereign would be given an absolute rather than suspensive veto over parliamentary resolutions. This too was an '*erbkaiserlich*' demand.

3. Elections to the *Volkshaus* would be carried out according to indirect three-class suffrage. This came closer to the '*erbkaiserlich*' requirements based on taxation than Frankfurt's direct and equal suffrage.

By the end of 1849, 26 German states had endorsed the union plan. It encountered an ambiguous response from the public. Opinions on the subject were inevitable, given the proposal for elections to a union parliament in Erfurt to be held in those states which were participating in the unification efforts. Debates on the draft constitution were to be held at a '*Reichstag*'.

The democratic people's associations and workers' associations protested against the plan. Their opposition to the suffrage regulations, which privileged the landowning classes, was particularly vehement. The constitutionalists on the other hand met for discussions from 25 to 27 June 1849 in Gotha, where they decided to take part in the elections. 150 of the 270 invited came; 'all the *erbkaiserlich* élite' (Huber), including the core of the 'Casino' faction, Bassermann, von Beckerath, Beseler, Dahlmann, von Gagern, Hergenhahn, von Mevissen and Simson. After this meeting they became known as the '*Gotha Party*'. The absolute veto, the reinforcement of federal arrangements and suffrage based on property-ownership had already been part of their programme in Frankfurt.

The *Erfurt Parliament* met on 20 March 1850 and accepted the draft constitution *en bloc*. The 'Gotha Party' formed the majority in the *Volkshaus* and the *Staatenhaus*. Suffrage and the democrats' boycott had turned them into 'leftists', while opposed to them on the 'right' were ultraroyalists who had not sat on the benches of the Paulskirche. They included representatives of the Prussian 'camarilla': Ernst Ludwig von Gerlach, Stahl and von Bismarck, who, already during the March revolution, had been no strangers to plans involving *coups d'état*. The core of the conflicts was now reduced to the alternatives 'royalist' or 'parliamentary' (Stahl).[1]

But the constitutional political unification of the *Reich* 'from above' turned out to be simply an instrument in the competing power politics between Austria, Prussia and the medium states, and it too failed. Following the defeat of Hungary in August 1849, Schwarzenberg's Austrian policies had room once more to attack the Prussian union plan as a contravention of the German Federal Act, which he still regarded as legally valid. Hanover and Saxony had in fact already left the union in October 1849. On 27 February the four medium states, Bavaria, Saxony, Hanover and Württemberg, formed an 'Alliance of Four Kings', which postulated the full annexation of the entire state of Austria, including all its non-German parts. This heralded the restoration of the *Bundestag*.

The Austrian government invited the German states to the reopening of the *Bundestag* in Frankfurt on 2 September 1850. However, a domestic crisis in Kurhesse threatened to turn the conflict between Austria and Prussia into a war. The government in Kurhesse had to ward off protest on the part of the *Stände*, the officers and the courts following a coup-like breach of the constitution. Formally, the state belonged to the Prussian-dominated union. However, it requested military intervention from the Austrian-led Rump Confederation. Given Frederick William's vacillating stance on whether or not to use military force, von Radowitz resigned, for he had demanded energetic reaction (2 November 1850). The intransigence of the Austrian government brought the conflict to a head, until finally, on 8 November 1850, Austrian and Bavarian troops in Kurhesse found themselves close enough to Prussian troops to shoot. The Tsar's readiness to intervene on the Austrian side was unmistakable.

The November crisis led to a general war-like atmosphere, vaguely reminiscent of the feelings whipped up by the Schleswig-Holstein issue, in which the nationalistically inclined constitutionalist and democratic groups in Prussia propagated its 'honour', the rescue of the Erfurt union and the fight against the powers of 'reaction'.

The tight-knit 'camarilla' circle, however, was in favour of an understanding with Austria; this came close to a capitulation, recorded in the Treaty of Olmütz (29 November 1850), in which Prussia renounced the union and declared itself ready to withdraw from Kurhesse and to surrender Schleswig-Holstein.

The Prussian policy of reaching agreement, vilified as the 'disgrace of Olmütz', ended the open rivalry between both states on the German question for a decade. Austria and Prussia's common and co-ordinated anti-revolutionary domestic policies dated from the

Olmütz Punctation. When von Brandenburg died he was replaced as Prussian Minister President by Otto von Manteuffel, who openly declared to the chamber on 19 December 1850 that there must now be 'a decisive break with the revolution'; the turning-point in the inner-German development, he said, had now been reached.[2] Before the reopening of the full *Bundestag*, Prussia, Austria, Hanover and Saxony reached an agreement on a secret organization of the political police in Germany, which in typical German officialese was called 'The police association of the more important German states' (*'Polizeiverein'*). By February 1852 Bavaria, Württemberg and Baden had also joined it. On 9 April 1851 the first of 20 police conferences met in Dresden, which, together with the vigorous exchange of information between state police forces, led to the monitoring, persecution and suppression of the political opposition in Germany.[3]

The 'police association' touched all areas which had become driving forces in the development of informed political opinion during the revolution: the publishing industry; book shops; journalism and political writing; literature; political associations; chambers; political refugees and former revolutionaries, individually and in entire groups, such as the 'tax boycotters' of the Berlin National Assembly or the members of the Stuttgart Rump Parliament. From now on, all public activity of those known to be members of the 'Gotha Party' was also monitored and the Workers' Fraternity was banned. Agents and envoys even submitted information on the plans and activities of German emigrants in London, Paris, Brussels and Switzerland. The 'police association' co-ordinated the anti-revolutionary policies amongst the seven states and also concentrated the state police within each state; the member states also monitored the small German states.

This secret police practice was supplemented by legal reaction on the part of the *Bundestag* from 1851 onwards. The middle-class movement, the Frankfurt National Assembly and the state parliaments had sought to legitimize the revolution. They had resolved legally binding laws and changes to the constitution. Most of this now had to be legally undone again. In the so-called Federal Reaction Decree of 23 August 1851, the *Bundestag* institutionalized the process of 'de-liberalization and de-democratization of the state constitutions'.[4] A Reaction Committee was appointed to oversee the task. The same day the *Bundestag* began revoking the Frankfurt Basic Rights. The system of legal restoration was concluded with the Federal Press Law of 6 July and the Federal Association Law of 13 July 1854.

Between 1849 and 1851 the confederation states had already individually undertaken the legal and political repression of these most
sensitive areas of public activity.

The social emancipation processes which had got off the ground
in 1848 were now delayed for the foreseeable future. The antagonisms within society which had begun in 1848–9 were once again
artificially and violently suppressed. In 1858, if a judgement had to be
made regarding employment or (re)instatement as a teacher, judge
or mayor in public service, a 'forty-eighter' was still regarded as
handicapped by the state authorities. Whenever the German public
became restless, as in 1859 in the context of the Italian War of Unity,
local police authorities in Saxony, Hanover, Bavaria or Prussia still
turned their attention to the former 'leaders of the revolutionary
party'. For years members of the 'Gotha Party' and to an even greater
extent democrats, came under this heading.

Conclusion: 1848–9 and the Crises
of Modernization

Accounts of the revolution of 1848–9 usually end with reflections on its 'failure'. Yet this would imply a monodimensional objective on the part of the revolution, which our observations on its dynamics have thrown into doubt. Actions occurred simultaneously and parallel to one another, on different levels, in different arenas, reinforcing or paralysing each other; in a context of reciprocal influences which far transcended the judgement and decision-making powers of all the participants. The search for 'the guilty parties', which is always associated with responses to the 'failure' of the revolution, is therefore also of debatable value. In 1848 no one knew what was happening at the same time in the provinces, at the ruler's residence, in competing party factions, in the newspapers, in the army or at rallies. Nor did they know where the leading actors in each case were at work. The actors of 1848–9 did not have a *single*, clearly determinable aim in which they subsequently 'failed'. It is not possible to summarize the revolution simply in terms of the Frankfurt Imperial Constitution of 28 March 1849, which did in fact fail, or in terms of the diverging aims of the Frankfurt Paulskirche, 'Germany's great hope' (F. Eyck), to which the image of the revolution is often abbreviated. The exclusive focus on failure detracts from the many problems of the year of the revolution; and it is vital to understand these problems.

The same process of change sometimes gave rise to apparently conflicting and contradictory responses. The accumulation of problems both provoked and paralysed the revolution, in that, at the end of the day, it proved to be too much for the participants. Hopes of change and 'progress' were raised. Yet when the changes were actually implemented, people from all social spheres began to experience deep-seated anxieties about threats to their position. The nature of Germany as a pre-industrial, agrarian country populated by small businesses and craftsmen, a land shaken by the crisis of 1845 to 1847, had a profound influence on the revolution. In March 1848 peasants set out in large groups. Quickly satisfied or disappointed, though usually not in a political sense, they then withdrew from events again. Small craftsmen, journeymen, apprentices and 'workers' fought on the barricades; many were permanently haunted by the nightmare of social demotion. Yet what appeared to be a struggle for new rights was often actually a fight against the decorporatization of society; against 'modernization'.

The dissolution of the old system of estates not only gave rise to back-ward-looking insecurities, but also unleashed the energy required for people to join together in forward-looking pressure groups and associations aimed at defending common interests; opportunities were also created for the formation of democratic groupings which were not necessarily linked to politics. There was now scope for groups of people to organize in accordance with statutes and rules, and to bring this shared opinion to the attention of the public in a more effective manner. Differences in the hierarchical *Stände* and cor-porations were levelled out and competing interest groups brought them closer together. When press freedom and the freedom to associ-ate were granted, it was this very *rapprochement* which allowed class barriers to emerge; acute divisions which the German population only became aware of for the first time in the year of the revolution. The rural worker found himself opposed to the peasant, the master craftsman to the journeyman, the factory worker to the day labourer, the independent freelancer to the civil servant, the constitutionalist noble landowner to the feudal mediatized prince, and, lastly and most importantly of all, the middle classes, with their property and civil servant status, found themselves opposed to the underclasses.

Defences were mobilized following the exposure of the class bar-riers: the traditional tendency to preserve the status quo as embodied by the old alliance between throne and altar and the new one between the army and the commercial middle class. A constant feature of the course of the revolution is that the realm of the citizen of the state was gradually contracted to that of the middle classes. This was clear in all the attempts to protect the state from the onslaught 'from below': in the efforts to restrict suffrage, to include the possibility of an emer-gency law in the Basic Rights, and to accept the imposition of the constitution as an emergency measure designed to protect the state;

and most starkly of all in the readiness to deploy military force against the lower middle-class and underclass movements, and the use of police methods against political associations, widely practised by the March ministries and the Provisional Central Power.

The use of the modern state's instruments of force gave rise to profound disagreements amongst the middle classes, who were divided on the issue of whether pacification or an appeal to 'the people' was the appropriate course of action. This rift extended from the March ministries down through the parliaments and to the civil guards, weakening the dynamics of the revolution as a whole.

Yet if we look solely at the crises and conflicts unleashed as a result of the modernization process, we are left with only a fragmentary picture. Equal attention should be paid to the methods and strategies adopted in the attempt to overcome these conflicts. These emerged in the spheres of the press, parties and parliaments. Once the protective shell of the *ständisch* order had lost its guiding function, a sophisticated and highly differentiated sphere of political associations sprang up in its place. On a national level, it gave rise to a basic five-part party system, which went on to develop and expand with all the refractions associated with the political press and parliamentary factions. The political associations came in wherever politics needed not simply action, but language and the formation of opinion and understanding too.

Despite the divisions exposed within it, society underwent a fundamental politicization during the year of the revolution; for the first time politics in its widest sense was brought to the lower orders, to 'popular culture' and 'everyday life', to the 'provinces' and to 'the man and woman on the street'. The elections to the parliaments, which revealed the extent of the sense of citizenship at local level, were unique in their attempts to harness political mobilization.

The assemblies formed after the elections, and above all the Frankfurt National Assembly, reflected many aspects of a fully developed parliamentary system. A parliamentary form of government was practised, factions were used to help shape opinion, extra-parliamentary influences were managed through effective committee work, and individual deputies acted as mediators for pressure groups. The ability to reach parliamentary compromise testifies to the remarkable 'maturity' of the middle classes in their dealings with political power in democratic institutions, the culmination of which was the drafting of the Basic Rights and the balanced structure of the Imperial Constitution.

Writing a constitution in 1848–9 also implied forming a nation. Here, too, the first all-German parliament was able to reach a compromise, although the original binding force of the national idea soon gave way to a juxtaposition of different competing groups. The decisions reached on the question of borders destroyed the 'Peoples' Spring' and unleashed the explosive force of the nationality principle. Nationalism began to shed its humanitarian origins and, if we are to take seriously the speeches of countless Paulskirche parliamentarians, the elected *Reichstage* of the future would be able to promise at best a hard-won co-existence, but hardly the harmonious co-operation of the future German *Reich* with its neighbouring states. The Schleswig-Holstein crisis foreshadowed events here; further conflicts were already on the horizon.

Of all the forces which were involved in the revolution, the most constant and persistent proved to be the princes and the bureaucratic and military state apparatus represented by them. References to traditional defensive attitudes apply above all to the pre-revolutionary ruling élites. Psychologically and politically, they proved to be no match for the pre-1848 crises or for the breakthrough of modernism during the revolution. Their backwardness was expressed in their refusal to surrender their monopoly on rule. After March they were able to veil this for a while in promises, in tactically determined concessions and even in conscious deception. None of the rulers of the leading German states were willing to make a constitutional compromise on the democratic basis of 1848. This was shown above all by the subsequent period of reaction, when they were able to build on the continuing 'resistance of the system consolidated between 1806 and 1815 of the monarchic administrative states and their driving forces' (Faber).[1] The royal and aristocratic apparatus of power – the state bureaucracy with the entire internal administration, diplomacy, and above all the armies of the major states – emerged from the revolution more or less intact.

The fact that the country was divided into states might, in March, have appeared to be a disadvantage for the assertion of state power. In subsequent months, however, it proved to be its greatest strength. Decentralized armies meant the revolutionaries could win apparent victory in some arenas, yet ultimately they were unable to assert themselves anywhere. One centre of action might be weakened, but the next remained sound. It was here that the European nature of the revolution's interactions and set-backs were highlighted most strikingly.

The participants in the revolution were well aware that their major problem was securing an internal loyal affirmation of the new state order from the army. However, the homage decree from the Frankfurt National Assembly and similar attempts on the part of the Berlin National Assembly, proved only that the modern state could not use legislative means to bring the instruments of militarily enforced power into the process of democratization.

With the exception of the Palatinate and Baden, certain isolated episodes in Württemberg and Saxony, and the particular situation of Vienna, the army showed itself to be inaccessible to the revolutionary challenge and superior in battle in every respect. To some extent this was already clear in the Badenese revolution in April 1848. By the autumn it was patently obvious in Frankfurt, Vienna and Berlin and, finally, in the campaign for the Imperial Constitution. This is equally true of the all European revolutionary arenas.[2] The main features of the modern state – the dependent bureaucracy and the standing armies – proved ultimately to be superior to the social emancipatory processes.

With the capitulation of the princes in 1848, and the apparently successful barricade battles in Vienna and Berlin, large sections of the public began to believe that they had been victorious. Blum's execution shattered this illusion in all political camps:

> The news that Robert Blum had been shot had the most appalling effect. Never have I seen people so utterly shocked and moved as in those days. They simply could not believe that such a thing might be possible. Such bloody justice for such a loved and illustrious victim had never been seen before, at least not in Germany. No death sentences had been passed after the uprisings in Baden or after the September uprising in Frankfurt. Because the freedom to write and speak and assemble had not been curtailed, a kind of innocent feeling of security reigned, in which even defeat in the fight against military force was not regarded as an offence which might be threatened by the most extreme consequences of retaliation.[3]

Ludwig Bamberger's memoirs, with all their personal involvement in events, reflect the fact that no one reckoned with the consistent deployment of military force against their own population; as if it might still be possible to negotiate after barricade battles, as if the March achievements could still be developed upon, despite all the evidence to the contrary from Prague and Paris after June 1848. Yet they could not conceive that this might possibly be Germany's fate too. Just as German rulers were so shocked by the unprecedented and fundamental politicization they witnessed that they kept silent in March 1848, so too did the population experience the systematic deployment of military force within the country as a break with the past. Not since the Peasant Wars had the armies of the German states been deployed in this way.

The ruling princes' backwardness was expressed in the fact that they required at least a decade after the revolution before they could begin to tolerate competing public opinion, to allow the formation of political associations, and to exploit the antagonisms within society in order to stabilize the system. Von Bismarck was a master of this kind of policy. But the society of 1862 was very different from that of the year of the revolution. The post-revolutionary policies of the governments prevented the evolutionary development of a restrictedly democratic parliamentary political system: it was simply impossible under the constitutionalist crypto-absolutism which prevailed after 1849. The breakthrough of industrialization which began in the 1850s, the so-called 'take-off', coincided with the period of most extreme reaction. Economic prosperity and domestic political suppression were not mutually exclusive. For now the apolitical *Bürger* and free economic citizen remained the official model.

Notes

Introduction: Coming to Terms with the German Revolution of 1848–9

1. Cf. W. Siemann (ed.), *Der 'Polizeiverein' deutscher Staaten, Eine Dokumentation zur Überwachung der Öffentlichkeit nach der Revolution von 1848/49* (Tübingen, 1983).
2. K. Biedermann, *Mein Leben und ein Stück Zeitgeschichte*, vol. I (Breslau, 1886), p. 344.
3. R. Haym, *Die deutsche Nationalversammlung*, 3 vols (Berlin, 1848–50).
4. Cf. L.A. von Rochau, *Grundsätze der Realpolitik*, ed. H.-U. Wehler (Frankfurt, 1972).
5. G.G. Gervinus, *Einleitung in die Geschichte des 19. Jahrhunderts*, ed. W. Boehlich (Frankfurt, 1967) p. 171; the trial is documented in detail in W. Boehlich (ed.), *Der Hochverratsprozeß gegen Gervinus* (Frankfurt, 1967); for L. Gall's biography see H.-U. Wehler (ed.), *Deutsche Historiker*, vol. 5 (Göttingen, 1972) pp. 7–26; G. Hübinger, *G.G. Gervinus* (Göttingen, 1984).
6. Wilhelm Hartwig Beseler, 20 January 1853, in Gervinus, op. cit., p. 205.
7. *MEW*, vol. 8 (1960) pp. 3–108.
8. W. Zimmermann, *Die Deutsche Revolution* (Karlsruhe, 1851, 2nd edn).
9. Cf. F. Baumgart, *Die verdrängte Revolution, Darstellung und Bewertung der Revolution von 1848 in der deutschen Geschichtsschreibung vor dem Ersten Weltkrieg* (Düsseldorf, 1976) p. 120f.; *Stenographische Berichte über die Verhandlungen des Reichstags, 9. Legislaturperiode, 5. Session* (1897/98), vol. 2, p. 1607.

10. W. Blos, *Die deutsche Revolution, Geschichte der deutschen Bewegung von 1848 und 1849*, ed. H.J. Schütz (Stuttgart, 1893; reprinted Berlin, 1978); E. Bernstein, *Geschichte der Berliner Arbeiterbewegung*, 3 vols (Berlin, 1907–10), especially vol. 1, pp. 1–68; F. Mehring, *Geschichte der deutschen Sozialdemokratie*, 2 vols (Stuttgart, 1921), especially vol. 2, pp. 1–194; cf. also Baumgart, op. cit., p. 158f.

11. H. Oncken, 'Zur Genesis der preußischen Revolution von 1848 (1900)', p. 3, in H. Oncken (ed.), *Historisch-politische Aufsätze und Reden*, vol. 2 (Munich, 1914), pp. 3–34.

12. B. Faulenbach, *Ideologie des deutschen Weges: Die deutsche Geschichte in der Historiographie zwischen Kaiserreich und Nationalsozialismus* (Munich, 1980), especially pp. 54–60 and 114–21.

13. E. Troeltsch, *Spektator-Briefe: Aufsätze über die deutsche Revolution und die Weltpolitik, 1918/22* (Tübingen, 1924), p. 16.

14. V. Valentin, *Geschichte der deutschen Revolution von 1848–1849*, 2 vols (Berlin, 1930–1; reprinted Cologne, 1970); for biographical details, see E. Fehrenbach in Wehler (ed.), *Historiker*, vol. 1 (1981), pp. 69–85; H.-U. Wehler, *Historische Sozialwissenschaft und Geschichtsforschung: Studien zu Aufgaben und Traditionen deutscher Geschichtswissenschaft* (Göttingen, 1980) pp. 292–7.

15. H. Rosenberg, *R. Haym und die Anfänge des klassischen Liberalismus* (Munich, 1933); H. Rosenberg, *Die Weltwirtschaftskrisis von 1857–1859* (Stuttgart, 1934; 2nd edn, Göttingen, 1974).

16. *Vormärz* literally means 'before March', meaning before the outbreak of the revolution in March 1848, and is used to describe the period leading up to the revolution, usually from about 1830, but sometimes extending back to 1815.

17. H. Stein, 'Pauperismus und Assoziation, Soziale Tatsachen und Ideen auf dem westeuropäischen Kontinent vom Ende des 18. bis Mitte des 19. Jahrhunderts', in *International Review for Social History*, 1 (1936) pp. 1–120.

18. Cf. introduction and examples of texts at the beginning of the collection edited by D. Langewiesche, *Die deutsche Revolution von 1848/49* (Darmstadt, 1983).

19. R. Stadelmann, *Soziale und politische Geschichte der Revolution von 1848* (Munich, 1948; 2nd edn, 1970); R. Stadelmann, 'Das Jahr 1848 und die deutsche Geschichte', in Langewiesche (ed.), *Revolution*, pp. 21–38.

20. G. Wollstein, '1848 – Streit um das Erbe', in *NPL*, 20 (1975), pp. 491–507; *NPL*, 21 (1976), pp. 89–106.

21. K. Obermann (ed.), *Flugblätter der Revolution: Eine Flugblattsammlung zur Geschichte der Revolution von 1848/49 in Deutschland* (Berlin, 1970; abridged paperback edn Munich, 1972).

22. *Illustrierte Geschichte der deutschen Revolution, 1848/49* (Berlin, 1973) p. 366; cf. also Langewiesche (ed.), *Revolution*, pp. 8f.

23. G.W. Heinemann, 'Die Freiheitsbewegung [!] in der deutschen Geschichte, Ansprache aus Anlaß der Eröffnung der Erinnerungsstätte in Rastatt, Rastatt 26. Juni 1974', in G.W. Heinemann (ed.), *Reden und Schriften*, vol. 1 (Frankfurt, 1975) p. 43; cf. P. Münch, 'Geschichte und Demokratie. Zu Inhalt und Funktion demokratischer Traditionen in den Reden des Bundespräsidenten Gustav W. Heinemann 1969–1974', in H. Rabe *et al.* (eds), *Festgabe E. W. Zeeden* (Münster, 1976) pp. 481–503, which also includes a letter by Heinemann on the issue of power (see ibid., p. 503).

24. Valentin, op. cit., vol. 2, p. 534.

25. All quotations from K.-G. Faber, *Deutsche Geschichte im 19. Jahrhundert: Restauration und Revolution, 1815–1851* (Wiesbaden, 1979) pp. 221, 271ff.

26. For an important early example, see K. Repgen, *Märzbewegung und Maiwahlen des Revolutionsjahres 1848 im Rheinland* (Bonn, 1955).

27. W. Conze (ed.), *Staat und Gesellschaft im deutschen Vormärz 1815–1848* (Stuttgart, 1962; 2nd edn, 1970); F. Balser, *Sozial-Demokratie 1848/49–1863, Die erste deutsche Arbeiterorganisation 'Allgemeine deutsche Arbeiterverbrüderung' nach der Revolution*, 2 vols (Stuttgart, 1962; 2nd edn, 1965).

28. Cf. H.-U. Wehler (ed.), *Sozialgeschichte Heute, Festschrift H. Rosenberg* (Göttingen, 1974).

29. C., L. and R. Tilly, *The Rebellious Century, 1830–1930* (London, 1975); R. Tilly, *Kapital, Staat und sozialer Protest in der deutschen Industrialisierung* (Göttingen, 1980); H. Volkmann and J. Bergmann (eds), *Sozialer Protest: Studien zu traditioneller Resistenz und kollektiver Gewalt in Deutschland vom Vormärz bis zur Reichsgründung* (Opladen, 1984); for an important example of the day-to-day history of the revolutionary period, see W. Kaschuba and C. Lipp, *1848 – Provinz und Revolution: Kultureller Wandel und soziale Bewegung im Königreich Württemberg* (Tübingen, 1979).

30. An excellent, comprehensive and informative survey of the current state of research, on-going debates and open research issues is given in D. Langewiesche, 'Die Deutsche Revolution von 1848/49 und die vorrevolutionäre Gesellschaft. Forschungsstand

und Forschungsperspektiven', in *AfS*, 21 (1981) pp. 458–98, continued in *AfS*, 31 (1991) pp. 331–443.

31. S. Schmidt (ed.), *Politik und Ideologie des bürgerlichen Liberalismus im Revolutionszyklus zwischen 1789 und 1917* (Jena, 1983); see also J. Schradi, *Die DDR-Geschichtswissenschaft und das bürgerliche Erbe: Das deutsche Bürgertum und die Revolution von 1848 im sozialistischen Geschichtsverständnis* (Frankfurt, 1984), especially pp. 217, 237–44.

32. Cf. G.P. Meyer, 'Revolutionstheorien heute: Ein kritischer Überblick in historischer Absicht', *GG Sonderheft*, 2 (1976) pp. 122–76.

33. Gervinus, op. cit., p. 170.

34. Langewiesche (ed.), *Revolution*, p. 11.

Chapter 1   German Society before 1848

1. Cf. W. Conze, 'Adel', in W. Conze *et al.* (eds), *Geschichtliche Grundbegriffe. Historisches Lexikon zur politisch-sozialen Sprache in Deutschland*, vol. 1 (Stuttgart, 1972) p. 28.

2. E.R. Huber (ed.), *Dokumente zur deutschen Verfassungsgeschichte*, vol. 1 (Stuttgart, 1978, 3rd edn) p. 88 (pagination differs in earlier editions); H. Gollwitzer, *Die Standesherren. Die politische und gesellschaftliche Stellung der Mediatisierten, 1815–1918* (Göttingen, 1964, 2nd edn).

3. E.R. Huber, *Deutsche Verfassungsgeschichte seit 1789*, vol. 2 (Stuttgart, 1960, 2nd edn, reprinted 1975) p. 483, cf. pp. 338f.

4. Cf. Gollwitzer, op. cit., pp. 83–97; C. Dipper, *Die Bauernbefreiung in Deutschland, 1790–1850* (Stuttgart, 1980) p. 68; for a discussion of the problems experienced by the aristocracy as a class in competition with the middle classes, whose behaviour conformed more readily to bureaucratic standards, see H. Reif, *Westfälischer Adel, 1770–1860: Vom Herrschaftsstand zur regionalen Elite* (Göttingen, 1979) esp. pp. 375–98.

5. Cf. R. Koselleck, *Preußen zwischen Reform und Revolution, Allgemeines Landrecht, Verwaltung und soziale Bewegung, 1791–1848* (Stuttgart, 1967, 1981 3rd edn) pp. 514–16.

6. For a general discussion, see J. Kocka, *Unternehmer in der deutschen Industrialisierung* (Göttingen, 1975).

7. *Die Gegenwart*, vol. 3 (Leipzig, 1849) p. 37.

8. Cf. H. Henning, *Die deutsche Beamtenschaft im 19. Jahrhundert* (Stuttgart, 1984); W. Heindl, 'Die österreichische Bürokratie.

Zwischen deutscher Vorherrschaft und österreichischer Staats-
idee (Vormärz und Neoabsolutismus)', in H. Lutz and H. Rumpler (eds), *Österreich und die deutsche Frage im 19. und 20. Jahrhundert*
(Munich, 1982) pp. 73–91.

9. For regional variations see Henning, op. cit., pp. 37–52, 149–51;
Dipper, op. cit., p. 62.

10. B. Schimetschek, *Der österreichische Beamte* (Munich, 1984) p. 150.

11. Valentin, op. cit., vol. 1, p. 110.

12. H. Brandt, *Landständische Repräsentation im deutschen Vormärz: Poli-
tisches Denken im Einflußfeld des monarchischen Prinzips* (Neuwied
1968) p. 36; cf. P.M. Ehrle, *Volksvertretung im Vormärz* (Frankfurt,
1979) pp. 789–817.

13. Quoted in Huber (ed.), *Dokumente*, vol. 1, pp. 324–6.

14. For a social history of the freelance intelligentsia, see H.H. Gerth,
*Bürgerliche Intelligenz um 1800. Zur Soziologie des deutschen Frühlibera-
lismus* (Göttingen, 1976); R. Engelsing, *Arbeit, Zeit und Werk im
literarischen Beruf* (Göttingen, 1976).

15. W.H. Riehl, *Die deutsche Gesellschaft* (Stuttgart, 1854, 2nd edn)
pp. 304–41.

16. Cf. W. Schieder, 'Der rheinpfälzische Liberalismus von 1832 als
politische Protestbewegung', esp. pp. 193f., in H. Berding *et al.*
(eds), *Festschrift T. Schieder* (Munich, 1978) pp. 169–95;
W. Schieder (ed.), *Liberalismus in der Gesellschaft des deutschen Vormärz* (Göttingen, 1983) (= *GG Sonderheft 9*).

17. Quoted in Huber (ed.), *Dokumente*, vol. 1, pp. 323f.

18. See the discussion in D. Fricke (ed.), *Deutsche Demokraten. Die
nichtproletarischen demokratischen Kräfte in Deutschland, 1830–1945*
(Berlin/Cologne, 1981), esp. pp. xi–xx, 26–31.

19. H. Sedatis, *Liberalismus und Handwerk Südwestdeutschland, Wirt-
schafts- und Gesellschaftskonzeptionen des Liberalismus und die Krise des
Handwerks im 19. Jahrhundert* (Stuttgart, 1979) p. 221; the distinction between 'Kleinbürger' and 'workers' is made by J. Bergmann, 'Soziallage, Selbstverständnis und Aktionsformen der
Arbeiter in der Revolution von 1848', p. 284, in Volkmann and
Bergmann (eds), op. cit., pp. 283–303.

20. Cf. J.J. Sheehan, *Der deutsche Liberalismus, 1770–1914* (Munich,
1983) pp. 29f.

21. Sedatis, op. cit., p. 122.

22. The standard work on this complex issue is U. Engelhardt
(ed.), *Handwerker in der Industrialisierung. Lage, Kultur und Politik
vom späten 18. bis ins frühe 20. Jahrhundert* (Stuttgart, 1984).

See also the sections in this work specifically on the *Vormärz* period and the revolution by J. Bergmann, C. Lipp and W. Kaschuba.

23. W. Conze, 'Sozialgeschichte, 1800–1850', p. 437, in H. Aubin and W. Zorn (eds), *Handbuch der deutschen Wirtschafts- und Sozialgeschichte*, vol. 2 (Stuttgart, 1976) pp. 426–94.

24. For a general discussion, see Dipper, op. cit., pp. 50–92; G. Franz, 'Die agrarische Bewegung im Jahre 1848', in *Zeitschrift für Agrargeschichte und Agrarsoziologie*, 7 (1959) pp. 176–93; R. Koch, 'Die Agrarrevolution in Deutschland 1848', in Langewiesche (ed.), *Revolution*, pp. 362–94.

25. Franz, 'Agrarbewegung', p. 186.

26. Ibid.

27. W. Conze, 'Vom "Pöbel" zum "Proletariat". Sozialgeschichtliche Voraussetzungen für den Sozialismus in Deutschland', in *VSWG*, 41(1954) pp. 332–64.

28. The seminal work on the subject is J. Kocka, *Lohnarbeit und Klassenbildung, Arbeiter und Arbeiterbewegung in Deutschland, 1800–1875* (Berlin, 1983), esp. pp. 71–123. A remarkable survey by a contemporary is cited in Reuter, 'Verhältnisse und Lage der handarbeitenden Volksklassen in den deutschen Gegenden des mittleren Rhein- und unteren Main- und Neckar-Gebietes', in *Zeitschrift des Vereins für Deutsche Statistik*, 1 (1847) pp. 359–81. For a social history of the lower orders, see also H. Mommsen and W. Schulze (eds), *Vom Elend der Handarbeit. Probleme historischer Unterschichtenforschung* (Stuttgart, 1981); R. Engelsing, *Zur Sozialgeschichte deutscher Mittel- und Unterschichten* (Göttingen, 1978, 2nd edn); for extensive source material and literary quotations, see J. Kuczynski, *Geschichte des Alltags des deutschen Volkes*, vol. 3: 1810–1870 (Cologne, 1981).

29. Conze, 'Sozialgeschichte', pp. 440f.; G. Hardach discusses the problems associated with previous statistics in 'Klassen und Schichten in Deutschland 1848–1970, Probleme einer historischen Strukturanalyse', in *GG*, 3 (1977) pp. 503–24.

30. Cf. H.-J. Ruckhäberle (ed.), *Frühproletarische Literatur. Die Flugschriften der deutschen Handwerksgesellenvereine in Paris, 1832–1839* (Kronberg, 1977); H.-J Ruckhäberle (ed.), *Bildung und Organisation in den deutschen Handwerksgesellen- und Arbeitervereinen in der Schweiz, Texte und Dokumente zur Kultur der deutschen Handwerker und Arbeiter 1834–1845* (Tübingen, 1983); see also Kocka, *Lohnarbeit*, pp. 96–110; Kocka (ed.), *Europäische Arbeiterbewegungen im 19.*

Jahrhundert, Deutschland, Österreich, England und Frankreich im Vergleich (Göttingen, 1983).

31. K. Tenfelde, *Sozialgeschichte der Bergarbeiterschaft an der Ruhr im 19. Jahrhundert* (Bonn-Bad Godesberg, 1977), esp. p. 160.

32. The recruitment of factory workers is discussed by H.-J. Rupieper, 'Regionale Herkunft, Fluktuation und innerbetriebliche Mobilität der Arbeiterschaft der Maschinenfabrik Augsburg-Nürnberg (MAN) 1844–1944', in W. Conze and U. Engelhardt (eds), *Arbeiter im Industrialisierungsprozeß. Herkunft, Lage und Verhalten* (Stuttgart, 1979) pp. 94–112; H. Zwahr, *Zur Konstituierung des Proletariats als Klasse, Strukturuntersuchung über das Leipziger Proletariat während der industriellen Revolution* (Berlin, 1978).

33. Cf. Kocka, *Lohnarbeit*, pp. 73–6; Reuter, op. cit., pp. 370–4; for a discussion of servants' protests see G. Hummel-Haasis (ed.), *Schwestern, zerreißt eure Ketten. Zeugnisse zur Geschichte der Frauen in der Revolution von 1848/49* (Munich, 1982) pp. 97, 172f.; see also H. Müller, *Dienstbare Geister, Leben und Arbeitswelt städtischer Dienstboten* (Berlin, 1981).

34. R. Wirtz, *'Widersetzlichkeiten, Excesse, Crawalle, Tumulte und Skandale'; Soziale Bewegung und gewalthafter sozialer Protest in Baden, 1815–1848* (Frankfurt, 1981).

Chapter 2   Middle-Class Organization and Social Protest

1. Cf. W. Siemann, *'Deutschlands Ruhe, Sicherheit und Ordnung': Die Anfänge der politischen Polizei, 1806–1866* (Tübingen, 1985).

2. Valentin, op. cit. vol. 1, p. 114.

3. Cf. Th. Nipperdey, 'Verein als soziale Struktur in Deutschland im späten 18. und frühen 19. Jahrhundert', in Th. Nipperdey, *Gesellschaft, Kultur, Theorie* (Göttingen, 1976) pp. 174–205. W. Hardtwig gives the standard account of the current state of research in 'Strukturmerkmale und Entwicklungstendenzen des Vereinswesens in Deutschland 1789–1848', in *HZ Beiheft*, 9 (1984) pp. 11–50.

4. E. Illner, *Bürgerliche Organisierung in Elberfeld, 1775–1850* (Neustadt/Aisch, 1982).

5. Ibid., p. 203.

6. H. Volkmann, 'Protestträger und Protestformen in den Unruhen 1830–1832', in Volkmann and Bergmann (eds), op. cit., pp. 56–75.

7. J. Bergmann, 'Ökonomische Voraussetzungen der Revolution von 1848. Zur Krise von 1845 bis 1848 in Deutschland', in *GG Sonderheft*, 2 (1976) pp. 254–87.

8. W. Conze, 'Sozialer und wirtschaftlicher Wandel', p. 34 in K.G.A. Jeserich *et al.* (eds), *Deutsche Verwaltungsgeschichte*, vol. 2 (Stuttgart, 1983) pp. 19–56; seminal as regards detail: R. Spree and J. Bergmann, 'Die konjunkturelle Entwicklung der deutschen Wirtschaft, 1840–1864', in Wehler (ed.), *Sozialgeschichte Heute*, pp. 289–325; R. Spree, *Die Wachstumszyklen der deutschen Wirtschaft 1840–1880* (Berlin, 1977); Bergmann, 'Voraussetzungen'.

9. Valentin, op. cit. vol. 1, p. 58.

10. D. Langewiesche, *Liberalismus und Demokratie in Württemberg zwischen Revolution und Reichsgründung* (Düsseldorf, 1974), 87.

11. Cf. K. Obermann, 'Wirtschafts- und sozialpolitische Aspekte der Krise von 1845–1847 in Deutschland, insbesondere in Preußen', in *Jahrbuch für Geschichte*, 7 (1972) pp. 141–74.

Chapter 3   The European Point of Departure, 1847–8

1. H. Stuke and W. Forstmann (eds), *Die europäischen Revolutionen von 1848* (Königstein, 1979); see also P.N. Stearns, *1848: The Revolutionary Tide in Europe* (New York, 1974); W. Schmidt *et al.*, 'Die europäischen Revolutionen 1848/49', in M. Kossok (ed.), *Revolutionen der Neuzeit, 1500–1917* (Berlin/Vaduz, 1982) pp. 271–348.

2. F. Engels, 6 March, 1895, Preface to K. Marx, *Die Klassenkämpfe in Frankreich, 1848–1850*, in *MEW*, vol. 7 (1960) p. 512.

3. Huber, *Verfassungsgeschichte*, vol. 2, pp. 661–6.

4. Quoted in Huber (ed.), *Dokumente*, vol. 1, pp. 589f.

5. *Neue Würzburger Zeitung*, no. 217, dated 7 August 1845, cited by D. Düding, *Organisierter gesellschaftlicher Nationalismus in Deutschland, 1808–1847. Bedeutung und Funktion der Turner- und Sängervereine für die deutsche Nationalbewegung* (Munich, 1984) p. 272. My remarks on the national song festivals are based on Düding.

6. Cf. E. Labrousse, 'Panorama der Krise', in *Stuke and Forstmann* (eds), op. cit., pp. 70–89; M. Agulhon, *The Republican Experiment, 1848–1852* (Cambridge, 1983; in French, Paris, 1973); R. Price (ed.), *Revolution and Reaction: 1848 and the Second French Republic* (London, 1975).

Chapter 4   The March and April Revolutions of 1848

1. Quoted in H. Fenske (ed.), *Vormärz und Revolution, 1840–1849* (Darmstadt, 1976) pp. 264f.
2. For revolutionary events in individual German states, see the relevant articles on each state in *Die Gegenwart*, 12 vols (Leipzig, 1848–56) (overall survey, vol. 12, pp. xiii–xviii).
3. See essays by Franz and Koch referred to above.
4. Valentin, op. cit., vol. 1, p. 357.
5. See Huber, *Verfassungsgeschichte*, vol. 2, pp. 666–8; Frederick VII's letter and the Kiel announcement are cited in Huber (ed.), *Dokumente*, vol. 1, pp. 591–93.
6. Cf. W. Häusler, *Von der Massenarmut zur Arbeiterbewegung. Demokratie und soziale Frage in der Wiener Revolution von 1848* (Vienna, 1976), esp. pp. 139–45.
7. D. Dowe discusses the events of 3 March in Cologne in *Aktion und Organisation, Arbeiterbewegung, sozialistische und kommunistische Bewegung in der preußischen Rheinprovinz 1820–1852* (Hanover, 1970) pp. 133–6.
8. Quoted in Huber (ed.), *Dokumente*, vol. 1, pp. 445f.
9. K.A. Varnhagen von Ense, *Tagebücher*, vol. 2 (Leipzig, 1863, 2nd edn) p. 291.
10. O. von Bismarck, 'Erinnerung und Gedanke', in O. v. Bismarck, *Die gesammelten Werke*, vol. 15, p. 22, cited in Huber (ed.), *Dokumente*, vol. 1, p. 450; text of address, ibid.
11. Ibid., p. 450.
12. Ibid., pp. 448f.
13. Cf. Koch, 'Agrarrevolution', pp. 371f.
14. Cf. W. Real, *Die Revolution in Baden 1848/49* (Stuttgart, 1983).
15. Valentin, op. cit., vol. 2, pp. 482f.
16. W. Boldt, *Die Anfänge des deutschen Parteiwesens. Fraktionen, politische Vereine und Parteien in der Revolution 1848* (Paderborn, 1971) pp. 148–50.

Chapter 5   The Legitimization of the Revolution

1. Wording of statutes and bans in Boldt, op. cit., pp. 147–50.
2. Valentin, op. cit., vol. 1, p. 352.
3. *Deutsche Chronik für das Jahr 1849 (1850)*, vol. 1, p. 144.
4. Quoted in Huber (ed.), *Dokumente*, vol. 1, pp. 325–28.

5. Letter of invitation of 12 March 1848, quoted ibid., p. 328.
6. Ibid., p. 327.
7. Cf. M. Botzenhart, *Deutscher Parlamentarismus in der Revolutionszeit 1848–1850* (Düsseldorf, 1977) p. 117.
8. Quoted in Huber (ed.), *Dokumente*, vol. 1, pp. 332–4; for the debate too, see Fenske (ed.), op. cit., pp. 276–94.
9. Cf. Botzenhart, op. cit., pp. 124f.
10. Cf. Huber, *Verfassungsgeschichte*, vol. 2, pp. 602f.
11. This takes into account the slight difference between Botzenhart's statements, p. 156: up to 25% of mature men were excluded, and p. 157: 'at least 80% were entitled to vote'.
12. Cf. ibid., pp. 152 and 157.
13. See the analysis of delegates in D. Langewiesche, 'Die politische Vereinsbewegung in Würzburg und in Unterfranken in den Revolutionsjahren 1848/49' (p. 205f.), in *Jahrbuch für fränkische Landesforschung*, 37 (1977) pp. 195–233.
14. Botzenhart, op. cit., p. 163.
15. Cf. Huber, *Verfassungsgeschichte*, vol. 2, p. 554.
16. Cf. K. Obermann, 'Die österreichischen Reichstagswahlen 1848. Eine Studie zu Fragen der sozialen Struktur und Wahlbeteiligung auf der Grundlage der Wahlakten', in *MÖStA*, 26 (1973) pp. 342–74.

Chapter 6 Political Associations and Middle-Class Pressure Groups

1. Cf. D. Langewiesche, 'Die Anfänge der deutschen Parteien. Partei, Fraktion und Verein in der Revolution von 1848/49', in *GG*, 4 (1978) pp. 324–61; Botzenhart, op. cit., pp. 315–414; Boldt, op. cit.
2. H. von Gagern, 8 November 1847 to R. Eigenbrodt, in P. Wentzcke and W. Klötzer (eds), *Deutscher Liberalismus im Vormärz. Heinrich von Gagern, Briefe und Reden, 1815–1848* (Göttingen, 1959) p. 405.
3. Langewiesche, 'Forschungsstand', p. 470.
4. W. Schieder, 'Die Rolle der deutschen Arbeiter in der Revolution von 1848/49', p. 46, in W. Klötzer *et al.* (eds) *Ideen und Strukturen der deutschen Revolution 1848* (Frankfurt, 1974) pp. 43–56; cf. also Bergmann, 'Arbeiter 1848'.

5. M. Simon, *Handwerk in Krise und Umbruch, Wirtschaftspolitische Forderungen und sozialpolitische Vorstellungen der Handwerksmeister im Revolutionsjahr 1848/49* (Cologne, 1983).

6. *Die Verbrüderung, Correspondenzblatt aller deutschen Arbeiter, 1848–50* (reprinted Leipzig, 1975), 3 October 1848, p. 2.

7. Its correspondence is included in H. Schlechte (ed.), *Die Allgemeine Deutsche Arbeiterverbrüderung, 1848–1850: Dokumente des Zentralkomitees für die deutschen Arbeiter in Leipzig* (Weimar, 1979).

8. Balser, op. cit., vol. 1, pp. 72–5.

9. Manifesto of 2nd September1848. Quoted in Huber (ed.), *Dokumente*, vol. 1, pp. 454–6.

10. All available texts are in *Der Bund der Kommunisten, Dokumente und Materialien*, 3 vols (Berlin, 1970–84; vol. 1, 2nd edn 1983).

11. Ibid., vol. 1, p. 626.

12. Ibid., vol. 1, p. 739–41.

13. Cf. E.G.Franz, 'Die Hessischen Arbeitervereine im Rahmen der politischen Arbeiterbewegung der Jahre 1848–1850', esp. pp. 174–97, in *Archiv für hess. Geschichte und Altertumskunde New Series*, 33 (1975) pp. 167–262.

14. Schlechte (ed.), op. cit., p. 26.

15. Dowe, op. cit., p. 291.

16. *Zeitung des Arbeiter-Vereines zu Köln* (1848; reprinted Glashütten, 1976).

17. Cf. survey in *Botzenhart*, op. cit., pp. 402f.

18. The *organizational* division into a democratic and republican party which is occasionally attempted is somewhat artificial for 1848; according to this scheme, neither of the democratic congresses would be classed as democratic, though the 'Central March Association' would.

19. Quoted in Boldt, op. cit., pp. 117–20.

20. Botzenhart, op. cit., p. 331.

21. Quoted in Boldt, op. cit., pp. 144–6.

22. Transcript of proceedings and list of participants in G. Becker, 'Das Protokoll des ersten Demokratenkongresses vom Juni 1848', in *Jahrbuch für Geschichte*, 8 (1973) pp. 379–405.

23. Cf. R. Koch, *Demokratie und Staat bei Julius Fröbel, 1805–1893: Liberales Denken zwischen Naturrecht und Sozialdarwinismus* (Wiesbaden, 1978).

24. Cf. J. Paschen, *Demokratische Vereine und preußischer Staat, Entwicklung und Unterdrückung der demokratischen Bewegung während der Revolution von 1848/49* (Munich, 1977) pp. 90f.

25. List of participants in G. Lüders, *Die demokratische Bewegung in Berlin im Oktober 1848* (Berlin, 1909) pp. 164–7.
26. Paschen, op. cit., pp. 98; for a general statement on the democratic congress, see also pp. 96–112.
27. Botzenhart, op. cit., pp. 402f.
28. Cf. Botzenhart, op. cit., p. 376; Langewiesche, 'Anfänge', p. 361.
29. Botzenhart, op. cit., p. 333.
30. Quoted ibid., p. 385.
31. Cf. H. Gebhardt, *Revolution und liberale Bewegung, Die nationale Organisation der konstitutionellen Partei in Deutschland 1848/49* (Bremen, 1974) pp. 36f.
32. Ibid., p. 86; Botzenhart, op. cit., p. 390.
33. 'Resolution des Nationalen Vereins 16.5.1849 an die Paulskirche', in F. Wigard (ed.), *Stenographischer Bericht über die Verhandlungen der deutschen constituirenden Nationalversammlung*, vol. 9 (Frankfurt, 1849) p. 6599.
34. Cited by Gebhardt, op. cit., p. 16.
35. Cf. Huber, *Verfassungsgeschichte*, vol. 2, pp. 685–7; F. Schnabel, *Der Zusammenschluß des politischen Katholizismus in Deutschland im Jahre 1848* (Heidelberg, 1910) pp. 44f.
36. Quoted in E.R. and W. Huber (eds), *Staat und Kirche im 19. und 20. Jahrhundert, Dokumente zur Geschichte des deutschen Staatskirchenrechts*, vol. 2 (Berlin, 1976) pp. 12–14.
37. Boldt's collection.
38. *Neue Preußische Zeitung*, no. 53, 31 August 1848, cited by Botzenhart, op. cit., p. 392.
39. Paschen, op. cit., p. 91.
40. Cf. Botzenhart, op. cit., p. 394.
41. From the Staatsarchiv Potsdam Pr.Br.Rep. 30 Berlin C Polizeipräsidium Tit.95 Sect. 5, no. 15476/77; cf. H. Fischer, 'Der "Treubund mit Gott für König und Vaterland", Ein Beitrag zur Reaktion in Preußen', in *Jahrbuch für die Geschichte Mittel- und Ostdeutschlands*, 24 (1975) pp. 60–127.
42. Botzenhart, op. cit., pp. 397f.
43. See the survey in Faber, *Geschichte*, pp. 235–7.
44. Cf. H. Thielbeer, *Universität und Politik in der Deutschen Revolution von 1848* (Bonn, 1983).
45. G. Schulz, 'Über Entstehung und Formen von Interessengruppen in Deutschland seit der Industrialisierung', in H.J. Varain (ed.), *Interessenverbände in Deutschland* (Cologne, 1973) pp. 25–54.
46. Conze, 'Sozialgeschichte', p. 471.

Chapter 7 Communication and the Public

1. Cf. Huber (ed.), *Dokumente*, vol. 1, p. 391.
2. Valentin, op. cit., vol. 1, p. 177.
3. *Börsenblatt für den deutschen Buchhandel*, no. 25 (28 March 1848) p. 355.
4. A. Prinz, *Der Buchhandel, 1843–1853* (Hamburg, 1855) pp. 26–8, cited by R. Wittmann, *Buchmarkt und Lektüre, Beiträge zum literarischen Leben, 1750–1880* (Tübingen, 1982) p. 118.
5. Cited by W. Schulte, *Volk und Staat: Westfalen im Vormärz und in der Revolution, 1848/49* (Münster, 1954) p. 251.
6. Cf. M. Scharfe, 'Revolution als Kommunikationsprozeß: 1848/49', in H. Bausinger and E. Moser-Rath (eds), *Direkte Kommunikation und Massenkommunikation* (Tübingen, 1976) pp. 59f.
7. Cf. H. Tauschwitz, *Presse und Revolution 1848/49 in Baden* (Heidelberg, 1981); Schulte, op. cit., pp. 251–58.
8. Cf. survey in H.D. Fischer, *Handbuch der politischen Presse in Deutschland, 1480–1980* (Düsseldorf, 1981) pp. 186–204.
9. *Das Volk, Organ des Central-Komitees für Arbeiter, Eine social-politische Zeitschrift* (Berlin, 1848; reprinted Glashütten, 1973).
10. For further information on the *Neue Rheinische Zeitung*, see *MEW* vols 5 and 6; K. Koszyk, *Deutsche Presse im 19. Jahrhundert* (Berlin, 1966) p. 116.
11. L. Bergsträßer, 'Entstehung und Entwicklung der Partei-Korrespondenzen in Deutschland im Jahre 1848/49', p. 22, in *Zeitungswissenschaft*, 8 (1933) pp. 12–25.
12. Cf. B. Mann, *Die Württemberger und die deutsche Nationalversammlung 1848/49* (Düsseldorf, 1975) p. 397; E. Sieber, *Stadt und Universität Tübingen, in der Revolution von 1848/49* (Tübingen, 1975) pp. 86f. See also the holdings of the reading room of the Würzburg Volksverein in Langewiesche, 'Vereinsbewegung', pp. 215f.
13. Cf. R. Engelsing, *Analphabetentum und Lektüre, Zur Sozialgeschichte des Lesens in Deutschland zwischen feudaler und industrieller Welt* (Stuttgart, 1973) p. 97.
14. Häusler, op. cit., p. 168; see also Obermann's collection; G. Otruba, *Wiener Flugschriften zur Sozialen Frage 1848*, 2 vols (Vienna, 1978/80); S. Weigel, *Flugschriftenliteratur 1848 in Berlin* (Stuttgart, 1979).
15. Cf. Huber, *Verfassungsgeschichte*, vol. 2, pp. 345 and 733.
16. Figures given by V. Valentin, *Frankfurt a.M. und die Revolution von 1848/49* (Stuttgart, 1908) pp. 536–8.

17. Cf. B. James and W. Mossmann (eds), *Glasbruch 1848, Flugblattlieder und Dokumente einer zerbrochenen Revolution* (Darmstadt, 1983); U. Otto, *Die historisch-politischen Lieder und Karikaturen des Vormärz und der Revolution von 1848/49* (Cologne, 1982).
18. Sieber, op. cit., p. 87.
19. Schulte, op. cit., pp. 307f.; cf. H. Denkler (ed.), *Der deutsche Michel. Revolutionskomödien der Achtundvierziger* (Stuttgart, 1979); H. Denkler (ed.), *Berliner Straßenecken-Literatur 1848/49* (Stuttgart, 1977).
20. E. Hilscher, *Die Bilderbogen im 19. Jahrhundert* (Munich, 1977).

Chapter 8   The Paulskirche and the Parliaments

1. Quoted in Boldt, op. cit., p. 200.
2. Zimmermann, op. cit., p. 743.
3. Cf. Botzenhart, op. cit., p. 705.
4. The generally acknowledged standard work on the subject is M. Schwarz, *MdR, Biographisches Handbuch der Reichstage* (Hanover, 1965) pp. 43–112; cf. Botzenhart, op. cit., p. 161.
5. Cf. W. Siemann, *Die Frankfurter Nationalversammlung 1848/49 zwischen demokratischem Liberalismus und konservativer Reform* (Frankfurt, 1976); W. Fiedler (ed.), *Die erste deutsche Nationalversammlung 1848/49, Handschriftliche Selbstzeugnisse ihrer Mitglieder* (Königstein, 1980), in particular the Introduction, pp. 10–41.
6. Cf. Langewiesche, 'Anfänge'; Botzenhart, op. cit.; Mann, op. cit.
7. Cf. G. Hildebrandt (ed.), *Opposition in der Paulskirche. Reden, Briefe und Berichte kleinbürgerlich-demokratischer Parlamentarier, 1848/49* (Berlin, 1981); G. Hildebrandt, *Parlamentsopposition auf Linkskurs* (Berlin, 1975).
8. G. Eisenmann, *Die Parteyen der teutschen Reichsversammlung, ihre Programme, Statuten und Mitgliederverzeichnisse* (Erlangen, 1848) p. 5.
9. Ibid., p. 6.
10. Cf. Botzenhart, op. cit., p. 162.
11. This vote is specifically dealt with by H. Best, *Interessenpolitik und nationale Integration 1848/49, Handelspolitische Konflikte im frühindustriellen Deutschland* (Göttingen, 1980) p. 272.
12. Analyses of votes in Siemann, *Nationalversammlung*, pp. 289–303.
13. Cf. M. Peter, 'Der Konflikt in Schleswig-Holstein (1846–1852) im Spiegel der englischen Presse', Dissertation (Würzburg, 1972).

14. Cf. H.-G. Kraume, *Außenpolitik 1848. Die holländische Provinz Limburg in der deutschen Revolution* (Düsseldorf, 1979) p. 223; Langewiesche, 'Forschungsstand', p. 462f.

15. Cited in Siemann, '*Deutschlands Ruhe*', p. 227.

16. Ibid., esp. pp. 223–6.

17. 'G. Beseler als Ausschußsprecher für die Grundrechte', in Wigard (ed.), op. cit., vol. 1, pp. 700f.

18. Cf. W. Siemann, 'Wirtschaftsliberalismus 1848/49 zwischen Sozialverpflichtung und Konkurrenzprinzip. Zur Debatte über das "Recht auf Arbeit" in der "Paulskirche"', in Rabe *et al.* (eds), op. cit., pp. 407–32.

19. Cf. L. Gall, 'Liberalismus und "bürgerliche Gesellschaft", Zu Charakter und Entwicklung der liberalen Bewegung in Deutschland', in *HZ*, 220 (1975) pp. 324–56.

20. Quoted in Huber (ed.), *Dokumente*, vol. 1, p. 348.

21. D. J. Mattheisen, 'Die Fraktionen der preußischen Nationalversammlung von 1848', p. 158, in K.H. Jarausch (ed.), *Quantifizierung in der Geschichtswissenschaft* (Düsseldorf, 1976) pp. 149–67.

22. Cited by Huber, *Verfassungsgeschichte*, vol. 2, p. 725.

23. Ibid., p. 585.

24. Wigard (ed.), op. cit., vol. 1, pp. 576–81, where it is mistakenly given as 577:31 (ibid., p. 581).

25. Huber, *Verfassungsgeschichte*, vol. 2, p. 743.

26. Valentin, op. cit., vol. 2, p. 88.

27. Ibid., p. 190; cf. *Das Jahr 1848 in Oberösterreich und Hans Kudlich*, 2 vols (Katalog/Berichte und Reflexionen) (Linz, 1978).

28. Botzenhart, op. cit., p. 193; for a discussion of constitutionalism in the medium and small states, see ibid., pp. 193–313.

Chapter 9   Nation-Building and the Crisis of Nationalities

1. O. Dann (ed.), *Nationalismus und sozialer Wandel* (Hamburg, 1978), pp. 115f.

2. Ibid., pp. 103f.

3. Quoted in Huber (ed.), *Dokumente*, vol. 1, p. 334.

4. Wigard (ed.), op. cit., vol. 2, p. 1131.

5. Cf. L.B. Namier, *The Revolution of the Intellectuals* (Oxford, 1946).

6. Wigard (ed.), op. cit., vol. 2, p. 1247.

7. Cf. G. Wollstein, *Das 'Großdeutschland' der Paulskirche, Nationale Ziele in der bürgerlichen Revolution, 1848/49* (Düsseldorf,1977) p. 234.

8. Wigard (ed.), op. cit., vol. 2, p. 1558.
9. Cf. Kraume, op. cit.
10. See, for example, the list of contributors in Wigard (ed.), op. cit., vol. 2, pp. 947f.
11. Kraume, op. cit., p. 226.
12. See the skilful analysis of the various possibilities in ibid., pp. 223–31.
13. See Wollstein, *'Großdeutschland'*, for a general discussion of the subject.

Chapter 10   The Turning Point in the European Revolutions, Summer/Autumn 1848

1. Cf. H. Kretzschmar and H. Schlechte (eds), *Französische und sächsische Gesandtschaftsberichte aus Dresden und Paris, 1848–1849* (Berlin, 1956).
2. Cf. H. Kretzschmar (ed.), *Lebenserinnerungen des Königs Johann von Sachsen. Eigene Aufzeichnungen des Königs, 1801–1854* (Göttingen, 1958) pp. 202f.
3. S. Kieniewicz, '1848 in Polen', p. 163, in Stuke and Forstmann (eds), op. cit., pp. 162–72.
4. S.Z. Pech, 'Arbeiter in der böhmischen Revolution von 1848', in Stuke and Forstmann (eds), op. cit., pp. 173–88; S.Z. Pech, 'Studenten in der böhmischen Revolution von 1848', ibid., pp. 189–97.
5. Cf. R. Price, 'Der Juniaufstand', in Stuke and Forstmann (eds), op. cit., pp. 123–61.
6. Wigard (ed.), op. cit., vol. 3, p. 2184; the submission suggests that there were at least 20,000 participants.
7. For details of events, see Valentin, op. cit., vol. 2, pp. 164–66.
8. Huber, *Verfassungsgeschichte*, op. cit., vol. 2, p. 699.
9. Quoted in Huber (ed.), *Dokumente*, vol. 1, pp. 350f.
10. Valentin, op. cit., vol. 2, pp. 167f.
11. Ibid., p. 170.
12. Ibid., p. 175.
13. Häusler, op. cit., p. 249.
14. Huber, *Verfassungsgeschichte*, vol. 2, p. 568; cf. A. Schmidt-Brentano, *Die Armee in Österreich. Staat und Gesellschaft, 1848–1867* (Boppard, 1975); the aspect mentioned is neglected there.

15. Cf. S. Schmidt, *R. Blum: Vom Leipziger Liberalen zum Märtyrer der deutschen Demokratie* (Weimar, 1971) p. 252.
16. Quoted in Huber (ed.), *Dokumente*, vol. 1, pp. 457f.
17. Quoted in ibid., pp. 459f.
18. Quoted in ibid., pp. 476f.
19. Cf. Huber's comments on the army's attitude, *Verfassungsgeschichte*, vol. 2, p. 734.
20. Valentin, op. cit., vol. 2, pp. 284 and 641, n. 172.
21. Botzenhart, op. cit., pp. 551 and 555.
22. Quoted in Huber (ed.), *Dokumente*, vol. 1, pp. 479f.

Chapter 11   The Dynamics of the Revolution

1. Cf. R. Wirtz, 'Zur Logik plebejischer und bürgerlicher Aufstandsbewegungen – Die gescheiterte Revolution von 1848', p. 83, in *SOWI*, 8 (1979) pp. 83–88.
2. Ibid., p. 84.
3. Cf. N. Deuchert, *Vom Hambacher Fest zur badischen Revolution, Politische Presse und Anfänge deutscher Demokratie, 1832–1848/49* (Stuttgart, 1983) p. 257.
4. Zimmermann, op. cit., p. 36.
5. Cf. Valentin, op. cit., vol. 1, p. 347, on the Offenburg Rally of 19 March 1848.
6. *Die Gegenwart*, vol. 10 (1855) p. 313f.
7. Cf. A Tapp, *Hanau im Vormärz und in der Revolution von 1848–1849* (Hanau, 1976) p. 255–8.
8. Cf. Scharfe, op. cit., pp. 62f.
9. Cf. Kaschuba and Lipp, *Provinz*, pp. 189–202; E.P. Thompson, ' "Rough Music" oder englische Katzenmusik', in E.P. Thompson, *Plebejische Kultur und moralische Ökonomie. Aufsätze zur englischen Sozialgeschichte des 18. und 19. Jahrhunderts* (Frankfurt, 1980) pp. 131–68.
10. Cf. M. Gailus, 'Soziale Protestbewegungen in Deutschland 1847–1849', in Volkmann and Bergmann (eds), op. cit., pp. 76–106.
11. *Die Gegenwart*, vol. 1 (1848) p. 423; see also Langewiesche, 'Forschungsstand', p. 496.
12. L. Bamberger, *Politische Schriften, 1848–1868* (= *Ges. Schriften*, vol. 3) (Berlin, no date) p. 14.
13. Cited by Gailus, op. cit., p. 105.
14. For a general discussion of types of sources, see R. Moldenhauer, 'Die jüdischen Petitionen an die Deutsche Nationalversammlung

in (Frankfurt, am Main 1848/49', in Klötzer *et al.* (eds), op. cit., pp. 177–208, see also ibid., pp. 209–35.

15. Wigard (ed.), op. cit., vol. 4, pp. 2388–403.
16. Cf. Simon, op. cit., pp. 101f.
17. Ibid., pp. 102 and 117.
18. Cited ibid., p. 121.
19. See the informative abstracts of petitions in ibid., pp. 457–652.
20. Best's analysis is standard, see in particular p. 131.
21. Cf. Schnabel, op. cit., p. 45.
22. Cf. L. Bergsträßer, *Studien zur Vorgeschichte der Zentrumspartei* (Tübingen, 1910) p. 184.
23. Cf. M. Brecht *et al.* (eds), *Pietismus und Neuzeit*, vol. 5 (1979; Göttingen, 1980); E. Schubert, *Die evangelische Predigt im Revolutionsjahr 1848* (Gießen, 1913) (includes numerous sermon extracts).
24. Dated 16 May 1848. Cited in Wirtz, 'Widersetzlichkeiten', p. 184.
25. Cited in Franz, 'Agrarbewegung', p. 186.
26. Cf. J. Mooser, *Ländliche Klassengesellschaft 1770- 1848, Bauern und Unterschichten, Landwirtschaft und Gewerbe im östlichen Westfalen*, (Göttingen, 1984) p. 356.
27. *Die Gegenwart*, vol. 5 (1850) p. 274f.
28. Cf. B. Parisius, ' "Daß die liebe alte Vorzeit wo möglich wieder hergestellt werde", Politische und soziokulturelle Reaktionen von oldenburgischen Landarbeitern auf ihren sozialen Abstieg 1800–1848', op. cit., p. 201f., in Volkmann and Bergmann (eds), op. cit., pp. 198–211.
29. Cf. H.-G. Husung, 'Eisenbahnarbeiter im Vormärz', in D. Langewiesche and K. Schönhoven (eds), *Arbeiter in Deutschland* (Paderborn, 1981) pp. 209–20.
30. Cf. Valentin, op. cit., vol. 2, pp. 252f.
31. Cited by Bergmann, 'Arbeiter 1848', p. 295.
32. *Zeitung des Arbeiter-Vereines zu Köln*, no. 6 (28 May 1848) pp. 54f.; cf. U. Engelhardt, 'Von der "Unruhe" zum "Strike" ', p. 239, in Volkmann and Bergmann (eds), op. cit., pp. 228–52.
33. *Börsenblatt für den deutschen Buchhandel*, no. 27 (dated 4 April 1848) p. 380.
34. In the July edition of *Westfalia*, cited by Schulte, op. cit., p. 262.
35. Printed by F. Frahm, 'Entstehungs- und Entwicklungsgeschichte der preußischen Verfassung (von März 1848 bis zum Januar 1850)', pp. 265f., in *FBPG*, 41 (1928) pp. 248–301.
36. Ibid.

37. *Börsenblatt für den deutschen Buchhandel*, no. 106 (dated 8 December 1848) p. 1297.
38. Cf. J. Toury, *Soziale und politische Geschichte der Juden in Deutschland, 1847–1871: Zwischen Revolution, Reaktion und Emanzipation* (Düsseldorf, 1977) pp. 290f.; W. E. Mosse *et al.* (eds), *Revolution and Evolution: 1848 in German-Jewish History* (Tübingen, 1981) is a seminal work on 1848 and contains a survey of research to date by R. Rürup, op. cit., pp. 1–53.
39. Cf. details in J. Toury, *Die politischen Orientierungen der Juden in Deutschland. Von Jena bis Weimar* (Tübingen, 1966) pp. 59–62, 345–50.
40. Cf. Toury, *Geschichte*, pp. 296f.
41. Cf. M. Twellmann-Schepp, *Die deutsche Frauenbewegung. Ihre Anfänge und erste Entwicklung, 1843–1889* (Meisenheim, 1972); U. Gerhard, 'Über die Anfänge der deutschen Frauenbewegung um 1848. Frauenpresse, Frauenpolitik, Frauenvereine', in K. Hausen (ed.), *Frauen suchen ihre Geschichte* (Munich, 1983) pp. 196–220; see also Hummel-Haasis (ed.), op. cit., and Langewiesche, 'Forschungsstand', pp. 487f.
42. Cited by Gerhard, op. cit., p. 202.
43. Cf. Weigel, op. cit., and Valentin, op. cit., vol. 2, pp. 581f.

Chapter 12 The Imperial Constitution and the Election of the Kaiser

1. Quoted in Huber (ed.), *Dokumente*, vol. 1, p. 360.
2. Ibid., pp. 362f.
3. Ibid., pp. 371–3.
4. Cited by Botzenhart, op. cit., p. 691.
5. Cf. ibid., p. 670.
6. H. Laube, *Das erste deutsche Parlament*, vol. 3 (Leipzig, 1849) p. 386.
7. Cf. Botzenhart, op. cit., p. 693.
8. Cf. Huber, *Verfassungsgeschichte*, vol. 2, p. 495.
9. Huber (ed.), *Dokumente*, vol. 1, pp. 402f.
10. Ibid., pp. 363–6.
11. Ibid., pp. 411f.
12. L. v. Ranke, *Aus dem Briefwechsel Friedrich Wilhelms IV. mit Bunsen* (Leipzig, 1873) p. 272.
13. Botzenhart, op. cit., p. 695.

Chapter 13 The Campaign for the Imperial Constitution, April–July 1849

1. Wigard (ed.), op. cit., vol. 9, p. 6256.
2. Cf. F. Engels, 'Die deutsche Reichsverfassungskampagne', in *MEW*, vol. 7, pp. 109–97; Valentin, op. cit., vol. 2, pp. 448–544; C. Kleßmann, 'Zur Sozialgeschichte der Reichsverfassungskampagne von 1849', in *HZ*, 218 (1974) pp. 283–337; B. Mann, 'Das Ende der Deutschen Nationalversammlung im Jahre 1849', in *HZ*, 214 (1972) pp. 265–309; B. Mann, *Württemberger*, pp. 293–351; H.-J. Rupieper, 'Die Sozialstruktur der Trägerschichten der Revolution von 1848/49 am Beispiel Sachsen', in H. Kaelble *et al.*, *Probleme der Modernisierung in Deutschland* (Opladen, 1978) pp. 80–109.
3. Huber (ed.), *Dokumente*, vol. 1, pp. 418f.; Wigard (ed.), op. cit., vol. 9, p. 6396, vote 6435.
4. Valentin, op. cit., vol. 2, p. 463.
5. Huber (ed.), *Dokumente*, vol. 1, pp. 435f.; Wigard (ed.), op. cit., vol. 9, pp. 6735f., passing of the resolution, ibid., p. 6761.
6. Huber, *Verfassungsgeschichte*, vol. 2, p. 860.
7. Cf. Kleßmann, op. cit., p. 334.
8. Cf. Valentin, op. cit., vol. 2, pp. 475f.
9. Cf. Mann, *Württemberger*, p. 316.
10. Cf. R. Weber, *Die Revolution in Sachsen 1848/49* (Berlin, 1970) p. 355.
11. Huber (ed.), *Dokumente*, vol. 1, p. 416.
12. K. Goebel and M. Wichelhaus (eds), *Aufstand der Bürger, Revolution 1849 im westdeutschen Industriezentrum* (Wuppertal, 1974, 3rd edn) p. 37.
13. Huber, *Verfassungsgeschichte*, vol. 2, pp. 864f.
14. Cf. Langewiesche, 'Vereinsbewegung', pp. 224f., 232f.
15. Cited by Valentin, op. cit., vol. 2, p. 493.
16. Cf. Botzenhart, p. 713.
17. Cf. Valentin, op. cit., vol. 2, pp. 540–42.

Chapter 14 From Erfurt Union to Reaction

1. Cf. Botzenhart, op. cit., p. 770.
2. Cf. Huber, *Verfassungsgeschichte*, vol. 2, p. 922.

3. Cf. Siemann, '*Polizeiverein*' and *Deutschlands Ruhe*, esp. pp. 242–304.
4. Huber, *Verfassungsgeschichte*, vol. 3, p. 134.

Conclusion   1848–9 and the Crisis of Modernization

1. Faber, op. cit., p. 283.
2. Cf. D. Langewiesche, 'Die Rolle des Militärs in den europäischen Revolutionen von 1848/49', in W. Bachofer and H. Fischer (eds), *Ungarn – Deutschland* (Munich, 1983) pp. 273–88.
3. L. Bamberger, *Erinnerungen*, ed. P. Nathan (Berlin, 1899) p. 138.

Select Bibliography with Commentary

This survey of literature is intended as a brief introduction which will facilitate a further, deeper engagement with the revolution of 1848–9. Particular attention has been paid to the practical needs of those studying the subject at university and school. Most of the books listed are easily accessible and provide an introduction to their subject with further references to enable the reader to explore the subject in greater depth. Additional references are to be found in the notes above.

Research reports, Aids to Further Research

Indispensable for anyone planning a doctoral thesis on the German revolution, the best statement on the current state of research is to be found in D. Langewiesche, 'Die deutsche Revolution von 1848/49 und die vorrevolutionäre Gesellschaft, Forschungsstand und Forschungsperspektiven', in *AfS* 21 (1981) pp. 458–98, continued in *AfS*, 31 (1991) pp. 331–443. This should be supplemented by G. Wollstein, '1848 – Streit um das Erbe', in *NPL*, 20 (1975) pp. 491–507; *NPL*, 21 (1976) pp. 89–106. W. Klötzer *et al.* (eds), *Ideen und Strukturen der deutschen Revolution 1848* (Frankfurt, 1974) was published on the occasion of the 125th anniversary of the revolution, and takes stock of research over that period. H. Bartel (ed.), *Die bürgerlich-demokratische Revolution von 1848/49 in Deutschland*, 2 vols (Berlin, 1972) examines research in the GDR; H. Müller, 'Forschungen zur deutschen Geschichte 1789–1848', in *ZfG* (1980) Sonderband, pp. 122–42; J. Hofmann and W. Schmidt, 'Forschungen zur Geschichte der Revolution von 1848/49', in ibid., pp. 143–68. Further references are to be found in the bibliographies in M. Botzenhart, *Deutscher Parlamentarismus in der Revolutionszeit, 1848–1850*

245

(Düsseldorf, 1977) pp. 800–43 (contains much on regional history); for the European situation, see H. Stuke and W. Forstmann (eds), *Die europäischen Revolutionen von 1848* (Königstein, 1979) pp. 211–32; V. Valentin lists older literature in *Geschichte der deutschen Revolution von 1848–1849*, 2 vols (Berlin, 1930/31; reprinted Cologne, 1970), vol. 1, pp. 611–62; vol. 2, pp. 687–97; access to numerous statistical documents is provided by W. Fischer *et al.* (eds), *Sozialgeschichtliches Arbeitsbuch*, vol. 1: *Materialien zur Statistik des Deutschen Bundes, 1815–1870* (Munich, 1982).

The best introduction to historiographical issues and changes in perspective is given by D. Langewiesche (ed.), *Die deutsche Revolution von 1848/49* (Darmstadt, 1983), which includes texts from 1948 to 1980. The following works are particularly useful for the *Kaiserzeit*: F. Baumgart, *Die verdrängte Revolution, Darstellung und Bewertung der Revolution von 1848 in der deutschen Geschichtsschreibung vor dem Ersten Weltkrieg* (Düsseldorf, 1976); M. Neumüller, *Liberalismus und Revolution, Das Problem der Revolution in der deutschen liberalen Geschichtsschreibung des 19. Jahrhunderts* (Düsseldorf, 1973); the Weimar period is dealt with by B. Faulenbach, *Ideologie des deutschen Weges, Die deutsche Historiographie zwischen Kaiserreich und Nationalsozialismus* (Munich, 1980); see also D. Blackbourn and G. Eley's controversial and stimulating *Mythen deutscher Geschichtsschreibung, Die gescheiterte bürgerliche Revolution von 1848* (Frankfurt, 1980).

The areas of controversy between research in the Federal Republic and in the former GDR are dealt with by A. Dorpalen, 'Die Revolution von 1848 in der Geschichtsschreibung der DDR', in *HZ*, 210 (1970) pp. 324–68; J. Schradi, *Die DDR-Geschichtswissenschaft und das bürgerliche Erbe, Das deutsche Bürgertum und die Revolution von 1848 im sozialistischen Geschichtsverständnis* (Frankfurt, 1984); H. Bleiber, 'Die bürgerlich-demokratische Revolution von 1848/49 in Deutschland in der bürgerlichen Geschichtsschreibung der BRD', in H. Bleiber (ed.), *Bourgeoisie und bürgerliche Umwälzung in Deutschland, 1789–1871* (Berlin, 1977) pp. 193–227.

General Works on the Period

Those wishing to further their knowledge of the wider historical background to the revolution of 1848–9 by means of works written in English should turn first to J. Sperber, *The European Revolutions, 1848–1851* (Cambridge, 1994); this thoroughly researched work is stimulating, precise, to the point and contains a current critical bibliography. It is also suitable for use as a textbook. J. Sperber, *Rhineland Radicals: The Democratic Movement and the Revolution of 1848–1849* (Princeton, NJ, 1991) focuses on the 'everyday events' of the German revolution, the background to it and its problems. James J. Sheehan, *German History, 1770–1866* (Oxford, 1989; paperback, 1993) provides an excellent survey, which analyses the long traditions in German history and also deals with German federalism.

The following excellent works also deal with the wider historical framework, and each contains a chapter on the revolution itself: K.G. Faber, *Deutsche Geschichte im 19. Jahrhundert, Restauration und Revolution, 1815–1851* (Wiesbaden, 1979); Th. Nipperdey, *Deutsche Geschichte, 1800–1866: Bürgerwelt und starker Staat* (Munich, 1983); for a socio-historical emphasis, see R. Rürup, *Deutschland im 19. Jahrhundert 1815–1871* (Göttingen, 1984); the most recent general GDR interpretation is to be found in W. Schmidt (ed.), *Die bürgerliche Umwälzung 1789–1871* (= *Deutsche Geschichte*, vol. 4) (Berlin/Cologne, 1984); in addition to the volume edited by Stuke and Fortsmann referred to above, the European perspective is examined in W. Bußmann (ed.), *Europa von der Französischen Revolution zu den nationalstaatlichen Bewegungen des 19. Jahrhunderts* (= *Handbuch der europäischen Geschichte*, vol. 5) (Stuttgart, 1981); D. Langewiesche, *Europa zwischen Restauration und Revolution, 1815–1849* (Munich, 1985) (includes an excellent survey of research problems and literature); a range of cultural historical perspectives are to be found in E.J. Hobsbawm, *Europäische Revolutionen, 1789–1848* (Zurich, 1962); E.J. Hobsbawm, *Die Blütezeit des Kapitals, Eine Kulturgeschichte der Jahre 1848–1875* (Munich, 1977); W. Siemann, *Vom Staatenbund zum Nationalstaat, Deutschland 1806–1871* (Munich, 1995).

The following works all examine issues which are of direct significance for the revolution; most of them include a chapter on the revolution: H. Aubin and W. Zorn (eds), *Handbuch der deutschen Wirtschafts- und Sozialgeschichte*, vol. 2 (Stuttgart, 1976); W. Conze, 'Sozialer und wirtschaftlicher Wandel', in K.G.A. Jeserich *et al.* (eds), *Deutsche Verwaltungsgeschichte*, vol. 2 (Stuttgart, 1983) pp. 19–56 (brief, but instructive); R. Spree, *Die Wachstumszyklen der deutschen Wirtschaft 1840–1864* (Berlin, 1977); H. Volkmann and J. Bergmann (eds), *Sozialer Protest, Studien zu traditioneller Resistenz und kollektiver Gewalt in Deutschland vom Vormärz bis zur Reichsgründung* (Opladen, 1984); W. Abel, *Massenarmut und Hungerkrisen im vorindustriellen Europa* (Hamburg, 1974); J. Kocka, *Lohnarbeit und Klassenbildung, Arbeiter und*

Arbeiterbewegung, 1800–1875 (Berlin, 1983); U. Engelhardt (ed.), *Handwerker in der Industrialisierung. Lage, Kultur und Politik vom späten 18. bis ins frühe 20. Jahrhundert* (Stuttgart, 1984); C. Dipper, *Die Bauernbefreiung in Deutschland 1790–1850* (Stuttgart, 1980); H. Henning, *Die deutsche Beamtenschaft im 19. Jahrhundert* (Stuttgart, 1984); O. Dann, 'Nationaler und sozialer Wandel in Deutschland 1806–1850', in O. Dann (ed.), *Nationalismus und sozialer Wandel* (Hamburg, 1978) pp. 77–128; W. Schieder (ed.), *Liberalismus in der Gesellschaft des deutschen Vormärz* (Göttingen, 1983) (= *GG Sonderheft* 9); E.R. Huber, *Deutsche Verfassungsgeschichte seit 1789*, vol. 2 (Stuttgart, 1960, 2nd edn; reprinted 1975) (contains a detailed section on the revolution, pp. 502–884); W. Siemann, *'Deutschlands Ruhe, Sicherheit und Ordnung'. Die Anfänge der politischen Polizei 1806–1866* (Tübingen, 1985) (chapter 4 deals specifically with the revolution).

Works on the Revolutionary Period

Valentin (op. cit.) is inexhaustible in terms of material, though rather unstructured; R. Stadelmann, *Soziale und politische Geschichte der Revolution von 1848* (Munich, 1948; 2nd edn, 1970) remains stimulating; the standard work on the growth of the parliamentary system and parties (with the exception of workers' societies) is Botzenhart (op. cit.); the Paulskirche is discussed by F. Eyck, *Deutschlands große Hoffnung, Die Frankfurter Nationalversammlung* (Munich, 1973) (holds 'the radicals' and 'the left' responsible for the 'failure of the moderate liberal governments'); W. Siemann, *Die Frankfurter Nationalversammlung 1848/49 zwischen demokratischem Liberalismus und konservativer Reform* (Frankfurt, 1976); biographical details of the deputies are to be found in M. Schwarz, *MdR, Biographisches Handbuch der Reichstage* (Hanover, 1965) pp. 43–112; the formation of parties is dealt with by D. Langewiesche, 'Die Anfänge der deutschen Parteien, Partei, Fraktion und Verein in der Revolution von 1848/49', in *GG*, 4 (1978) pp. 324–61 (includes numerous regional historical references); W. Boldt, *Die Anfänge des deutschen Parteiwesens, Fraktionen, politische Vereine und Parteien in der Revolution 1848* (Paderborn, 1971); H. Gebhardt, *Revolution und liberale Bewegung. Die nationale Organisation der konstitutionellen Partei in Deutschland 1848/49* (Bremen, 1974); G. Hildebrandt, *Parlamentsopposition auf Linkskurs, Die kleinbürgerlich-demokratische Fraktion Donnersberg in der Frankfurter Nationalversammlung 1848/49* (Berlin, 1975). The

German question in the European power play is the subject of G. Wollstein, *Das 'Großdeutschland' der Paulskirche, Nationale Ziele in der bürgerlichen Revolution 1848/49* (Düsseldorf, 1977); H.-G. Kraume, *Außenpolitik 1848, Die holländische Provinz Limburg in der deutschen Revolution* (Düsseldorf, 1979) (deals with wider national issues too); H. Rumpler, *Die deutsche Politik des Freiherrn von Beust 1848–1850* (Vienna, 1972). The best works on economic and socio-historical aspects are H. Best, *Interessenpolitik und nationale Integration 1848/49. Handelspolitische Konflikte im frühindustriellen Deutschland* (Göttingen, 1980); P.H. Noyes, *Organization and Revolution: Working-Class Association in the German Revolutions of 1848–1849* (Princeton, NJ, 1966); F. Balser, *Sozial-Demokratie 1848/49–1863: Die erste deutsche Arbeiterorganisation 'Allgemeine deutsche Arbeiterverbrüderung' nach der Revolution*, 2 vols (Stuttgart, 1962; 2nd edn, 1965); J. Bergmann, 'Ökonomische Voraussetzungen der Revolution von 1848, Zur Krise von 1845 bis 1848 in Deutschland', in *GG Sonderheft*, 2 (1976) pp. 254–87.

Many of the analyses of individual states discuss the broader dimensions of the revolution. A new general examination of the *Austrian* situation has not yet been published, although A. Springer's work remains important and contains a wealth of material: *Geschichte Österreichs seit dem Wiener Frieden 1809*, 2 parts (Leipzig, 1863/65) (Part 2 deals exclusively with 1848/49); an excellent account of the Vienna revolution is given by W. Häusler, *Von der Massenarmut zur Arbeiterbewegung, Demokratie und soziale Frage in der Wiener Revolution von 1848* (Munich, 1979); A. Sked, *The Survival of the Habsburg Empire: Radetzky, the Imperial Army and the Class War 1848* (London, 1979); for *Prussia*, see G. Grünthal, *Parlamentarismus in Preußen 1848/49–1857/58* (Düsseldorf, 1982); J. Hofmann, *Das Ministerium Camphausen–Hansemann, Zur Politik der preußischen Bourgeoisie in der Revolution 1848/49* (Berlin, 1981); J. Paschen, *Demokratische Vereine und preußischer Staat, Entwicklung und Unterdrückung der demokratischen Bewegung während der Revolution von 1848/49* (Munich, 1977); K.-G. Faber, *Die Rheinlande zwischen Restauration und Revolution, Probleme der rheinischen Geschichte von 1814 bis 1848 im Spiegel der zeitgenössichen Publizistik* (Wiesbaden, 1966); K. Repgen, *Märzbewegung und Maiwahlen des Revolutionsjahres 1848 im Rheinland* (Bonn, 1955); D. Dowe, *Aktion und Organisation. Arbeiterbewegung, sozialistische und kommunistische Bewegung in der preußischen Rheinprovinz, 1820–1852* (Hanover, 1970); W. Schulte, *Volk und Staat, Westfalen im Vormärz und in der Revolution 1848/49* (Münster 1954); for *Saxony*, see Rumpler (op. cit.) and R. Weber, *Die Revolution in Sachsen 1848/49* (Berlin, 1970); for *Württemberg*, see

D. Langewiesche, *Liberalismus und Demokratie in Württemberg zwischen Revolution und Reichsgründung* (Düsseldorf, 1974); B. Mann, *Die Württemberger und die deutsche Nationalversammlung 1848/49* (Düsseldorf, 1975); W. Kaschuba and C. Lipp, *1848 – Provinz und Revolution, Kultureller Wandel und soziale Bewegung im Königreich Württemberg* (Tübingen, 1979); for *Bavaria*, see M. Spindler (ed.), *Handbuch der bayerischen Geschichte*, vol. 4/1–2 (Munich, 1974/75); L. Zimmermann, *Die Einheits- und Freiheitsbewegung und die Revolution von 1848 in Franken* (Würzburg, 1951); D. Nickel, *Die Revolution 1848/49 in Augsburg und Bayerisch-Schwaben* (Erlangen, 1965); for *Baden*, see L. Gall, *Der Liberalismus als regierende Partei. Das Großherzogtum Baden zwischen Restauration und Reichsgründung* (Wiesbaden, 1968); W. Real, *Die Revolution in Baden 1848/49* (Stuttgart, 1983); the *city republics* are dealt with by V. Valentin, *Frankfurt a. M. und die Revolution von 1848/49* (Stuttgart, 1908); W. Biebusch, *Revolution und Staatsstreich, Verfassungskämpfe in Bremen 1848–1854* (Bremen, 1973).

Source Collections

The revolution left behind an almost impenetrable mass of official records and personal testimonies (memoirs, letters, memories of the revolution), a guide to which is provided in the commentated source collection by W. Siemann, *Restauration, Liberalismus und nationale Bewegung 1815–1870, Akten, Urkunden und persönliche Quellen* (Darmstadt, 1982) (with references to larger collections of source material, works by the major participants in the revolution and parliamentary records). The most important and comprehensive contemporary editions are: F. Wigard (ed.), *Stenographischer Bericht über die Verhandlungen der deutschen constituirenden Nationalversammlung*, 9 vols, plus index (Frankfurt, 1848–50); *Die Gegenwart, Eine encyklopädische Darstellung der neuesten Zeitgeschichte für alle Stände*, 12 vols (Leipzig, 1848–56) (with excellent articles on states, overview in vol. 12 pp. xiii–xviii); A. Wolff, *Berliner Revolutions-Chronik*, 3 vols (Berlin, 1851–54; reprinted Vaduz, 1979).

The following collections are useful as an introduction: W. Grab (ed.), *Die Revolution von 1848/49* (Munich, 1980) (appendix contains a detailed chronicle of the revolution); K. Obermann (ed.), *Flugblätter der Revolution, Eine Flugblattsammlung zur Geschichte der Revolution von 1848/49 in Deutschland* (Berlin, 1970; abridged paperback edition, Munich, 1972); K. Obermann (ed.), *Einheit und Freiheit, Die deutsche Geschichte 1815–1849 in zeitgenössischen Dokumenten* (Berlin, 1950) (three-quarters of which is devoted to 1848–9, reproduces many original documents); H. Fenske (ed.), *Vormärz und Revolution 1840–1849* (Darmstadt, 1976); T. Klein (ed.), *1848. Der Vorkampf deutscher Einheit und Freiheit, Erinnerungen, Urkunden, Berichte, Briefe* (Leipzig, 1914).

Documentation relating to individual aspects of the revolution is included in E.R. Huber (ed.), *Dokumente zur deutschen Verfassungsgeschichte*, vol. 1 (Stuttgart, 3rd edn, 1978) (expanded, pagination differs in older editions; standard work on the policies of the March governments, the Central Power, parliaments and associations); H. Scholler (ed.), *Die Grundrechtsdiskussionen in der Paulskirche, eine Dokumentation* (Darmstadt, 2nd edn, 1982); G. Hildebrandt (ed.), *Opposition in der Paulskirche. Reden, Briefe und Berichte kleinbürgerlich-demokratischer Parlamentarier 1848/49* (Berlin, 1981) (the first comprehensive collection on the democrats and the republicans); H. Schlechte (ed.), *Die Allgemeine Deutsche Arbeiterverbrüderung 1848/1850, Dokumente des Zentralkomitees für die deutschen Arbeiter in Leipzig* (Weimar, 1979); *Der Bund der Kommunisten, Dokumente und Materialien*, 3 vols (Berlin, 1970–84; vol. 1, 2nd edn, 1983); G. Hummel-Haasis (ed.), *Schwestern, zerreißt eure Ketten. Zeugnisse zur Geschichte der Frauen in der Revolution von 1848/49* (Munich, 1982); J. Hansen (ed.), *Rheinische Briefe und Akten zur Geschichte der politischen Bewegung 1830–1850*, vols 1, 2.1 and 2.2 (Essen/Bonn/Cologne, 1919/42/76). Vol. 2.2, edited by H. Boberach, is particularly important on the subject of the formation of parties and the popular movement.

Newspapers provide accounts which are particularly close to revolutionary events; several have been reprinted and are easily accessible, primarily those published by workers' societies. They include *Die Verbrüderung* (Berlin, 1848–50; reprinted Leipzig, 1975); *Das Volk* (Berlin, 1848; reprinted Glashütten, 1973); *Zeitung des Arbeiter-Vereines zu Köln* (1848; reprinted Glashütten, 1976); *Freiheit, Brüderlichkeit, Arbeit* (Cologne, 1848–9; reprint, ed. D. Dowe, Berlin, 1980); *Die Allgemeine Frankfurter Arbeiter-Zeitung* (1848, ed. M. Quarck, 1925; reprinted Frankfurt, 1968); *Neue Rheinische Zeitung* (Cologne, 1848–9; reprinted, 2 vols, Glashütten, 1973). As yet the only source collection dealing with post-revolutionary domestic politics is W. Siemann (ed.), *Der 'Polizeiverein' deutscher Staaten, Eine Dokumentation zur Überwachung der Öffentlichkeit nach der Revolution von 1848/49* (Tübingen, 1983).

Illustrations, facsimiles of original documents and caricatures on the revolutionary era are to be found in particular in F. Vollmer, *Der Traum von der Freiheit, Vormärz und 48er Revolution in Süddeutschland in zeitgenössischen Bildern* (Stuttgart, 1983); H. Blum, *Die deutsche Revolution 1848–49* (Leipzig, 1898) (useless as an account of events); W. Schmidt (ed.), *Illustrierte Geschichte der deutschen Revolution von 1848/49* (Berlin, 1973); K. Mellach (ed.), *1848, Protokolle einer Revolution, Eine Dokumentation* (Vienna, 1968) (includes excellent illustrations and reproductions on the subject of the Vienna revolution); S. Wolf, *Politische Karikatur in Deutschland 1848–49* (Mittenwald, 1982); H. Hartwig and K. Riha, *Politische Ästhetik und Öffentlichkeit, 1848 im Spaltungsprozeß des historischen Bewußtseins* (Fernwald, 1974) (excessively topical, but with numerous caricatures); U. Otto, *Die historisch-politischen Lieder und Karikaturen des Vormärz und der Revolution von 1848/49* (Cologne, 1982); S. Weigel, *Flugschriften 1848 in Berlin, Geschichte und Öffentlichkeit einer volkstümlichen Gattung* (Stuttgart, 1979); numerous illustrations are also to be found in Obermann, Einheit (op. cit.) and Häusler (op. cit.); P. Lahnstein, *Die unvollendete Revolution 1848–49: Badener und Württemberger in der Paulskirche* (Stuttgart, 1981) (includes illustrations of the revolution in general, with examples of the Neuruppin illustrated broadsheets, but as an account of the revolution is uninformed and full of errors); A. Briggs (ed.), *Das neunzehnte Jahrhundert, Politik, Wirtschaft, Wissenschaft und Kunst im Zeitalter des Imperialismus* (Munich, 1972) (extremely comprehensive, compares various European countries, with an emphasis on cultural history).

Index